Presidents, Parties, and Prime Ministers

How the Separation of Powers Affects Party Organization and Behavior

This book provides a framework for analyzing the impact of the separation of powers on party politics. Conventional political science wisdom assumes that democracy is impossible without political parties, because parties fulfill all the key functions of democratic governance. They nominate candidates, coordinate campaigns, aggregate interests, formulate and implement policy, and manage government power. When scholars first asserted the essential connection between parties and democracy, most of the world's democracies were parliamentary. Yet by the dawn of the 21st century, most democracies had directly elected presidents. Given this, if parties are truly critical to democracy, then a systematic understanding of how the separation of powers shapes parties is long overdue. David J. Samuels and Matthew S. Shugart provide a theoretical framework for analyzing variation in the relationships among presidents, parties, and prime ministers across the world's democracies, revealing the important ways in which the separation of powers alters party organization and behavior – thereby changing the nature of democratic representation and accountability.

David J. Samuels is the Benjamin E. Lippincott Professor of Political Science at the University of Minnesota. He is the author of *Ambition, Federalism, and Legislative Politics in Brazil* (Cambridge University Press, 2003) and the coeditor of *Decentralization and Democracy in Latin America* (2004). He has published articles in the *American Political Science Review*, the *Journal of Politics, Comparative Politics, Comparative Political Studies, Legislative Studies Quarterly*, and the *British Journal of Political Science*.

Matthew S. Shugart is Professor in the Department of Political Science and the School of International Relations and Pacific Studies, University of California, San Diego. Among his books are *Seats and Votes* (with Rein Taagepera, 1989), *Presidents and Assemblies* (with John Carey, Cambridge University Press, 1992), *Presidentialism and Democracy in Latin America* (coedited with Scott Mainwaring, Cambridge University Press, 1997), *Executive Decree Authority* (coedited with John Carey, Cambridge University Press, 1998), and *Mixed-Member Electoral Systems* (coedited with Martin Wattenberg, 2001). His articles have appeared in numerous journals, including the *American Journal of Political Science*, the *American Political Science Review*, the *British Journal of Political Science*, and *Electoral Studies*.

Presidents, Parties, and Prime Ministers

How the Separation of Powers Affects Party Organization and Behavior

DAVID J. SAMUELS
University of Minnesota

MATTHEW S. SHUGART
University of California, San Diego

CAMBRIDGE
UNIVERSITY PRESS

CAMBRIDGE UNIVERSITY PRESS
Cambridge, New York, Melbourne, Madrid, Cape Town,
Singapore, São Paulo, Delhi, Tokyo, Mexico City

Cambridge University Press
32 Avenue of the Americas, New York, NY 10013-2473, USA

www.cambridge.org
Information on this title: www.cambridge.org/9780521689687

First published 2010
Reprinted 2011

A catalog record for this publication is available from the British Library.

Library of Congress Cataloging in Publication Data

Samuels, David, 1967–
Presidents, parties, and prime ministers : how the separation of powers affects
party organization and behavior / David J. Samuels, Matthew S. Shugart.
    p. cm.
Includes bibliographical references and index.
ISBN 978-0-521-86954-6 (hardback) – ISBN 978-0-521-68968-7 (pbk.)
    1. Separation of powers – Cross-cultural studies. 2. Heads of state – Crosscultural
studies. 3. Political parties – Cross-cultural studies. 4. Democracy –
Cross-cultural studies. I. Shugart, Matthew Soberg, 1960– II. Title.
JF229.S26   2010
324.2'1–dc22   2009038313

ISBN 978-0-521-86954-6 Hardback
ISBN 978-0-521-68968-7 Paperback

To our families, for all their support

Contents

Preface and Acknowledgments

This book brings together strands each of us has been thinking about for many years. Shugart's interest in the "distinctiveness" of presidential democracy and its impact on legislative elections and political parties began as he was working on his dissertation at the University of California, Irvine. In the dissertation, inspired largely by the work of Leon Epstein as well as by his own observations of politics in the United States and several Latin American countries, Shugart (1988) noted that presidentialism had an impact on both the number of parties and their "nature." Yet developing just what that nature might be would lie dormant while he focused for a time on the number of parties and worked on other aspects of comparative presidentialism. Later, after taking up a faculty position at the University of California, San Diego, Shugart would begin exploring the "intraparty dimension" of parties – the idea that electoral institutions would shape the behavior and organization of parties as much as, and maybe even more profoundly than, they shape their number. However, he would not put together these two strands – that both presidentialism and *legislative* electoral institutions shape political parties – until some years later, in collaboration with Samuels.

In 1993, in his first semester of graduate school at the University of California, San Diego, Samuels scribbled a comment in the margins of Kaare Strøm's 1990 article, "A Behavioral Theory of Competitive Political Parties" (*American Journal of Political Science* 34: 565–98). Samuels wrote, "But that is not how parties behave in presidential systems." Eventually, he tried to explain the sorts of behavioral incentives parties actually face in presidential systems in his 2002 article, "Presidentialized

Parties: The Separation of Powers and Party Organization and Behavior"
(*Comparative Political Studies* 35(4): 461–83), traces of which the reader
will find in Chapter 5 of this book.

After publishing that article, Samuels realized that an article
Shugart had published in 1998, "The Inverse Relationship between
Party Strength and Executive Strength: A Theory of Politicians' Constitutional Choices" (*British Journal of Political Science* 28: 1–29),
essentially told the flip side of the story he'd articulated in his 2002
article. As Shugart told it, party organization influences the structure
of executive-legislative relations when politicians get to rewrite the
political rules of the game. And as Samuels told it, the structure of
executive-legislative relations then influences party organization and
behavior. Samuels then approached Shugart with the idea of building
on their shared view that scholars had largely ignored the relationship
between the separation of powers and political party organization and
behavior.

Several years later, this book is the product of tying together the
strands of our earlier work and graduate-seminar inspiration. For
helping us along the way, we would like to thank the following people.
For research assistance: Jason Arnold, Andrew Dickinson (in memo-
riam), Fernando Furquim, Michelle Hogler, Catalina Hotung, Kevin
Lucas, Mihaela Mihailescu, Will Moody, Kuniaki Nemoto, Stephanie
Payne, Matthew Roberts, Amit Ron, Jessica Schroeder, Kevin Watt,
and Kimberly Wydeen. For comments and inspiration: Matthew
Cleary, Scott Desposato, James Druckman, Leon Epstein, Jen Gandhi,
Henry Hale, Reuven Hazan, Gretchen Helmke, Kathy Hochstetler,
Yuko Kasuya, Ofer Kenig, Scott Mainwaring, Tom Round, Phil
Shively, Georg Vanberg, Alisa Voznaya, and Erik Wibbels. Participants
in Shugart's graduate seminar on legislative and party organization in
the spring of 2009 offered comments that helped improve the book,
and the anonymous reviewer for Cambridge University Press helped
us strengthen several of our arguments. We are also grateful to Robert
Elgie for regularly answering queries about semi-presidential systems
and cohabitation and to Eduardo Leoni for sharing his data on Brazilian roll-call votes. A grant from the National Science Foundation to
Samuels made possible the collection of the district-level presidential
election results used in Chapter 5.

We are indebted to Arend Lijphart, Gary Cox, and Kaare Strøm for
their inspiration and comments on our work over many years. Shugart
is particularly grateful to Rein Taagepera, not only for comments that

improved this book, but also for more than 25 years of guidance. Finally, the field of comparative executive-legislative systems would never have enjoyed its resurgence without the contributions of Juan Linz, whose intellectual impact is felt throughout this book.

Minneapolis, Minnesota, and Ladera Frutal, California

August 20, 2009

Presidents, Parties, and Prime Ministers

How the Separation of Powers Affects Party Organization and Behavior

I

Introduction

In every pure parliamentary system a vote for any particular legislator – or for the party's list – is indirectly a vote for that party's leader as candidate for prime minister. In a sense, a "perfect correlation" exists between that party's votes for executive and legislative candidates. Yet in systems with popularly elected presidents, parties cannot take for granted the automatic alignment of the electoral bases of their executive and legislative "branches." Indeed, the notion of presidential coattail effects – well known to even casual observers of elections in presidential democracies – suggests that in such systems parties *expect* variation between their executive and legislative vote totals. When voters have two ballots, parties must hope that their presidential candidates encourage voters to *also* cast votes for their candidates in the legislative race.

In light of this fact, consider the 2006 reelection of Brazil's incumbent president, Luis Inácio Lula da Silva. At the same election, the party that Lula had helped found in the late 1970s and had led for over a decade, the Partido dos Trabalhadores (Workers' Party, PT), won the largest share of votes in Brazil's legislative elections. Yet while Lula won 49% of the votes, his party won only 15% that same day. Even more remarkably, in constituencies where Lula did well, the PT did poorly. That is, in 2006 there was a *negative* correlation between Lula's performance and the PT's performance, wholly contradicting the notion of presidential coattails. As we show in more detail in Chapter 5, a result as divergent as this is unusual but not unheard of. Such electoral outcomes reveal that under presidentialism the electoral bases – and presumably the policy preferences – of different "branches" of the same party can diverge widely. In parliamentary systems such electoral divergence – and the resulting policy divergence between a prime minister and his or her party's median member – is, quite simply, impossible to imagine.[1]

Separate presidential and legislative elections can also cause partisan forces to realign in ways they would not in a pure parliamentary system. Consider the process of government formation after Romania's 2004 elections. Prior to the election the ruling Social Democratic Party and the Humanist Party joined forces in a coalition and explicitly agreed to form a government if they were to win the elections (BBC Monitoring Europe 2004c). Such pre-electoral alliances are common in parliamentary democracies; parties typically honor these agreements by apportioning ministries and other portfolios (Carroll 2007). Together these two parties won a plurality of 40% of the seats, and their presidential candidate emerged in the first round with an eight-point lead over the candidate from the opposition Democratic Party. Given the results, these parties immediately prepared to form a government, with the aid of several smaller parties.

However, Romania's requirement that presidents obtain an electoral majority threw a wrench into those plans, because the Democratic candidate, Traian Băsescu, came from behind to beat the Social Democrats' candidate in the runoff. The Democratic Party had won only 14% of the seats, and its own coalition partner – the National Liberal Party – had won another 19%. Băsescu became president but appeared headed for a situation of "cohabitation" in which he would have confronted an assembly controlled by the Social Democrats and the Humanists. However, he avoided cohabitation by first nominating as premier the leader of the National Liberals and then by convincing the Humanists to break their agreement with the Social Democrats and join his government. The results of the direct presidential election thus not only took government formation out of the hands of the largest parliamentary party and the largest parliamentary coalition, but also served to break a pre-election agreement, altering the partisan balance of forces that *parliamentary* coalitions and *parliamentary* elections had established.

In these two examples, direct presidential elections produced results that are unthinkable in pure parliamentary systems. A party as small as Lula's Workers Party likely could not have headed a parliamentary government and certainly could not have done so had there been a negative

---

[1] In Brazil, tension between presidents and their parties is not new: President Getúlio Vargas (1950–54) went so far as to commit suicide in the presidential palace because he felt betrayed by his allies.

correlation between its leader's popularity and the party's popularity. Similarly, without a presidential runoff election, a small party like the Democrats or Liberals in Romania would have almost no chance to form a government, since two larger parties had already formed a coalition and were close to reaching a majority.

Now consider a case of parliamentary democracy, and of a prime minister – Margaret Thatcher – who was so famous for her strong-willed leadership that she was known as the Iron Lady and was sometimes said to exert a presidential style of leadership.[2] Despite the moniker, Thatcher's political authority vanished in 1990, three and a half years after her third-straight landslide election win, when her Conservative Party colleague Michael Heseltine challenged her in the Conservative Party's annual internal leadership election – a process that normally simply reaffirms the incumbent's leadership for another year. Heseltine's challenge failed, but his effort served to expose Thatcher as politically vulnerable – and led her to resign as Conservative leader.

Because the leader of the majority party in the British parliament automatically becomes prime minister, Thatcher also immediately resigned from that position, more than two years before the next scheduled parliamentary election. That is, the UK changed its national executive because of a regularly scheduled *intraparty* leadership election, outside of any formal parliamentary procedure and without any direct public input. Such events are fairly common in parliamentary systems. However, as we detail in Chapter 4, we found only one case in the modern history of democratic government in which purely intraparty squabbles forced an incumbent president from office early. After a presidential election, intraparty accountability virtually ceases, because once in office parties cannot "fire" their leaders as presidents.

These three examples illustrate the main point of this book: *parties and party politics differ under different constitutional formats.* Conventional political science wisdom preaches that mass democracy is impossible without political parties. We agree, because parties – defined as organizations that "seek benefits derived from public office by gaining representation in elections" (Strøm 1990, 574) – fulfill all the key functions of democratic governance. They nominate candidates, coordinate election campaigns, aggregate interests, formulate and implement policy proposals, and manage government power. When scholars first asserted the essential connection between political parties and modern

---

[2] See for example, Poguntke and Webb eds. (2005), p. 21.

democracy, most of the world's democracies were parliamentary. Yet, as we shall see below, by the end of the 20th century most democracies had directly elected presidents. Given this, if parties are truly critical to democracy, then a systematic understanding of how presidencies shape parties is long overdue. Providing a framework for analysis that fills this gap is the reason we wrote this book.

DEMOCRACIES WITH ELECTED PRESIDENTS ARE NOW IN THE MAJORITY

The great increase in the number of democracies in recent decades is by now well known and much celebrated (Huntington 1991; Geddes 1999). What is less well recognized is the dramatic evolution of the types of democracy throughout this period: where parliamentarism once was the rule and presidentialism the exception, forms of presidentialism now dominate. Throughout this book, we consider a country democratic if it scores at least 5 on the Polity IV scale for five or more years (a typical term length) in the post-war era.[3] Before proceeding further, we provide working definitions of each type of democratic regime. We develop these definitions more fully in Chapter 2, but by way of introduction we summarize the basic distinctions as follows: In a "pure" parliamentary democracy the executive branch consists of a prime minister and cabinet who are collectively responsible to parliament through the confidence mechanism, by which a parliamentary majority may remove and replace the executive between elections.

The other "pure" type, presidentialism, features both separate origin and separate survival of the executive branch. Separate origin means citizens separately elect both the executive and legislative branches of government – usually through direct universal suffrage.[4] Separate survival means that an assembly majority cannot remove the head of the executive branch. In other words, the executive's term in office is fixed – as is the legislature's term, unlike in most parliamentary systems.

---

[3] As of 2007; see http://www.systemicpeace.org/polity/polity4.htm.

[4] An electoral college that consists of legislators or other politicians would not qualify as either direct or separate. However, an electoral college that mediates between popular votes and the final selection of a president (i.e., one that cannot propose candidates who did not seek popular votes) is still "separate election" for our purposes. Among the countries covered in this book, only the United States still has an electoral college and thus we frequently use the term "directly elected" to emphasize the absence of a role for legislators or other officials in the determination of a president (with occasional exceptions noted).

The third main type, semi-presidentialism, shares with pure presidentialism the separate election of a president who is head of state, but also shares with parliamentarism a prime minister who is head of government and who is, along with the cabinet, responsible to the assembly majority (Duverger 1980). In Chapter 2 we provide more details about all three of these democratic regime-types and various hybrids; for now, the key point is that semi-presidential systems share two critical characteristics with pure presidential systems: separate election and separate survival of the president.

As we discuss in detail in Chapter 2, the differences among these three regime-types have important implications for political parties. Changes in the distribution of democratic regime-types in the past few decades provide good reason to pursue the connection between democratic regime-type and party politics. Figure 1.1 shows that parliamentarism has lost its dominance among the world's growing number of democracies relative to pure and semi-presidentialism. In 1950 there were 20 democracies, twelve of which were parliamentary. The number of democracies doubled by 1983, and fully half remained parliamentary. Yet since that year the percentage of parliamentary democracies has never exceeded 50%. Democratization in Latin America in the 1980s moved presidentialism into second place among the three main types, but democratization in Eastern Europe in the early 1990s gave semi-presidentialism the lead among democracies with elected presidencies. As the 21st century dawned, semi-presidentialism gained a narrow plurality of all the world's democracies, and by 2005, there were eighty-one democracies by our criteria, of which 29 were semi-presidential, 28 parliamentary, and 24 pure presidential – meaning 65.4% of all democracies had directly elected presidents.

Despite the sustained growth in the absolute and relative number of democracies with elected presidencies, comparativists lack theoretical understanding of how political parties operate in such systems. Scholars have paid considerable attention to the ways in which different democratic regimes impact politics. Major topics in this literature include whether differences between presidentialism, parliamentarism, and semi-presidentialism affect regime survival, policy stability or change, or the possibilities of democratic representation and accountability.[5] Yet scholars of political parties have yet to focus much attention on how, why,

---

[5] See e.g. Cheibub (2006); Haggard and McCubbins (2001); Persson and Tabellini (2002); Samuels and Shugart (2003); Samuels (2007).

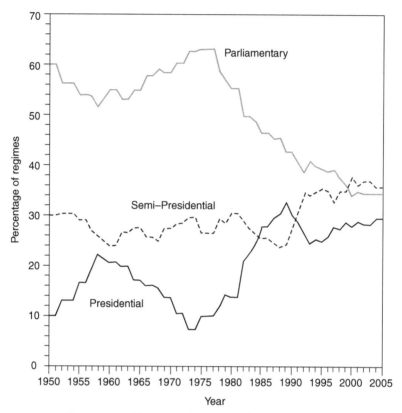

FIGURE I.I. Percentage of Democratic Regimes by Executive–Legislative Structure, 1950–2005.

and to what extent *political parties themselves* differ under different democratic institutional contexts.

This book focuses on the phenomenon we call the "presidentialization" of political parties. We define presidentialization as *the way the separation of powers fundamentally shapes parties' organizational and behavioral characteristics, in ways that are distinct from the organization and behavior of parties in parliamentary systems.* Before explaining this concept in more detail, we briefly review scholarship on comparative political parties, focusing on the ways scholars have both ignored and taken into account variation in executive–legislative structure.

THE COMPARATIVE STUDY OF POLITICAL PARTIES AND
THE MISSING VARIABLE OF REGIME-TYPE

Scholars have been exploring party politics for over a century. Yet most comparative scholarship on parties, party systems, and party-voter linkages has little or even nothing to say about the relationship between democratic regime-type and the parties that operate within those institutions.[6] Some scholarship goes so far as to explicitly dismiss the potential impact of constitutional structure on party politics or party-system development. Even Maurice Duverger (1954) – though remembered as a founder of modern institutionalist research in political science – ignored the separation of powers in his classic book, a fact that attracted prominent criticism at the time (Beer 1953) but has gone largely unexplored since.[7] Duverger even ignored the impact of regime-type on parties in the widely cited article in which he introduced the concept of "semi-presidential" government (Duverger 1980).

The most important reason scholars have not considered the influence of the separation of powers on parties is because comparative research on parties is intellectually rooted in the historical experience of Western Europe, where parliamentarism dominates (Janda 1993). The classics in the literature on parties all implicitly assume that the study of parliamentary parties *is* the study of political parties.[8] Even when such research focuses on party organizations as institutions, by omission it assumes away the possibility that the separation of powers might matter.[9] In any case, the starting point for much research is not *institutional* structure but rather *social* structure, focusing on how cultural and economic cleavages translate into parties and party systems. Research on the emergence and evolution of party "types" reflects this focus. Thus, regardless of the geographic or institutional context,

---

[6] See e.g. Janda (1993); Ware (1996); Stokes (1999); Diamond and Gunther (2001); Gunther, Montero, and Linz (2002); Katz and Crotty (2006); Boix (2007); Kitschelt (2007); Hagopian (2007).

[7] Beer was reviewing the French edition of Duverger's book. McCormick (1966, 4) made essentially the same point about scholars' tendency to erase the presidency from the study of American political parties.

[8] See e.g. Michels [1911] (1962); Weber [1919] (1958); Duverger (1954); Lipset and Rokkan (1967); Sartori (1976); Panebianco (1988); Strøm (1990); Kitschelt (1994).

[9] As Ware (1996, 270–1) notes, "Panebianco (1988, xv) famously excluded American parties from his analysis by asserting that the factors affecting their emergence and development were different, but without discussing what the difference actually was."

political scientists have long referred to "elite," "mass," and "cadre" party types, formulated specifically for the late-19th- and early-20th-century Western European context, and then to "catch-all" and later "cartel" parties, which emerged largely as a function of socioeconomic transformations in that same European context in the second half of the 20th century.[10]

Research on party *systems'* emergence and consolidation has also reflected scholars' concern with the impact of social-structural change – in particular industrialization, urbanization, and technological modernization – on political mobilization and competition, and on the ability of social groups to win parliamentary representation. Lipset and Rokkan (1967), building on concepts from Marx, Weber, Parsons, and others, inferred the development of both parties and party systems from the consequences of political, social, and economic modernization in Western Europe. Subsequent scholarship echoes this emphasis on how sociocultural cleavages impact party emergence and evolution (e.g. Inglehart 1987; Dalton 2008; Kitschelt 1994). Even today, somewhat ironically, research on the alleged "presidentialization" of parties (Poguntke and Webb 2005a) downplays variation in executive-legislative institutions across Europe and focuses instead on the impact of long-term structural and social change.

A second reason scholarship has yet to fully appreciate the potential impact of the separation of powers is due to a tension in the study of political parties in the United States. American parties have been subject to scrutiny since the late 19th century (Bryce 1888) and were the object of the first explicitly comparative study (Ostrogorski [1902] 1964). On the one hand, some scholars of US political parties give the separation of powers pride of place. For example, McCormick (1966; 1979), Burnham (1979), and Epstein (1967) observed long ago that American parties did not emerge from societal cleavages or legislative divisions, as theories developed for Europe suggest.[11] Instead, they noted that party competition in the United States first emerged and consolidated around presidential elections (Epstein 1986, 84; see also Davis 1992; Milkis 1993; Rae 2006). This view highlights the powerful impact separate executive elections have on party emergence, organization, and behavior. According to Philip Klinkner (1994, 2),

---

[10] See e.g. Duverger (1954); LaPalombara and Weiner (1966); Kirchheimer (1966); Katz and Mair (1995); Diamond and Gunther (2001); Wolinetz (2002).
[11] Epstein's (1967) fundamental point was to dispute Duverger's claim that the "mass" party was the modern norm.

in such an environment parties suffer "at best benign neglect and at worst outright hostility" from presidents and presidential candidates, who take it upon themselves to articulate the party's policy positions. Candidates and incumbent presidents can do this because they know that their separate election gives them "their own political constituencies and power bases, apart from those of Congress" (Epstein 1986, 87).

This separate election of the executive and legislative branches *of government* enhances the incentives for politicians in different branches *of the same party* to go their own way. Legislative majorities can defeat presidents without driving them from office – but they cannot force presidents to abandon their proposals. And presidents, for their part, can veto legislative proposals – but they cannot threaten legislators with parliamentary dissolution and new elections. This mutually assured survival in office means that neither "branch" of a single party is bound to support the other as in a parliamentary system. In this way, the constitutional separation of powers provides a recipe for intraparty conflict.

Given these electoral and institutional incentives, scholars such as Steven Skowronek (1997, 49) have concluded that "the institutional imperatives of the presidency lie on the side of independent political action, and that independence drives a wedge between partisanship and presidential conceptions of political responsibility." The same holds true for legislators: the institutional context generates incentives to protect legislative autonomy from executive encroachment. Thus Robin Kolodny suggests that comparing legislators' incentives across democratic regimes is an exercise in comparing apples and oranges, because under the separation of powers legislators' primary interest is serving in the majority in their legislative chamber, *regardless of whether their party's presidential candidate wins or not* (1998, 5).

In short, for many scholars of American politics the presidential and congressional branches of a single political party cannot be considered a single actor. As Richard Neustadt astutely observed, "What the Constitution separates, our political parties do not combine" (1960, 33–34). Given this, many prominent scholars blame the separation of powers for American democracy's shortcomings, suggesting that presidentialism frustrates "responsible" party government, again in contrast to European parliamentary systems. It was for this reason that Woodrow Wilson (1908), in his capacity as political scientist and not as US president, urged amending the US constitution to adopt parliamentarism.

E. E. Schattschneider repeated Wilson's lament decades later (1942), and his view gained an enduring readership in the form of the statement by the American Political Science Association's Committee on Political Parties (1950), which appears on course syllabi to this day. The critique of "irresponsible" parties resurges intermittently in discussions of American politics.[12]

If this view of American parties were consensual, we would simply ask why comparativists have failed to learn anything from the US experience. Yet despite these scholars' eminence and the prominence of their arguments, the separation of powers vanishes entirely from some discussions of American political parties. Indeed, the influential treatment inspired by V. O. Key (1952) and Frank Sorauf (1968) draws attention to the "three faces" of parties – in government, in the electorate, and as organizations – but largely ignores the separation of powers.[13] (See Hershey 2008 for the 13th edition of the undergraduate textbook built around this conceptualization.) The high profile and theoretically sophisticated debate about the status of *legislative* parties in the United States also ignores the separation of powers. For example, Aldrich's *Why Parties?* (1995) and Cox and McCubbins' two books (1993; 2005), among the most-cited books on American parties – and ones which comparativists frequently cite and use for teaching purposes – all treat American parties as if they existed in a unicameral parliamentary system and discuss the separation of powers hardly at all.

Given this intellectual schizophrenia, comparative scholars of political parties rarely seek – much less derive – lessons from the US experience. To our knowledge, only Leon Epstein (1967; 1986) has explicitly and systematically placed American parties *as institutions or organizations* in comparative perspective.[14] Epstein argued that constitutional structure conditions party development and that party leaders must adapt to this institutional context. He focused on the implications of the

---

[12] See e.g. Helms (1949); Long (1951); Cutler (1980); Fiorina (1988); Katz (1987); Janda (1992); Sundquist (1992); Katz and Kolodny (1994).

[13] Poguntke and Webb (2005) essentially replicate, without acknowledgment, the tripartite nature of political parties that Key and Sorauf articulated so long ago.

[14] However, see also Cain, Ferejohn, and Fiorina (1987), which focuses on the difference in party appeals to the electorate between the United States and the UK and which has inspired substantial comparative research (e.g. Carey and Shugart 1995). A few scholars have also begun to respond to Poguntke and Webb's (2005) characterizations (e.g. Heffernan 2005).

fact that presidentialism offers parties two electoral prizes, arguing that the methods for winning each prize may conflict and generate intraparty dilemmas that are specific to separation of powers systems.

For whatever reason, comparative scholars of political parties have largely ignored this insight and have paid scant attention to the experience of the world's oldest presidential democracy. Instead, they have returned again and again to questions originally postulated for the study of European parliamentary parties. Party scholars thus tend to privilege sociological variables and ignore or downplay the impact of the type of executive on party organization and behavior, notwithstanding the enormous differences on this variable between Europe and much of the rest of the world. As a result, attention to the separation of powers remains inconsistent even in regions where it might matter most. For example, in Latin America, the region of the world with the most experience with presidentialism outside the United States, scholars have explored the tension between presidentialism and party *systems* but have yet to consider the relationship between presidentialism and the parties themselves.[15]

Even within Europe, there are now major differences in constitutional structure that merit attention. For example, Portugal's democratic experience since the mid-1970s and the emergence of several democracies in the wake of the collapse of the Soviet empire have increased the number of elected presidencies on a continent where such an institution for decades was a French and Finnish aberration. Although scholars of postcommunist Eastern Europe have addressed the role of presidencies for understanding party-system evolution,[16] this growing body of literature has only rarely treated the organization and behavior of parties themselves as outcomes the separation of powers might shape. As we noted in our discussion of Figure 1.1, democratization in Europe pushed semi-presidentialism into the leading position among the world's democratic regimes. However, comparative research on political parties has yet to systematically investigate the potential importance of the separation of powers, despite the growing importance of elected presidencies for democratic governance around the world.

---

[15] See e.g. Scott (1969); Dix (1989); Scully (1992); Shugart and Carey (1992); Mainwaring (1993); Linz (1994); Mainwaring and Scully (1995); Torcal and Mainwaring (2003); Alcántara Sáez and Freidenberg (2001a; 2001b; 2001c); Mainwaring and Torcal (2006). However, see Coppedge (1994) and Romero (2005).

[16] See e.g. Kitschelt et al. (1999, 55–56); Ordeshook (1995); Filippov, Ordeshook, and Shvetsova (1999); Remington, (2002; 2006); Hale (2005); Meleshevich (2007).

CLUES FROM EXISTING RESEARCH

Perhaps comparative scholars have yet to fully incorporate the separation of powers into the study of parties because there is no need to – that is, because the separation of powers is in fact unimportant and the American case is sui generis. As comparativists, we reject national exceptionalism arguments on principle. In any case, consider the long-standing notion shared by party scholars of methodological orientations as varied as Joseph Schlesinger (1984; 1991), Leon Epstein (1967; 1986), Angelo Panebianco (1988), and Kaare Strøm (1990) that *political opportunity structures shape parties' emergence, evolution, and strategy.* When one combines this idea with Paul Pierson's (2000) notion that political institutions tend to generate incentives that induce the formation of new and complementary institutions, we can hypothesize that *presidential constitutions encourage the development of specifically presidentialized parties* (Samuels 2002). And despite our conclusion about the general direction of comparative research on political parties, scholars have offered important insights that support our hypothesis.[17]

Indeed, we were inspired to write this book because of mounting evidence – some of it indirect – that the separation of powers affects not only the number but also the nature of the parties in a political system. For example, extending the argument that electoral institutions shape party-system fragmentation,[18] scholars have found that presidentialism tends to reduce the number of parties, at least if presidential elections are held using plurality rules (as opposed to a two-round majority system) and held simultaneously with legislative elections.[19] The dependent variable in this literature is the degree of fragmentation in the party system, and as such this research only indirectly explores political parties themselves. After all, the effective number of parties is empirically and theoretically ambiguous as anything more than a summary index of the relative size of the largest parties and the fragmentation of the overall field (Taagepera and Shugart 1989, 259–60; Taagepera 2007). It tells us nothing about parties' ideological commitments, internal organizational structures, or behavioral imperatives. Yet if presidential elections can

---

[17] See e.g. Willey (1998); Geddes (2004); and Kasuya (2004).

[18] See e.g. Rae (1971); Riker (1982); Taagepera and Shugart (1989); Lijphart (1994); Cox (1997); Taagepera (2007).

[19] Lijphart (1994); Jones (1995); Shugart (1995); Cox (1997); Coppedge (2002); Golder (2006); Hicken and Stoll (2007).

reduce the fragmentation of the party system and thus the number of important partisan actors, logically they must also generate incentives for parties to aggregate into relatively larger organizations, with broader appeals. And if that is the case, then the separation of powers not only leads to *fewer* parties but also to parties of a *different nature* – a point that has been made before, if only in passing (e.g. Epstein 1967; Shugart 1988, 10–12; Sartori 1994, 101).

How might parties' "nature" differ under the separation of powers? First, presidentialism tends to *hinder parties' organizational development* (Colton 1995; Mainwaring and Scully 1995; Fish 2000; 2005; Ishiyama and Kennedy 2001). Yet second, the separation of powers also tends to generate *nationalized* parties. In the United States, repeated presidential elections nationalized the party system starting in the 1830s (McCormick 1979). Cox (1997) generalized this hypothesis, suggesting that "pursuit of the presidency" encourages nationalization because "would-be executives have an incentive to orchestrate cross-district coalitions of would-be legislators" (201) in order to build support for their own candidacy. The impact of presidential elections on nationalization may in turn be a function of the powers of the presidency, because as the presidency becomes more powerful, candidates for legislative office across different constituencies face stronger incentives to link with a presidential candidate.[20] The extent of nationalization might also be a function of the concurrence of executive and legislative elections (Shugart 1995; Mainwaring and Jones 2003). When elections are concurrent, they will be "presidentialized," at least to some degree, because attention shifts to the executive race and away from legislative elections.

Perhaps because the separation of powers impedes strong party organizations and forces candidates to appeal to broad, national electoral coalitions, scholars have also recently suggested that *mass partisanship is weaker* in presidential systems (Dalton, McCallister, and Wattenberg 2000; Huber, Kernell, and Leoni 2005). There is no necessary contradiction between "nationalized" and "weak" parties, whether organizationally or in the electorate: a party can be structured to aggregate votes throughout the national territory yet have low levels of membership and interelection commitment of activists. The point remains that the separation of powers imposes electoral incentives that affect party organization

[20] Riker (1987); Cox (1997); Ehrlich (2000); Chhibber and Kollman (2004); Hale (2005); Clark and Wittrock (2005).

in particular ways, shaping parties' number and their nature. Compared to "parliamentarized" parties, broad coalitions with diffuse ideological commitments may be precisely the sorts of characteristics that describe the DNA of "presidentialized" parties.

Evidence from research on legislative politics also bolsters the notion that parties' nature differs under the separation of powers. Most important, given the long-standing allegation that presidentialism and "party government" are incompatible, John Carey (2009) has recently confirmed the long-held supposition (e.g. Janda and Colman 1998) that *legislative parties are less cohesive* on roll-call votes under the separation of powers. Perhaps because of this, presidents are also able to *implement less of their legislative agenda* than prime ministers, controlling for the size of the executive's legislative coalition (Cheibub, Przeworski, and Saiegh 2004).

These findings from comparative research on elections and legislative politics indirectly support our main theoretical point: *intraparty politics differs substantially under separation of powers*, whether under single-party majority or multiparty government, because the separation of powers affects not only relations between branches of government but also between the executive and legislative branches of a single political party. We aim to move beyond this indirect evidence and provide both a theoretical framework as well as direct empirical support for understanding how and why the strategic dilemmas that party politicians face differ as a function of variation in the institutional context – and thus support the notion that the constitutional separation of executive and legislative powers fundamentally affects parties themselves.

"PRESIDENTIALIZED" VERSUS "PARLIAMENTARIZED" PARTIES

The central question in this book is, To what extent does the presence of constitutionally separate executive authority "presidentialize" political parties? We are interested in explaining how the constitutional structure of executive-legislative relations affects party organization and behavior. In any democratic regime, situations frequently arise in which the goals of the executive and legislative elements of the same party come into conflict (Laver 1999). Such conflict is a function of incentive incompatibility in the electoral and governing arenas between a party's executive and legislative elements, and of a party's relative ability to hold its own executive to account. Our core argument, which we elaborate in Chapter 2, suggests that both incentive incompatibility and the extent of intraparty accountability vary more *across* than *within* democratic regime-types, due to the constitutional separation of origin and survival.

Separate *origin* means that politicians from the same party can face different and even conflicting incentives in the electoral arena. The separation of powers implies that parties face distinct dilemmas of executive candidate selection and campaign strategy under different constitutional regimes, because the characteristics that facilitate winning a direct presidential campaign differ from the characteristics of a good legislative leader. In contrast, the fused origin of the executive from within a party's legislative contingent under parliamentarism necessarily implies that the executive is a direct agent of the party, thereby minimizing incentive incompatibility between branches of the same party.

Likewise, the distinction between fused and separate *survival* of executive authority has important ramifications for internal party politics, particularly in the governing arena. Separate survival means that a party or legislative majority cannot remove a sitting president, absent an extraordinary constitutional crisis. Numerous scholars have considered how fixed terms influence *interbranch* relations (e.g. Mainwaring 1993; Linz 1994; Cheibub 2007), but scholars have largely ignored the implications of fixed terms for *intraparty* relations. The checks and balances built into the separation of powers are supposed to constrain politicians from abusing their powers by setting "ambition against ambition." This may be true of *inter*party politics, where a president faces an opposition majority in the legislature. However, separate survival means that presidents have little to fear from their own colleagues – a fact that results in qualitatively different barriers to intraparty cohesion and alters the intraparty balance of power in favor of directly elected executives in terms of cabinet and bureaucratic appointments and policy proposals. Our theoretical argument, which we elaborate in Chapter 2, suggests that Madison's theory of incentive-based accountability in separate powers systems contains an unrealized tension: while checks and balances might hold *across branches*, they do not hold *within parties*.

In short, the separation of powers changes how parties engage in all of their key tasks: nominating, electing, and governing. Given this, our argument suggests that *to the extent that capture of a separately elected presidency is important for control over the distribution of the spoils of office and/or the policy process, party behavior and organization will tend to mimic constitutional structure, giving rise to "presidentialized" parties.* Such parties will exhibit greater incentive incompatibility between their executive and legislative "branches," and less intraparty leadership accountability. This means, not surprisingly, that "presidentialization" is minimized under parliamentarism. And as we discuss in Chapter 2, party presidentialization is likely not only under the "pure" regime-type, but also under semi-presidential systems. This is because in these regimes, pursuit of the presidency also tends to become parties' overriding organizational and behavioral imperative.

What is the distinction between "presidentialized" and "parliamentarized" parties? These are ideal types. We start with the assumption that parties are teams of politicians who (1) cooperate in elections under a common label to recruit candidates that they seek to elect to office and (2) coordinate the process of governing and policymaking between elections. A parliamentarized party fuses its executive and legislative functions, by selecting its leader and holding him or her accountable through an internal deselection process. This means that intraparty accountability over a leader in parliamentary parties mimics parliamentary accountability over a prime minister, which occurs through the confidence procedure. In the language of principal-agent theory, which we employ extensively in subsequent chapters, the party is the principal and the national chief executive is the agent, accountable to that principal.

Given the differences in democratic constitutional regimes, a presidentialized party is therefore one that delegates far greater discretion to the leader that it selects, in terms of how to seek and win the national chief executive position and how to govern. Discretion in the electoral and governing arenas follows from the separation of origin of executive authority in a separate election process – the hallmark of presidential forms of government. And upon election, the separation of survival also affords the party leader additional discretion in selecting cabinet and other executive personnel and in policy initiation and management – because after the election, the party that nominated the presidential candidate can no longer hold that person immediately accountable.

We do not claim that these ideal-type parties follow rigidly from regime-type. Some parties in parliamentary systems may exhibit presidentialized features – a dynamic that has attracted attention in recent years (Poguntke and Webb 2005a). That is, we agree that under some conditions, parties in parliamentary systems will choose leaders with personal charisma and suprapartisan appeal, and that these leaders may then use their personal popularity to distance themselves from party constraints. If this leader remains popular while the party loses popularity, he or she will retain more freedom to direct the executive branch than a leader who enjoys less personal support. This seems to have been the case, for example, of the highly personalized tenure of Japanese prime minister Junichiro Koizumi (Krauss and Nyblade 2005), who famously vowed to "destroy" the Liberal Democratic Party (LDP) upon assuming its leadership in April 2001 and whose tenure was marked by repeated battles with party insiders.[21] Other examples of parties closely identified with their leader exist, such as the dependence of Forza Italia on Silvio Berlusconi.

Nonetheless, the theoretical logic and evidence we present in this book suggest that one should not exaggerate this sort of party presidentialization in parliamentary systems. Party presidentialization is at odds with the core logic of parliamentarism, and it is likely the exception rather than the rule or a trend across all systems, as Poguntke and Webb imply. This follows from the inescapable fact that under parliamentarism voters cannot vote *against* a party while voting *for* its leader – and it is impossible for a politician, no matter how personally popular, to ascend to the top executive post and remain there without ongoing support from the legislative majority.

Our argument also allows for parties in presidential systems to exhibit "parliamentarized" characteristics. For example, some parties in presidential systems impose rules seeking to limit the discretion and independence of their leaders who become president. Some parties also seek to maximize control over the presidential candidates by tightly controlling candidate selection and maintaining highly partisan rather than personalized presidential campaigns, and some attempt to rein in their candidates who win the presidency by insisting that they regularly consult with top party leaders while in office. Such mechanisms appear to have existed, for example, in Venezuela's Acción Democrática (Democratic Action, AD) in the 1960s and 1970s (Coppedge 1994; Crisp 2000), suggesting that this party was relatively parliamentarized.

---

[21] For an overview, see Mazami Ito, "Koizumi leaves LDP factions in tatters," *Japan Times Online*, June 26, 2006. http://search.japantimes.co.jp/print/nn20060626f1. html (accessed December 30, 2008).

However, like presidentialization in parliamentary systems, parliamentarization in presidential systems is usually ephemeral, again because of the inescapable logic of such regimes: a politician can ascend to and remain in the top executive post *even if* his or her party performs poorly in legislative elections or declines to support the president's policies once in office, and can remain in office *despite* the desires of his or her party. And even in allegedly parliamentarized parties such as AD, presidents can and do repudiate their parties – as evidenced by the battles between Venezuelan President Carlos Andrés Pérez and his party in the early 1990s (Stokes 2001; Corrales 2002) (see Chapters 4 and 8).

The separation of powers creates the conditions for the emergence of presidentialized parties. We do not claim that our argument supersedes or supplants the importance of social, economic, or cultural forces that drive party formation, evolution, and behavior. We only suggest that the separation of powers provides a necessary addition to the comparative study of parties. There may be many reasons that parties differ across countries, but analysis of these differences should begin with the difference in constitutional design.

OUTLINE OF THE BOOK

Chapter 2 presents our theoretical framework, based on principles derived from the *Federalist Papers* and framed in the language of collective action and principal-agent theory. The principles underlying these theories teach us that political institutions shape individual politicians' incentives. Membership in a political party confers collective benefits to all individual members. Yet maintaining the reputation of the party poses collective action problems, which politicians resolve through delegation and other mechanisms to enforce coordinated action. All parties face these dilemmas, regardless of the institutional context. However, we claim that variation in the relationship between the executive and legislative branches of government impacts parties' organizational and behavioral imperatives, because such variation complicates resolution of these delegation and collective action problems.

Chapters 3 and 4 elaborate on the challenges of delegation between principals (parties) and agents (their leaders) across constitutional formats. Inherent in all principal-agent relationships are potential conflicts of interest between contracting parties: leaders can employ delegated resources or authority to further their own interests, which may conflict with the principals' collective interests. This problem is exacerbated to the extent that the principal cannot overcome the problems of *adverse selection*, the notion that people with undesirable characteristics are more likely to seek and obtain certain positions, and *moral hazard*, the notion that maintaining the letter and the spirit of a contract is difficult once it is signed.

In Chapter 3 we argue that parties face greater adverse selection problems under the separation of powers because the best potential agent from the party's point of view may be incapable of winning a direct presidential election, while the candidate most likely to win a direct national election may be less likely to serve as a faithful party agent. Using a global database of national executives, we show that presidents, although not the stereotypical "outsiders" many have assumed, do have less *partisan* experience than prime ministers, on average. Such experience is the primary signal that parties-as-principals seek when hiring agents to reduce the danger of adverse selection. We also show that prime ministers in semi-presidential systems are less likely to be party insiders than those in pure parliamentary systems, and present evidence suggesting that presidents in such systems may be able to *reverse* the principal-agent relationship, making the prime minister an agent of the president rather than the party.

Chapter 4 turns to the question of moral hazard. Careful selection of agents – the power to *hire* – may mitigate adverse selection problems. However, to contain the problem of moral hazard, the power to *fire* an agent is more important. Principals who cannot fire their agents cannot control their agents at all, while principals who can easily fire their agents will find those agents highly responsive. Deselection mechanisms are thus critical tools for enforcing intraparty accountability. We show that in parliamentary systems, parties regularly remove their own leaders as prime minister between elections. In contrast, in semi-presidential systems *presidents* frequently remove the prime minister – even when the constitution does not clearly afford them such a right – again suggesting a reversal of the principal-agent relationship. And in both pure and semi-presidential systems, parties almost never initiate proceedings to remove their own sitting president. This inability to "fire" a leader under the separation of powers creates serious intraparty moral hazard problems.

Chapters 5 through 7 move into the electoral and governing arenas, to explore the nature and potential extent of incentive incompatibility between parties' executive and legislative branches. Separate origin means that members of the executive and legislative branches of a single party can be motivated by different political incentives. This can occur because different branches of the same party can derive electoral support from different bases – either for geographic or policy reasons, or both. To the extent that this "electoral separation of purpose" can be observed, it suggests that the president and his or her party are not a single (if highly imperfect) electoral agent of the legislative party's voters, as we assume under parliamentarism. The greater the electoral separation of purpose, the greater the intraparty conflict.

Chapter 5 thus examines the degree of overlap between constituency-level election returns for presidential candidates and their parties in 53 presidential and semi-presidential systems between 1946 and 2007. Despite the unifying effect of "presidential coattails," this survey shows that electoral separation of purpose is both normal and often extensive – and that purely intraparty factors, rather than cross-national and largely unchanging institutional factors, account for much of the variation over time in the relationship between a party's executive and legislative vote totals.

Chapters 6 and 7 turn to qualitative case studies of the impact of separation of origin and survival on incentive incompatibility between parties' executive and legislative branches, in both the electoral and governing arenas. To test the hypothesis that parties organize and behave differently under different constitutional designs, we would ideally compare how parties fared in countries that have shifted from one "pure type" democratic regime to the other. Only two democracies have undertaken institutional changes close to this ideal: France in 1958 and Israel in 1992 and again in 2001. In Chapter 6 we therefore explore the impact of constitutional change on party organization and behavior in these two quasi-experimental cases, explaining how a shift toward an autonomous executive presidentialized the parties in those two countries.

Following the exploration of parties in two hybrid democratic regimes in Chapter 6, Chapter 7 turns to two pure presidential systems, exploring the sources of separation of purpose in the conservative Mexican National Action Party (PAN) and the leftist Brazilian Workers' Party (PT). This contrast between two ideologically distinct parties shows that controlling for a country's institutional context, intraparty battles from election to election over presidential nominations, campaign strategies, and policy platforms affects the extent of incentive incompatibility between a party and its candidate for executive office.

Finally, in Chapter 8 we consider the implications of our theoretical framework for the study of political representation and governance. This chapter offers the first global test of the hypothesis that "responsible party government" is less likely under the separation of powers. Our framework suggests that responsible parties are a function of the degree of incentive incompatibility between the executive and his or her party. Building on research by Susan Stokes (2001), we explore the incidence of "policy-switching" under different democratic regimes, comparing incumbent executives' policy preferences before and after every democratic election in the world between 1978 and 2002. We confirm that "mandate representation" is less likely when executive elections are competitive and when executives do not control a legislative majority – but find that these conditions hold *only* in pure and semi-presidential systems, implying that the factors Stokes (2001) identified as causally important in Latin America cannot be generalized. In short, our findings do suggest that "responsible" party government is less likely under separate-powers systems.

Our argument and findings carry wide-ranging implications for understanding comparative politics. Most broadly, this book suggests that many of the alleged differences in governance between democratic regimes arise as a function of the ways in which regime-type interacts with parties – not with the *number* of parties, as much previous research has claimed, but with their *nature* – the ways parties organize and behave strategically.[22] Systems with presidentialized parties will see different patterns of party organization and behavior because the separation of origin and survival of the executive and legislative branches of government affects party strategy about whom to nominate for both executive and legislative office, about whether to form electoral and/or governing coalitions, about the content of political campaigns, and about the content of and degree of support for executive policy proposals. To the extent that a separately elected presidency exerts influence over any of the things that parties seek – votes, office, or policy – then the separation of powers does not merely split one branch from the other; it splits parties *internally*, posing particular dilemmas for members of the same party who occupy or seek to occupy different branches of government.

---

[22] It also suggests that the separation of powers is conceptually prior to any analysis of "veto players" (Tsebelis 2002), because the separation of powers not only affects the number of veto players, but also their nature.

2

Political Parties in the Neo-Madisonian
Theoretical Framework

Our theoretical approach for thinking about how variation in the structure of executive-legislative relations affects political parties is rooted in the *Federalist Papers*. The Federalists advocated on behalf of the proposed US Constitution, and offered a theory of how institutions shape politicians' behavior. Contemporary rational choice and institutionalist political science provide a modern synthesis of key concepts from the Federalists, and result in what we call the *neo-Madisonian* theoretical perspective (Carroll and Shugart 2007).

This framework starts from the Federalists' core hypothesis: the extent to which government ensures liberty or gives way to tyranny is directly related to the manner in which the institutions of government structure the representation of societal interests and channel political ambition. In *Federalist #10*, James Madison articulated the core problem all democracies face: representative government necessarily entails delegation of power from voters to a small number of politicians, yet politicians can turn this delegated power against voters. Madison feared that tyranny would result if politicians' selfish motivations, which he took for granted, were not held in check. To preserve liberty, Madison favored the establishment of an "extensive republic" in which a diversity of interests would gain representation and be pitted against one another, thereby preventing a single faction from dominating the entire political system.

What is often forgotten is that Madison's original constitutional proposal for achieving this goal bore scant resemblance to the theory of government that is most widely associated with him today, separation of powers and institutional checks and balances. He only articulated this latter conception of a republican constitution – in which the executive originates and survives independently of the legislature – in *Federalist* #51, which informed the final draft of the US Constitution and which forms the basis of what we now call pure presidentialism.

Madison's initial draft constitution, known as the "Virginia Plan," made the House of Representatives the dominant institution and contained no provision for separate origin of the executive. As Kernell (2003) has noted, the theory of *factional* checks and balances Madison articulated in *Federalist* #10 logically required that the House – the body most capable of representing the diverse factions of the extensive republic – dominate government institutions. Only later did Madison develop the conception of *institutional* checks and balances, adding a differently constituted Senate and a powerful, independent executive, both of which were designed to impede the House's political dominance. This model emerged later in the Constitutional Convention partly because smaller states adamantly opposed the principle that state population alone should determine legislative representation.

Madison's two theoretical constructs – the dominant assembly of *Federalist* #10 and the Virginia Plan versus the institutional checks and balances of *Federalist* #51 and the Constitution – echo the distinction between pure parliamentarism and pure presidentialism. Yet despite this clear difference, Madison's two models share a key feature that is highly relevant for our purposes: both assume that nothing akin to the modern national political party would emerge. In *Federalist* #10 Madison assumed that each member of the assembly would represent his constituency's "local and particular" interests. Legislative majorities would therefore inspire little fear of tyranny – or so Madison believed – because the degree of internal diversity in the legislature would make oppression of minorities impossible, and because no single faction (whether a minority or majority) would be able to dominate long enough to entrench itself at the expense of other minorities. Madison never considered the possibility that a single majority party could control the legislature for an entire term.

Of course, parties have emerged in democracies of every kind, and these parties do compete to control legislative majorities – either on their own or in coalition with other parties. In particular, when the executive originates from within the legislative majority, competition for control of the executive is a direct function of parties' competition in legislative elections. Madison's Virginia Plan called for the legislature to select the executive – a concept that has emerged as the core feature of parliamentarism. Had the Constitutional Convention adopted the Virginia Plan the United States might never have incubated the separation-of-powers model that eventually became modern presidential democracy. Instead, American government might have developed a parliamentary system like those that eventually emerged in the UK, Canada, Australia, and elsewhere in the British Commonwealth. And had this occurred, political parties might have evolved in the United States as they have in many parliamentary systems, embodying the "responsible party government" model. Such parties tend to be highly institutionalized, organized nationally, and focused on national policy concerns, in contrast to Madison's expectation that politicians would organize ad hoc coalitions along merely local and particular interests.

This thought experiment – and the argument of this book – suggests that parties have developed in distinct ways in parliamentary and non-parliamentary democracies. As noted in Chapter 1, comparativists have paid scant attention to the potential impact of the separation of powers on party emergence, evolution, and behavior, even though Americanists have long lamented the absence of "responsible" parties in the United States. The very notion of a responsible party implies that party organizations dominate all aspects of the democratic process – candidate selection, campaigning and elections, formation of government, and policymaking. The "responsible" party is an ideal-type, one that no party ever completely embodies. Nonetheless, the notion of a responsible party erects a normative standard by which scholars judge the quality of collective representation and accountability under democracy. Thus, throughout this book we will ask how the separation of powers systematically changes the ways in which parties engage in each of those key aspects of the democratic process.

At one level, the differences in parties' roles across democratic regimes are obvious: in separate powers systems, legislative parties do not select or deselect the executive and have far less influence over the national policy agenda. Moreover, national electoral competition focuses on the popular election of the executive rather than on legislative elections. This may offer greater space for Madison's local and particular interests in legislative races (Shugart 1999; Samuels and Shugart 2003), but Madison's effort to counteract ambition with ambition as fully realized in the US Constitution also severs the connection between legislative electoral competition and the selection and deselection of the national executive – a connection that describes the very essence of parliamentarism. Although Madison did not intend it, this separation carries enormous implications for the political parties that have emerged in the system that evolved from his constitutional design.

In the remainder of this chapter, we develop a theoretical framework useful for understanding and explaining how differences between democratic regime types affect political parties. In the next section we describe differences in the chain of delegation from voters to elected officials across the world's democracies. We then describe how this focus on collective action problems and principal-agent relationships as key elements of democratic politics applies fruitfully to the study of political parties across these regimes. Put most simply, we argue that variation in institutional context shapes how – and even whether – party politicians resolve these delegation and collective action problems. Given this theoretical framework, we then describe these partisan dilemmas concretely, in three core activities that all parties undertake: (1) leadership selection and deselection; (2) electoral competition; and (3) governing.

DEMOCRATIC REGIMES AND THE NEO-MADISONIAN FRAMEWORK

Our theoretical framework begins with Madison's insight that institutions channel political ambition. Modern theories of collective action and delegation are contemporary emendations of Madison's intuitions about how institutional context shapes politicians' behavior, and such theories provide the foundation for our argument. All organizations must coordinate collective action in order to prevent free riding and to generate incentives for individual members to work on the group's behalf (Olson 1965). The tension between individual and collective interests can be addressed by delegating authority from principals ("rank and file") to agents ("leaders"). Delegation permeates all organizations, including political parties. Yet inherent in all relationships between principals and agents are potential conflicts of interest. Just as Madison feared politicians could use delegated power to oppress citizens, leaders of any organization can use the resources or authority they have been delegated to further their own private interests, which may be at odds with their principal's collective, organizational interests.

The idea that institutional design is central to understanding accountability relationships between citizens and elected officials is central to the ideas Madison articulated in *Federalist #51* to support his theory of checks and balances. For this reason, Kiewiet and McCubbins (1991) refer to the tension between the potential benefits and costs of delegation as "Madison's Dilemma." Our theoretical framework focuses on how differences in democratic regimes shape the ways parties attempt to resolve Madison's Dilemma – how they both delegate authority to a leader while simultaneously attempting to hold that leader accountable.

We employ a heuristic device to understand how institutional context shapes the ways party politicians address Madison's Dilemma. Think of representative democracy as a "chain of delegation" between principals and agents. Democracy requires that the first link in the chain connect voters to elected officials, and that those officials be accountable back to their principals, who can reelect them, or not.[1] Once in office, elected officials themselves become principals, because they delegate the responsibility to execute or implement policy to government bureaucrats – although this latter stage is beyond the scope of our analysis. We shall first describe the different chains of delegation that characterize democratic regimes. Once we have done this, we can explain why party organization and behavior will differ as a function of such variations in institutional context. In the remainder of this section we therefore compare and contrast the chains of democratic delegation in the two pure regime-types – presidentialism and parliamentarism – and then explore hybrid regimes such as semi-presidentialism.

The Chain of Delegation in "Pure" Types: Parliamentarism and Presidentialism

The key difference in the chain of delegation between "pure" types of democracy – parliamentarism and presidentialism – derives from the relationship between voters and the executive branch. In parliamentary democracy the voters elect a legislature. The members of the legislature, in turn, elect the executive.[2] Executive authority, vested in a cabinet headed by a prime minister, derives from the results of parliamentary elections, and not directly from the voice of the people. Moreover, the prime minister and the cabinet are agents of the parliamentary majority, to whom they are accountable: that is, the executive serves at the pleasure of the legislative majority.

---

[1] Persson and Tabellini's (2002, 239–44) discussion of accountability ignores parties – and thus ignores the fact that parties act distinctly within particular institutional environments. This is an unreasonable assumption given the centrality of parties to democratic politics and to any theory of accountability. Even so, their theoretical results implicitly require the executive and the median legislator to come from distinct parties.

[2] For present purposes it does not matter if the legislature is unicameral or bicameral.

Executive origin

		Fused (from assembly majority)	Separate (popularly elected)
Executive survival	Fused (subject to assembly confidence)	Parliamentary	Elected prime-ministerial
	Separate (fixed term)	Assembly-independent	Presidential

FIGURE 2.1. Two Dimensions of Executive Relationship to the Legislative Assembly.

The contrast with pure presidentialism is straightforward: in these latter systems the voters directly elect the executive, and the cabinet is an agent of the president, not the legislature. Moreover, the president is not an agent of the legislative majority; both the president and the legislature sit for fixed terms.

This distinction between the pure parliamentary and presidential types thus focuses our attention on two core dimensions of authority relations, as depicted in Figure 2.1: how executive authority *originates*, and how executive authority *survives*. Both origin and survival are defined with reference to the legislature, which means we can say that executive origin and survival are either *fused* or *separated*. As seen in the shaded cells of Figure 2.1, presidential and parliamentary systems are pure types because they have the same relationship to the legislature on both aspects of executive authority. That is, origin and survival are both either fused (parliamentary) or separated (presidential).

The Chain of Delegation in Hybrid Democracies with Single Executives

Executive authority can be constituted differently, in one of several hybrid constitutional formats. Two breeds of hybrid constitutional formats exist: those with a single executive, and those with a dual executive – and each breed has subtypes. Figure 2.1 includes the single-executive hybrid regimes in the clear cells; we shall focus on these relatively rare and poorly understood regimes first, and then consider the better known dual-executive hybrids, commonly known as semi-presidential systems.

As Figure 2.1 implies, both breeds of single-executive hybrids can be compared against the single-executive pure-type regimes. The differences between the pure and hybrid single-executive regimes derive from the way each system combines the dimensions of executive origin and survival. Thus in the lower left cell we have *assembly-independent* regimes (Shugart and Carey 1992), the best-known example of which is Switzerland.[3] In such systems, origin is fused but survival is separate. That is, the executive emerges from the legislature but is not accountable to the parliamentary majority for the duration of the term. Because there are so few real-world assembly-independent regimes apart from Switzerland (in which an informal "grand coalition" has governed for most of the last 60 years, neutralizing the potential effects that separate survival might have on the parties), they will not concern us further in this book.

The other single-executive hybrid, in the upper right cell of Figure 2.1, combines the dimensions of executive origin and survival in the opposite way from an assembly-independent regime. In these systems, which we call *elected prime-ministerial* regimes, origin is separate but survival is fused. That is, the prime minister is popularly elected like a president, yet he or she (along with the cabinet) remains accountable to and can be dismissed by the assembly majority. This sort of regime existed briefly in Israel, and it has been proposed in several other countries (Maddens and Fiers 2004), in particular the Netherlands (Lijphart 1984, 77; Andeweg 1997). Although this hybrid is also uncommon, we shall pay it considerable attention in this book. This is both because separate origin is critical to shaping party organization and behavior and because the Israeli experiment with this format provides the basis for a "natural experiment" discussed in Chapter 6, where we explore the partisan consequences of changes in the origin and survival of executive authority in Israel and France – two of the rare historical cases of constitutional reform away from pure parliamentarism and toward either a single- or a dual-executive hybrid.

[3] Sporadically, there have been other examples. Bolivia is sometimes classified as an assembly-independent regime because the Bolivian Congress frequently selects as president the head of one of the top two (formerly three) lists running in elections – unless one list obtains a majority of votes (as happened in 2005). Bolivia and Switzerland are frequently misclassified, and inconsistently so. For instance, both countries are "semi-presidential" to Gerring and Thacker (2004) but "presidential" to Cheibub (2002). Cheibub's classification is particularly odd given the absence of any process in Switzerland for directly electing the executive. As for Bolivia, because parties select presidential candidates who run in a potentially decisive direct national election, we lose little by classifying the country as presidential. Bolivia is most definitely *not* semi-presidential, since it has no prime minister accountable to the assembly majority (as does Peru, for example).

The Chain of Delegation in Dual-Executive Hybrids:
Semi-Presidentialism

Thus far we have described the chain of delegation in all single-executive forms of democracy: presidentialism and parliamentarism, which are quite common, and the rare assembly-independent and elected prime-ministerial regimes. A more common hybrid form of democracy involves a dual executive: semi-presidentialism (Blondel 1984). According to Duverger's (1980) influential definition, these systems have the following features:

1. A popularly elected president
2. Considerable constitutional authority vested in the president
3. A prime minister and a cabinet, subject to the confidence of the assembly majority

The key to semi-presidentialism is the juxtaposition of a president who enjoys separate origin with a prime minister accountable to the assembly majority. Yet as several scholars have pointed out (e.g. Elgie 1999, 13), Duverger's definition is vague. For example, what should we regard as "considerable" authority? More fundamentally, while the definition is clear about the origin of the president (through direct election, and thus separate from the assembly) and the survival of the prime minister and the cabinet (subject to parliamentary confidence), it is vague about (1) the *survival* of the president; (2) the *origin* of the prime minister and the cabinet; and (3) the sources of prime-ministerial and cabinet *survival*.

In terms of the president's survival, Duverger and others assume that the president's term is fixed, and thus that presidents in semi-presidential regimes enjoy separation of survival as well as origin. This is relatively unproblematic.

However, Duverger's silence on prime-ministerial and cabinet origin raises several issues, because presidents in many semi-presidential systems possess either formal, constitutional authority or (as we show in later chapters) informal, partisan authority to appoint both the prime minister and/or the cabinet. To the extent that this is the case, then prime ministers actually owe their *origin* to the results of the direct presidential election, even if – following Duverger – they owe their *survival* in office to the confidence of the assembly majority. As we explain in greater detail below, presidents' appointment powers enhance the importance to parties of the direct presidential election relative to parliamentary elections, infusing semi-presidential regimes (and the parties in those regimes) with a substantial presidential tilt.

Finally, in terms of prime ministers' survival in office, Duverger's definition missed the fact that many semi-presidential regimes afford presidents not only appointment but also either formal or informal dismissal power – of the prime minister, the cabinet, and in some cases the entire assembly. If presidents' "considerable authority" includes dismissal, then – contra the third element in Duverger's definition – the survival of the prime minister does not depend exclusively on the confidence of the assembly majority. In some cases losing such confidence would be a *sufficient* condition for removing the prime minister and cabinet,[4] but it would not be a *necessary* condition – because the prime minister and/or cabinet could also be dismissed if it lost the confidence of *the president*.

Given the vagueness of the role of the presidency in early definitions of semi-presidentialism, Shugart and Carey (1992) introduced the concepts of *premier-presidential* and *president-parliamentary* subtypes of semi-presidentialism. A simple way to differentiate these two subtypes is that the former have relatively "weaker" presidents. The key distinction in the chain of democratic delegation between these two regime subtypes derives from the way that the constitution inserts the president into the survival of the prime minister and cabinet:

- In premier-presidential regimes, the prime minister and cabinet are formally accountable *exclusively* to the assembly majority – and thus *not* to the president.
- In president-parliamentary regimes, the prime minister and cabinet are *dually* accountable to the president and the assembly majority.

As we discuss in Chapter 4, presidents possess only informal, partisan authority to fire the prime minister in premier-presidential systems. In contrast, in president-parliamentary systems presidents possess formal, constitutional authority to dismiss the premier and/or the cabinet. Still,

---

[4] To qualify as semi-presidential, the cabinet must be *collectively* accountable to the assembly *majority*. Scholars' typologies have not always respected this key condition. For example, Argentina since 1995 has had the post of the Cabinet Coordinator, subject to removal by the congress. However, the rest of the cabinet is not subject to confidence, so this system is presidential. Similarly, a few countries have a prime minister and cabinet that may be removed by an extraordinary majority (e.g. two-thirds), including Madagascar after 1997 and Taiwan before 1997. We do not classify these countries as semi-presidential during those time periods due to the supermajority requirement.

this means that both subtypes provide opportunities for presidentialization of the parties and the entire political system.

These subtypes clarify constitutional differences about prime ministers' *survival* in office. However, they retain Duverger's silence about
prime ministers' *origin*. Duverger's silence on this subject may stem from
his assumption, which he shared with other "founding fathers" of semi-
presidentialism, that separately elected presidents would be "above" the
assembly parties and remain distant from them. Likewise, Shugart and
Carey were unconcerned about the relationship between presidents and
parties in semi-presidential regimes. However, the extent to which presidents remain above or distant from *their own political parties* is an open
empirical question – and is the main focus of this book. We return to this
question in Chapter 3.

In this section we outlined the different chains of delegation
between voters and elected officials in the world's democracies. The
core institutional differences across democracies derive from whether
there is a single or dual executive and whether executive origin and
survival are fused or separate. Table 2.1 lists the democracies that
qualify under each regime-type. A country enters our sample when it
scores 5 or greater on the Polity IV scale of democracy (Marshall and
Jaggers 2008) for five or more years during the period 1945–2004.[5]
For each country we indicate the years the country was democratic
and the years the country qualified as having a given constitutional
format. Some countries changed format during this time period, and
thus have more than one entry. For these cases a number follows the
country name, indicating the chronological order of the country's different regimes.[6]

Much research has explored the consequences of differences between
presidential, parliamentary, and semi-presidential regimes, but few
scholars have explored how political parties operate within these different systems. We now turn our attention to this question of how constitutional format shapes the key tasks that all parties undertake.

---

[5] A country leaves the database if its democracy rating falls below five, but it can
reenter later if it again fulfills the basic conditions. For countries that qualified, we
gathered data up through 2007 (we conducted this research in 2008), for reasons
we discuss in Chapter 3 having to do with presidents' and prime ministers' post-
executive careers.

[6] Given our interest in different *types* of democracy, we do not divide into separate cases
countries where democracy of the same executive form has been interrupted by an
authoritarian interlude.

TABLE 2.1. *Countries Included, by Democratic Regime-Type*

Parliamentary	Premier-Presidential	President-Parliamentary	Presidential
Albania (1997–2007)	Armenia 2 (2005–07)	Armenia 1 (1998–2005)	Argentina (1983–2007)
Australia (1946–2007)	Bulgaria (1990–2007)	Austria (1946–2007)	Benin (1991–2007)
Bangladesh (1991–2007)	Croatia (2000–07)	Georgia 2 (2004–07)	Bolivia (1982–2007)
Belgium (1946–2007)	Finland (1945–2007)	Madagascar 2 (1993–97)	Brazil (1946–64, 1985–2007)
Botswana (1966–2007)	France 2 (1962–2007)	Mozambique (1994–2007)	Chile (1955–73, 1989–2007)
Canada (1946–2007)	Ireland (1952–2007)	Namibia (1990–2007)	Colombia (1957–2007)
Czech Republic (1993–2007)	Lithuania (1991–2007)	Peru (1980–92, 2000–07)	Costa Rica (1949–2007)
Denmark (1946–2007)	Macedonia (1991–2007)	Portugal 1 (1978–80)	Cyprus (1975–2007)
Estonia (1991–2007)	Madagascar 1 (1991–93)	Russia (1992–2007)	Dominican Republic (1978–2007)
France 1 (1946–62)	Mali (1992–2007)	Senegal (2000–07)	Ecuador (1979–2007)
Gambia 1 (1966–82)	Moldova 1 (1991–2001)	Sri Lanka 2 (1978–2007)	El Salvador (1984–2007)
Germany (1949–2007)	Mongolia (1992–2007)	Taiwan 2 (1997–2007)	Gambia 2 (1982–93)
Greece (1975–2007)	Poland (1989–2007)	Ukraine 1 (1992–2005)	Georgia 1 (1995–2004)
Hungary (1990–2007)	Portugal 2 (1980–2007)		Ghana (2001–07)
India (1950–2007)	Romania (1990–2007)		Guatemala (1996–2007)
Israel 1 (1948–96) and 3 (2001–07)[*]	Slovak Republic 2 (1998–2007)		Honduras (1982–2007)
Italy (1948–2007)	Slovenia (1991–2007)		Indonesia (2002–07)
Jamaica (1959–2007)	Ukraine 2 (2005–07)		Korea (1988–2007)

Parliamentary	Premier-Presidential	President-Parliamentary	Presidential
Japan (1952–2007)			Madagascar 3 (1997–2007)
Latvia (1991–2007)			Malawi (1994–2007)
Malaysia (1957–69)			Mexico (1997–2007)
Mauritius (1968–2007)			Nicaragua (1990–2007)
Moldova 2 (2001–07)			Panama (1989–2007)
Nepal (1990–2002)			Paraguay (1992–2007)
Netherlands (1945–2007)			Philippines (1950–69, 1987–2007)
New Zealand (1945–2007)			Taiwan 1 (1992–97)
Norway (1945–2007)			United States (1946–2007)
Pakistan (1988–99)			Uruguay (1952–71, 1985–2007)
Papua New Guinea (1975–2007)			Venezuela (1958–2007)
Slovak Republic 1 (1993–98)			Zambia (1991–2007)
Solomon Islands (1978–2000)			
Somalia (1960–69)			
South Africa (1990–2007)			
Spain (1978–2007)			
Sri Lanka 1 (1948–78)			
Sweden (1945–2007)			
Thailand (1992–2006)			

(continued)

TABLE 2.1 *(continued)*

Parliamentary	Premier-Presidential	President-Parliamentary	Presidential
Trinidad & Tobago (1962–2007)			
Turkey (1983–2007)			
UK (1946–2007)			

Note: The table lists the years for which we gathered political career data, as used in Chapters 3 and 4. Please see Chapter 3 for a discussion of the Austrian case.
* Israel 2 (1996–2001) was an elected prime-ministerial system.

PARTIES IN THE NEO-MADISONIAN FRAMEWORK

In the previous section we described how different democratic constitutional formats structure the relationship between voters and elected officials. The main point of this book is to explain how and why these differences influence party politics. Yet before doing so, we must lay out our assumptions about what parties are and what they do. Scholars working in what we call the neo-Madisonian theoretical framework assume that ambitious politicians have strong incentives to join forces in a political party, so as to solve the collective dilemmas they encounter in their quest to formulate public policies, win (re)election, and secure institutional posts.

Such collective dilemmas can emerge within the context of legislative politics, as in Cox and McCubbins (1993 or 2005) or Aldrich (1995), or they can emerge external to the legislature, as in Cox (1987). The first view draws attention to the social-choice problem of majority rule instability: a party-free legislature would be chaotic, meaning that individual legislators would be unable to get anything done. Legislators thus have strong incentives to band together into durable legislative coalitions. The second view suggests that politicians have strong electoral incentives to join forces to benefit from economies of scale, because as individuals they lack resources to adequately mobilize voters on their own behalf. Banding together thus not only helps induce policy stability on the floor of the legislature but also helps individuals develop and maintain a collective public image in the electoral arena. In this view, politicians form parties because they come to regard a collective good, their party's public reputation or "brand name," as critical to their individual success.

Whether for internal or external reasons, political parties provide ambitious politicians with collective benefits that they would not obtain in the absence of party affiliation. Yet the provision of collective benefits confronts parties with a particular problem. Collective benefits – whether gains from trade within the legislature or the collective reputation that accrues from working as a group – are public goods. The value of a party's brand name is a function of its platform and its success or failure in government; voters form an impression of a party based on the policies it favors and opposes, and on its ability to effectively enact policies it favors or impede policies it opposes. Thus when the party wins or loses, all members win or lose to some varying degree, regardless of whether they personally contributed to victory or defeat. Because the party's reputation is a public good, the party's effort to maintain and enhance that reputation confronts the problem of free riding. That is, in every party, individual politicians face the dilemma of whether to pursue their individual interests or to devote resources to maintaining the party's collective reputation.

According to scholars who adopt this approach, the key to understanding party politics generally lies with understanding how parties address this tension between individual and collective incentives.[7] Political parties seek to solve this problem by creating institutional mechanisms that commit individual politicians to act in the party's collective interest. Scholars here turn to the literature on delegation and principal-agent theory, derived from the theory of the firm (e.g. Alchian and Demsetz 1972). In firms and parties, "principals" (party rank and file) delegate formal and informal power to central "agents" (party leaders) to solve collective action problems and reduce transaction costs.

Delegation tasks party leaders with protecting the party reputation and thus maintaining the value of the party label. To do so, leaders can impose discipline or other sanctions on individual politicians whose behavior threatens the party's collective image, and they can reward politicians whose behavior helps the group. Aldrich (1995) suggests that the most important tools party leaders possess include control over candidate selection and the distribution of resources such as campaign finance; Cox

---

[7] In addition to the references already cited, see for example Döring (2001), Rohde (1991), or Strøm (1990).

and McCubbins (1993) add to this list leaders' control over allocation of legislative resources and over the party's legislative activity.

Successful delegation generates incentives for leaders to concentrate on solving the party's collective dilemmas. Yet delegation creates potential problems. Everyone – both leaders and followers – gains from delegation, but principals must beware the danger of *agency losses* due to agents' opportunistic behavior (Kiewiet and McCubbins 1991). In any process of delegation, conflicts of interest between principal and agent inevitably arise unless both parties have perfectly aligned interests and are acting under perfect information – conditions unlikely ever to hold. Given this, rank-and-file party members in any political system have powerful incentives to balance empowering a leader with attempting to minimize that leader's opportunistic behavior.

Our neo-Madisonian framework for studying political parties begins with the assumption that all parties face the challenge of engineering mechanisms that foster collective action. Parties pursue multiple and often conflicting goals – including votes, office, and policy – and the pursuit of those goals necessarily entails trade-offs (Strøm 1990). To resolve internal tensions and address the challenges of collective action in the electoral and governing arenas, parties delegate authority to a single person *who will stand as the party's candidate for national executive office.* Whether or not a presidential or prime-ministerial candidate is also de jure the head of the party organization, party organizations entrust prospective presidents and prime ministers with the parties' collective reputation – meaning that party members entrust leaders with their individual and collective political fates.[8] As Strøm suggested, a country's institutional context powerfully shapes how parties resolve such dilemmas. The next section follows up on this intuition and connects variation in democratic regime-type to variation in the ways in which parties resolve their collective dilemmas.

SITUATING PARTIES WITHIN THE SEPARATION OF POWERS

The notion that political parties serve primarily to solve politicians' problems of collective action and delegation has proven enormously influential in political science. Yet such theories have never considered

---

[8] Not all elected officials are party members, but our theory concentrates on parties and their members. Countries in which independent candidates win substantial seat shares (e.g. Russia and Ukraine before the move to fully party-list systems) are relatively uncommon.

how the separation of powers impacts the way politicians resolve these problems. This is especially puzzling given the intellectual tradition that fostered the development of these approaches in the first place. That is, the institutionalist literature in political science holds that political parties are endogenous creations of ambitious politicians and suggests that institutional context shapes the way politicians resolve their collective dilemmas. To the extent that scholars take this approach seriously, then any comparative theory of political parties must account for the way in which government institutions shape how party politicians resolve collective action and delegation problems.

Stated most generally, our main theoretical claim is the following: *to the extent that the constitutional structure separates executive and legislative origin and/or survival, parties will tend to be presidentialized.* As we explained in Chapter 1, presidentialization implies that parties delegate considerable discretion to their leaders-as-executives to shape their electoral and governing strategies, and that parties lose the ability to hold their agents to accounts. Parties can delegate more or less willingly; the question we consider is the extent to which a country's executive–legislative structure imposes higher or lower hurdles on parties' ability to hold their leaders to account.

Different democratic regimes enact different democratic chains of delegation. The simplest chain of delegation, which runs from voters to legislators to the executive, is a shorthand description of a parliamentary regime – and it is also a shorthand description of the relationships between voters, parties, and party leaders in a parliamentary regime. Moreover, due to the fusion of survival, parliamentarism imposes a relationship of symbiotic mutual dependence between branches of government – which also means that a relationship of symbiotic mutual dependence exists within parliamentarized parties. Given this, obstacles to holding party leaders-as-executives to account are minimized in parliamentary systems. Similarly, parliamentarism means that for any political party, a single electoral goal drives the resolution of any and all collective action problems: winning legislative seats. All collective decisions regarding delegation to a leader focus on what the party needs to accomplish in the legislature and in legislative elections to maintain its brand name and its ability to access executive positions.[9]

---

[9] Parties need not maximize seats; they may only seek to obtain enough seats to keep control of a particular ministry.

If, however, a direct election fully or partly constitutes executive authority independently of the will of the assembly majority, then the chain of delegation grows more complex. Our approach emphasizes the fact – one that party scholars have largely overlooked – that *separating the executive and legislative elements of government into two independent branches also breaks parties into two separate branches*, one in the legislature and one in the executive.

When executives enjoy separate origin and survival, parties' collective action and delegation problems differ in fundamental ways. First, in contrast to parliamentarism, separation of origin means that party politicians no longer have a single goal in mind – winning legislative seats – when considering how to resolve their collective action problems. Instead, parties have two potentially incompatible goals: winning a direct executive election *and* winning legislative seats. These goals are potentially incompatible because (as we detail below and in subsequent chapters) the qualities of potential prime-ministerial and presidential candidates do not necessarily overlap and because the separate executive electoral process means that presidential candidates can campaign on and win election for different reasons – or even be elected by a different set of voters – than their legislative parties. Such intrapartisan divergence of electoral incentives is impossible under parliamentarism.

The separation of survival also has powerful implications for intraparty politics. The separation of survival means that whether or not presidents and their parties were elected for similar reasons and by similar vote bases, once in office presidents can take policy stands that differ from their party's, without fear of dismissal. In such situations, branches of the same party confront each other from positions of mutual independence and must therefore negotiate. However, relative to prime ministers under parliamentarism, presidents negotiate from a position of relative advantage because a party cannot fire its leader-as-president.

In short, the separation of powers makes resolving coordination and delegation problems more complicated and confronts parties with particular organizational dilemmas. Separation of executive and legislative authority means that political parties cannot guarantee control over the things that they value – including access to cabinet and subcabinet executive-branch positions and influence over policy – by competing exclusively in legislative elections. Winning control of the executive branch directly offers the only guaranteed path to office and policy payoffs. Given this, to the extent that pursuit of a directly elected national executive improves parties' chances to access and/or control any of the things that they seek, then organizing to win executive elections rather than legislative elections will shape party organization and behavior.

PRESIDENT-PARTY RELATIONSHIPS UNDER SEMI-PRESIDENTIALISM

The ideas presented in the previous section provide grounds to believe that parties in pure presidential systems will differ fundamentally from parties in pure parliamentary systems. Yet what about hybrid formats? Here we consider in greater depth the ways in which the dual executive of semi-presidentialism impacts political parties. Semi-presidential systems merit scrutiny because their complexity leaves room for ambiguity as to whether they should be classified as sitting midway on a hypothetical continuum between the two pure types or whether the separate presidency implies parties will tend toward presidentialization, even in premier-presidential systems with "weaker" presidents. In what follows we provide theoretical reasons to expect party presidentialization across *all* semi-presidential systems.

Semi-Presidentialism: Designed to Change the Parties

The idea that semi-presidentialism impacts political parties by altering their relationship to government formation is hardly new, even if party scholars have tended to overlook it. Semi-presidentialism originates with the 1919 Finnish and German constitutions. The hybrid nature of the Weimar constitution, for example, owes much to the advice of several eminent social scientists.[10] Max Weber ([1917] 1978) suggested that the German constitution should empower an agent of the entire electorate in order to check and balance parties' legislative influence; influential jurist Hugo Preuss justified the hybrid regime by stating that such a constitution would provide the president and parliament with "autonomous sources of legitimacy" (Stirk 2002, 514).

These notions represent a 20th-century continental European echo of Madison's call for ambition to counteract ambition. Yet different from the context of the *Federalist Papers*, these "founding fathers" of semi-presidentialism wrote in an era in which mass parties already existed. That is, unlike Madison, these scholars articulated and advocated their model of government *precisely under the assumption that an elected*

---

[10] See e.g. Mommsen (1984), Myerson (1999), Stirk (2002), or Shugart (2005).

presidency would alter parties' role, relative to their role under pure parliamentarism. Weber ([1917] 1978, 1452–53), for example, mistrusted
parties' capacity to govern and assumed that a "plebiscitary" presidential election would force parties "to submit more or less unconditionally
to leaders who held the confidence of the masses."

The collapse of Weimar democracy with Hitler's rise to power could
have completely discredited this model of government. Yet the appeal of
a system that combines a popularly elected, powerful president with a
cabinet responsible to parliament continues to resonate powerfully. We
owe the spread of semi-presidentialism around the world not to Weimar's
disastrous experience but to France's rather more successful reinvention
of the regime-type a few decades later. In his Bayeux Manifesto of 1946,
Charles de Gaulle called for a "chief of state, placed above the parties"
(Lijphart 1992, 140–41). France's 1958 constitution elected the president
indirectly, through an electoral college that included the legislature, and
thus can be seen as a reform of the 4th Republic's pure parliamentary
model (1946–58) rather than as an entirely new political system. Yet
with his 1962 plebiscite de Gaulle gained approval for direct presidential elections, thereby recreating a key element of the Weimar constitution and establishing what has become the most-emulated democratic
regime-type in the world.

These two cases exemplify each semi-presidential subtype: Weimar
Germany was president-parliamentary, while France V is premier-
presidential. Of course, in contrast to Weimar's experience, 5th Republic
France has grown stable – even though the irony that de Gaulle's system recreated a key element of the Weimar constitution has gone mostly
unnoticed (but see Skach 2005). Party scholars have also largely failed to
appreciate that advocates of semi-presidentialism offered fundamentally
similar theoretical justifications for their proposed reforms in both countries: to create a system that would simultaneously change the parties
and change the relationship between parties and government. In both
countries, constitutional engineers understood that altering the chain of
delegation between voters and their agents in government would change
the organizational and behavioral natures of the parties that mediate
between voters and government.

We now explore how both subtypes "presidentialize" political parties. Presidentialization is embedded in the very constitutional design of
the president-parliamentary subtype. However, we also argue that parties are likely to be presidentialized under premier-presidentialism, due
to the importance parties place on winning the presidency.

Presidentialized Parties in President-Parliamentary Regimes

In a typical president-parliamentary system, the presidentialization of parties presents no puzzle. By definition, presidents in these systems have constitutional authority to both appoint and dismiss the premier – a power they do not possess in premier-presidential systems.[11] Given this, presidents are both the dominant executive official as well as the dominant actor in the entire system. Even when the assembly majority is sharply opposed to the president, the constant threat that the president will dismiss the premier gives presidents powerful political leverage (Shugart and Carey 1992, 121–26). This constitutional format makes this hybrid regime closely resemble pure presidentialism in terms of the president's authority over the cabinet. In some cases, presidents in president-parliamentary systems possess even *greater* authority than their counterparts in pure presidential systems, because under certain conditions they can dissolve the assembly.[12] Presidents' considerably formal authority in president-parliamentary systems suggests that the parties in such systems should tend to be highly presidentialized.

Presidentialized Parties in Premier-Presidential Regimes

In contrast to the situation in president-parliamentary regimes, the presidentialization of parties in premier-presidential systems poses a larger intellectual puzzle because in such systems the cabinet is formally accountable only to the assembly majority. In theory, this constitutional structure should weaken presidential influence in legislative politics, thereby limiting the presidentialization of the parties. Nonetheless, we argue that presidents' formal and informal influence works to presidentialize the parties in such systems.

In terms of formal institutional influence, Shugart (2005) noted that presidents in most premier-presidential systems do have the right to *propose* a prime minister, subject to an investiture vote, and some

---

[11] In all cases, the entire cabinet is required to resign if the prime minister resigns or is dismissed.

[12] While dissolution power also exists in some premier-presidential systems, the leverage it offers is tempered by the weaker leverage presidents in those systems enjoy over the cabinet – especially if, as happened in France in 1997, voters fail to give the president a legislative majority. That is, in president-parliamentary systems, dissolution clearly augments presidential powers, whereas in premier-presidential systems, dissolution balances the president's more restrictive executive authority. See Shugart (2005) for further discussion.

have the power to *appoint* the prime minister unilaterally. Only a few premier-presidential constitutions completely deny the president a formal role in initiating a premier's appointment.[13] To the extent that the president has formal authority to select the premier, then pursuit of the presidency will influence party organization. And as we show in Chapter 6, parties that focus on electoral pursuit of even relatively weak presidencies gain advantages over other parties. In this way, even relatively minimal formal presidential powers can induce party presidentialization.

We recognize that if presidents' formal authority to appoint the prime minister were their only source of political influence, party presidentialization would be quite limited. This is because after appointment, presidents have no formal authority to *dismiss* the prime minister or the cabinet in these regimes. Unless presidents possess some other source of political influence, parties might downplay the presidency and concentrate on capturing the assembly majority and, through it, control of the cabinet. However, presidents typically enjoy an additional source of political power beyond their formal constitutional authority: their informal partisan influence.

The importance of presidents' informal partisan authority in premier-presidential systems focuses our attention away from premiers' origin and toward their survival. As noted, in premier-presidential systems presidents have no *formal* authority to dismiss a prime minister or the cabinet. Thus, whether they like the incumbent PM or not, even a newly elected president in a premier-presidential system has no formal authority to dismiss the sitting premier.[14] These rules should, in principle, limit presidents' power over parliamentary parties and should give premier-

---

[13] These are Bulgaria, Croatia, Madagascar (formerly), and Ukraine (Shugart 2005, Table 2).

[14] After examining the constitutional provisions of all semi-presidential systems (see Table 2.2) regarding the conditions under which a government must resign, we determined that among the premier-presidential systems, only Armenia and Lithuania explicitly require a cabinet to resign upon the inauguration of a newly elected president, giving the latter the power to form a new government. However, most premier-presidential constitutions do contain a clause requiring the prime minister and cabinet to resign upon the swearing-in of a newly elected assembly. (Finland and France are prominent cases with no such provision.) This requirement is in any case implicit in the more fundamental requirement that the cabinet maintain parliamentary confidence. Notably, few president-parliamentary constitutions explicitly require cabinets to resign when a new president is inaugurated, yet presidents' unrestricted authority to dismiss a prime minister and the cabinet in such systems means that stipulating such authority is unnecessary.

parliamentary systems – and the parties that operate within them – a strong parliamentary "lean."[15] Yet as we demonstrate in subsequent chapters, parties in premier-presidential systems are remarkably presidentialized. For example, observers of French politics understand that the president is the dominant political player both within his party and within the entire system, even though the presidency is comparatively weak in terms of formal, constitutional authority. A strictly institutional interpretation of France's constitution, compared to other hybrid formats, would render this fact puzzling.

Presidents acquire informal political influence in premier-presidential systems if (1) the president and the assembly majority come from the same side of an ideological divide and (2) the president is the de facto head of his or her party. The first condition holds about 80% of the time (discussed later in the chapter). As for the second condition, presidents in premier-presidential systems are frequently the de facto leaders of their party even if they are not their party's formal leader. When presidents are de facto party leaders, the importance of parliamentary confidence to the chain of delegation – the third element of Duverger's definition of semi-presidentialism – vanishes, because the premier becomes an agent of the president. If presidents possess this sort of intraparty authority, then parties will become presidentialized regardless of the president's constitutional powers. This means that premier-presidential constitutions do not provide necessary conditions for presidentialized parties, only sufficient conditions. In such regimes the extent of presidential influence is a function of the way parties resolve their own internal problems of delegation and coordination, and not simply of the constitutional rules.

Of course, in a premier-presidential system there is no guarantee that elections and intralegislative bargaining will produce a legislative majority compatible with the president. When the president and the assembly majority come from opposing sides of an ideological divide the formal constitutional structure of authority should reign, and deprive the president of influence over the cabinet. This expectation derives from the fact that under premier-presidentialism the cabinet depends on the exclusive confidence of the (opposing) majority, which in turn eliminates the intrapartisan sources of presidential influence over legislative politics. Given this, the implications of cohabitation merit further exploration.

---

[15] Except, perhaps, after an assembly election or the breakup of an assembly majority coalition, in which case the president has influence over the nomination of the next prime minister and cabinet.

The Impact of Cohabitation

The definition of semi-presidentialism requires that the premier and cabinet be responsible to the assembly majority. However, the separate election of president and assembly makes possible an "executive divided against itself" (Pierce 2005) when an election results in an assembly majority that is opposed to the president, or vice-versa. Such situations are called "cohabitation," and are defined specifically as cases in which

1. The president and prime minister are from opposing parties
2. The president's party is not represented in the cabinet

Both conditions must hold for cohabitation to result. This restricts cases of cohabitation to those in which the president and prime minister come from *opposing* parties, not merely *different* parties. Thus the first condition rules out not only those cases in which the president and prime minister might be fierce rivals within the same party, but also cases in which the president and prime minister come from distinct yet allied parties – even if the alliance is an uneasy one. We also insist that the definition of cohabitation include the second criterion: there must be partisan opposition between the president and the entire cabinet, and not merely the head of the cabinet.

Consider the following two examples. First, given the dual executive, two parties might jointly pursue executive power, forming a coalition in which one of them would get the presidency and the other the premiership. In such cases it is likely that the two parties would also divide up cabinet positions. This is a *governing alliance*, not cohabitation. Second, two opposing parties (or blocs) might forge a "grand coalition" cabinet, again splitting the presidency and the premiership. This example is functionally equivalent to the first because in both cases parties agree to divide up the top executive posts. It is also not cohabitation because in both cases the presence of the president's party indicates a "division of the spoils." Our definition confines cohabitation to clear cases of partisan division between the presidency and the cabinet. Cohabitation cannot result merely from conflict between two officials; it must come from unresolved conflict between two officials from two opposing parties.

With this definition in mind, to the extent that our neo-Madisonian framework is useful, then we should observe differences in the frequency of cohabitation across the two subtypes. Cohabitation should occur from time to time under premier-presidentialism. In such systems, the success

TABLE 2.2. *Rate of Cohabitation by Semi-Presidential Subtypes*

	Duration of Cohabitation	Total Presidential Tenure	Percent of Cohabitation
Premier-Presidential	69 years, 9.7 months	315 years, 7.3 months	22.1
President-Parliamentary	2 years, 4 months	163 years, 6.2 months	1.4
Semi-Presidential Total	72 years, 1.6 months	479 years, 1.7 months	15.1

Note: See Table 2.A.1 for a complete list of cases of cohabitation.

of all parties in legislative elections depends in part on the electoral calendar (concurrent or not) and on the incumbent president's popularity at the time of the legislative election. Because the president can determine the premier only through informal, intrapartisan authority, elections that result in an opposition majority should result in cohabitation. To be sure, parties will pursue the presidency in premier-presidential regimes, and party presidentialization will result. Still, cohabitation should occur on a regular, if relatively infrequent, basis. In contrast, we expect cohabitation to almost never occur under president-parliamentarism. In such systems, by definition presidents have the authority to dismiss the cabinet. This gives presidents far greater influence over legislative parties. Indeed, parties in president-parliamentary systems should be more highly presidentialized than in the other subtype because they have such powerful incentives to focus on pursuit of the presidency.

The relative frequency of cohabitation across the two subtypes of semi-presidentialism offers a useful first test of our neo-Madisonian framework. We determined which prime ministers in our database led cohabitation cabinets. The dataset encompasses 25 countries with semi-presidential systems and includes 66 presidents and 209 prime ministers. (Our analysis included changes in cabinet composition.) Table 2.2 summarizes our findings, which strongly support our theoretical expectations. Across all semi-presidential systems, cohabitation occurred about 15% of the time. However, sharp differences by subtype emerge: cohabitation occurred just over 20% of the time under premier-presidentialism, but less than 1.5% of the time under president-parliamentarism. Indeed, we found only one case of cohabitation in this latter subtype – a brief period in Sri Lanka. The appendix to this chapter contains a complete list of all cases of cohabitation, by president and prime minister.

Our neo-Madisonian framework suggests that cohabitation should limit party presidentialization in semi-presidential systems. We shall explore this hypothesis in more detail in later chapters. At this point, we simply note that cohabitation is relatively infrequent to begin with and almost unknown in president-parliamentary systems. Consequently, given that presidents in both president-parliamentary and premier-presidential regimes enjoy substantial formal and informal political influence over the premier, the cabinet, and the assembly, party presidentialization should be substantial in all semi-presidential systems. After all, winning the presidency is critical for parties' pursuit of their policy and office goals, even where presidents are relatively weak.

In sum, parties face similar dilemmas of collective action and delegation under both pure *and* semi-presidential regimes. We now describe more precisely the sorts of dilemmas that presidentialized parties confront.

PARTY DILEMMAS UNDER THE SEPARATION OF POWERS

Our theoretical framework suggests that party structure should mimic constitutional structure, and that party behavior should follow from the incentives that constitutional structure generates. To the extent that a separately elected presidency influences parties' ability to obtain what they want – votes, office, and/or policy influence – party behavior and organization will become "presidentialized." At this point we derive observable implications from this theoretical framework. We focus on three core activities parties undertake in all democracies: leadership selection and deselection, campaigning, and governing.

Leadership Selection and Deselection

Variation in the structure of principal-agent relationships across democracies suggests that we should see differences in the process of party leadership selection and deselection across democratic regimes. In the neo-Madisonian perspective, once politicians have resolved to join forces, the key problem they confront is one of delegation to a leader. Successful principal-agent contracts generate positive externalities for all party members, while unsuccessful delegation can damage the party's fortunes.

We know a good deal about principal-agent relationships within legislative parties themselves (e.g. Aldrich 1995; Cox and McCubbins 2005), and about relationships between *legislatures and executives* (e.g. Shugart and Carey 1992; Strøm 2003), but we know little about how different democratic regimes shape the way parties structure the internal agency relationship with their leaders.[16] This is a critical question: after all, a party leader who also has won direct election as president or selection as prime minister will act in the party's collective interest only if he or she is truly an agent of the party. How does variation in the chain of delegation shape the way parties structure their leadership selection processes as well as their ability to hold leaders to account through the possibility of *de*-selection?

Our framework suggests the following hypotheses: to the extent that parties regard the presidency as a valuable prize, the separation of powers exacerbates Madison's Dilemma by (1) enhancing agent opportunism and (2) complicating principals' ability to rein in their agents. Agency losses are potentially greater in systems with separate executive origin and survival because both adverse selection and moral hazard problems are worse, and because the proposed organizational solutions party leaders could enact to hold their agents more accountable are more difficult, entail greater costs, or are simply impossible to achieve.

Adverse selection problems result from the likelihood that agents possess hidden information. In any institutional context, individuals who seek leadership positions have incentives to overstate their experience and qualifications or misrepresent their true preferences, particularly if their true preferences clash with those of the organization. Upon appointment or election to the leadership post, agents who have engaged in misrepresentation can make Madison's worst nightmare come true by pursuing their own goals or their own vision of what the party's "true" goals ought to be.

Systems with direct presidential elections exacerbate the problem of adverse selection. A party seeking to place its candidate as a nation's chief executive must select a leader who will be competitive in a national election. However, the pool of candidates who can appeal to voters directly and the pool of candidates who can implement the collective

---

[16] Comparative treatments include Davis (1992), Kenig (2006), Freidenberg and Sánchez López (2001), and Siavelis and Morgenstern (2008a). A special issue of the *European Journal of Political Research* in 1993 also explored this question. Several single-country studies exist; see for example Punnett (1992), Courtney (1995), or Stark (1996). However, none of these studies consider differences across democratic regimes.

"will" of the party organization might only weakly overlap. Parties may have to settle for suboptimal agents at the candidate-selection stage: the best potential agents from the party's point of view may be incapable of winning a presidential election, while candidates who can win such an election may not share the party's goals fully.

As for moral hazard, this problem arises from the possibility of hidden action. After a principal and agent sign a contract, the principal cannot observe every action the agent takes and cannot know whether all those actions conform precisely to the contract's terms. For political parties-as-principals, the danger is that leaders-as-agents might use their authority to advance their own personal goals rather than work toward their party's collective goals. This problem is minimized under parliamentarism because parties can "hire" a leader knowing that they can also "fire" that leader if he or she acts contrary to the organization's interests.

However, parties in pure presidential systems know that they cannot dismiss their agent if he or she exploits Madison's Dilemma. And in semi-presidential systems, the dual executive structure implies that parties have one agent they can freely fire and another that they cannot. Given this, to the extent that presidents influence prime-ministerial and/or cabinet selection and deselection, moral hazard can pose a considerable danger to parties' interests. In fact, semi-presidential systems that function as "parliamentary systems with an elected head of state" appear to be the exception rather than the norm, and our theoretical framework explains why: national electoral competition for the presidency provides an alternative path to power for ambitious politicians aside from legislative elections, and competition in direct presidential elections tends to shape legislative electoral competition in ways not possible in parliamentary systems (Tavits 2008). Once parties organize to pursue a presidency, presidentialization has begun; parties then face the dilemma of potentially empowering an agent whose preferences may imperfectly align with their own, but whom they are unable to dismiss.

Parties delegate to their leaders the tasks of promoting the group's collective benefit, protecting the party's reputation, and coordinating intra- and interparty negotiations over policy, appointments, and election campaigns. Their very survival depends on the ability to find and cultivate leaders who will internalize the party's collective dilemmas. Yet that task is fraught with potential agency problems, encapsulated in Madison's Dilemma. The trick is to induce those who seek to occupy leadership positions to work only toward the party's collective interests and to refrain from abusing delegated authority. As we show in detail in later chapters, this task is trickier for presidentialized parties.

Dilemmas of Electoral Competition

Principal-agent theory suggests that when Madison's Dilemma becomes too severe, delegation should not happen at all. Yet in a very real sense, parties in presidential and semi-presidential systems do not have the option of not delegating, at least if they want to remain politically relevant over the long term. Choosing not to delegate would mean not participating in presidential elections. To the extent that presidents influence cabinet composition and/or the legislative agenda, or possess a veto, parties that decide to compete only in legislative elections are imposing limits on their ability to access "office" and "policy" benefits, compared to parties that stand a good chance of entering a government coalition in a parliamentary system. Such parties relegate themselves to secondary positions in the political system and adopt self-imposed limits on their ability to achieve collective goals. Quite simply, operating in a separation of powers system as a strictly "parliamentary" party that only runs candidates for legislative seats is not likely to be a politically profitable strategy. Given this, parties rarely choose this path. (See Chapter 6.)

The need to win a popular presidential election focuses attention on parties' subjective evaluations of their viability in the presidential race, on which all their subsequent electoral strategy will be based, rather than on strategy for winning parliamentary seats. Parties become presidentialized when the elected presidency is valuable because the types of parties that are likely to form and prosper are precisely those that can field competitive candidates in national executive elections. To accomplish collective goals under parliamentarism, parties organize to capture a share of legislative seats sufficient to control the executive, or to bargain with other parties over shared control of the executive. Yet under the separation of powers, winning the executive branch, not legislative seats, becomes parties' driving goal. Any party that seeks to be a major player on the national scene must organize to compete in a national executive electoral contest or else be content to bargain with the winner of that contest from a subordinate position in the legislature.

The opportunity – and desire – to capture the executive branch directly provides parties with different organizational and behavioral imperatives, and confronts parties with situations they never encounter in a parliamentary system. As noted, parties face the challenge – unknown in parliamentary systems – of *whom* to nominate as a presidential candidate. This choice is fraught with potential difficulties for parties' collective action and delegation problems, because the need to organize and compete effectively in both executive and legislative races means that parties face the problem – also unknown in parliamentary systems – of having to *coordinate* electoral strategy across races for two institutions. The requirements for running a successful campaign will not necessarily overlap in both races, meaning that parties in separation of powers systems confront potentially conflicting incentives from two kinds of elections. This challenge is further complicated by the fact that the constituency of the median party legislator may differ substantially from the constituency necessary to win a direct presidential election.

The separation of powers thus forces parties to make hard choices in the electoral arena about candidate nomination, resource allocation (e.g. campaign finance and party personnel), and electoral coalitions that parliamentary parties do not face. The impact of coattail effects and the electoral cycle (the possibility of nonconcurrent executive and legislative elections) – both of which by definition do not exist in parliamentary systems – exacerbate these organizational, financial, informational, and strategic challenges. To the extent that a presidency is electorally valuable, direct executive elections – whether held concurrently or not – can strongly influence legislative elections.

Our argument suggests that as they attempt to resolve problems of candidate choice and campaign content, parties operating under separate executive origin will adopt a vote-seeking strategy as opposed to an office- or policy-seeking electoral strategy, relative to parties operating under parliamentarism (Samuels 2002). The separation of powers thus affects how parties articulate the content of their platforms: policy concerns will be sacrificed, and party organizations will be marginalized in setting the party's agenda and establishing the party's public image. This also implies that party campaign organizations will evolve differently under the separation of powers: parties will develop separate nuclei devoted to electing the chief executive in presidential systems, but central party organizations are more likely to retain control over the campaign in parliamentary systems.

Within separate powers systems, the degree of a party's behavioral and organizational presidentialization depends on both relatively constant factors and on the changing political context: the more-or-less objective value of the presidency for pursuing the party's broad goals, and the party's subjective evaluation of its chances of winning the presidency.

These evaluations affect how parties organize to win both the executive and legislative elections. Parties that believe they can compete for the presidency have relatively stronger incentives to invest their resources heavily in that race and to adopt a broad, vote-seeking strategy.

Governing Dilemmas

Just as they do in the electoral arena, governing parties confront distinct dilemmas in different institutional contexts. For parties in government, the separation of origin and survival generates distinct organizational and behavioral patterns unknown in parliamentary systems. In terms of the separation of origin, the potential electoral divergence between a party's executive and legislative branches can spill over into the policy-making process. Successful presidential candidates typically campaign on a platform that appeals to a wide swath of the electorate. Once in office, the president cannot simply revert to his party's potentially narrower core constituency, nor can he or she simply work to deliver policy that will help the party win legislative elections.

The separation of origin creates an agent of the citizenry specifically responsible for the "health of the nation," predisposed to care about the provision of public goods. Presidents know that history will judge them based on their ability to fulfill this role. However, legislators from a president's party may be judged on entirely different bases. For example, their electoral success may depend on the provision of goods to narrower constituencies, whether geographical or not. The degree to which one sees cooperation or conflict between the executive and the legislative branches of a party in a presidential system is partly a function of the degree to which the policies and goods of their respective constituencies overlap. Such overlap is maximized in pure parliamentary systems, but preference incompatibility varies considerably across presidential systems (Samuels and Shugart 2003).

The dynamics of intraparty negotiations over new policy directions will also differ across democratic regimes. In a parliamentary system, because survival is mutually dependent, the party and the prime minister have greater incentives to support each other. In presidential systems, the separation of survival makes intraparty negotiation over any policy differences more difficult. A party may choose to accept presidential proposals, or it may choose to ignore or even resist them. After all, there is no confidence vote to whip the party into line. Depending on the president's autonomous powers, the separation of survival may also let presidents achieve many of their policy goals *without* their party, a situation that never occurs in any parliamentary system. Moreover, presidential popularity and coattail effects mean that a party may find that its fate depends on what the president does independently of what the party wants him or her to do, another situation that is impossible under parliamentarism.

Another important difference for parties across political systems derives from the extent to which presidents autonomously control the policy and office benefits of holding power. Presidents' independent authority matters for intraparty politics no matter the number of parties in the system, but it is particularly relevant in multiparty situations. This is because if a president serves as cabinet *formateur*, party decisions to enter and leave a coalition will differ substantially across democratic regimes. Under parliamentarism the prime minister may have to concede de facto control over certain ministries to his or her cabinet partners (Laver and Shepsle 1996). In contrast, the separation of survival means that parties considering joining a cabinet have greater cause to fear an inability to transform participation in the government into real policy influence (Carroll 2007), and implies that cabinet coalitions will be more costly for the chief executive to maintain (Altman 2001).

The impact of the separation of powers on cabinet dynamics, and consequently on party organization and behavior, ranges beyond entry and exit decisions. Amorim Neto (2006b) notes that in pure parliamentarism, the *size* of the coalition (the number of legislative seats its controls) and the *number* of coalition partners are the critical variables in terms of governance outcomes such as cabinet stability and legislative success. Yet under pure presidentialism these two variables are relatively less important compared to the *proportion of partisan ministers* (versus the proportion of presidential cronies or of nonpartisan technocrats) and the *extent to which portfolios are proportionally distributed* across coalition partners. That is, in parliamentary systems, cabinets are nearly always fully partisan and cabinet portfolios are almost always distributed proportionally to the share of the coalition's seats each party controls. Yet both partisanship and proportionality decline as the government system moves away from the pure parliamentary model.[17] Differences in cabinet politics

---

[17] The clear importance of cabinet partisanship and proportionality under pure presidentialism calls into question cross-regime research that highlights the impact of the *number* and relative *size* of parties in legislative coalitions (e.g. Cheibub and Limongi 2002; Cheibub, Przeworski, and Saiegh 2004). The importance of cabinet partisanship and proportionality also suggest that a "veto players" framework (Tsebelis 2002) cannot adequately explain governance in separation of power systems.

illustrate another way in which the dynamics of "party government" diverge as one moves from a pure parliamentary to a pure presidential system of government. Autonomous *or* shared control over the cabinet, combined with presidents' separate survival, gives presidents a distinct advantage over prime ministers and works against parties' interests.

Finally, because presidents' electoral incentives may diverge from their party's, and because of the separation of survival, presidents are more likely to betray their party's principles than prime ministers. Theories of political representation and traditional notions of "responsible party government" suggest that parties' promises to enact new policies and preserve certain established policies are the main normative criteria by which we should judge whether party government is operating success- fully. We have already suggested elsewhere (Samuels and Shugart 2003) that presidents are less likely than prime ministers to act as faithful agents of their party in terms of mandate representation. They are less likely to implement the party's platform and are more likely to engage in "policy-switching" (Stokes 2001) than prime ministers. A president may choose to propose policies in the party's interest or not; the fact that the party nominated an individual and helped him or her win executive office does not automatically mean that the president is beholden to the party's wishes. In short, executives are less accountable *to their party* in presidential systems, even though they may be more accountable to *voters* (Hellwig and Samuels 2008). We explore this dynamic in depth in Chapter 8.

CONCLUSION

Constitutional systems with directly elected executives now comprise a majority of all democracies around the globe, yet the comparative study of political parties remains wedded to its roots in the European par- liamentary experience. At the core of this book is the question of how political parties organize and behave differently according to whether they are structuring electoral choice only for legislative offices, or for both legislative offices and a popularly elected executive office. We have argued that the collective action and delegation problems that parties face vary as a function of differences in the executive-legislative struc- ture of government.

Variation in parties' organization and behavior is a function of varia- tion in the institutions of democratic government. In pure presidential systems, the direct election of the executive implies that parties have

distinct challenges in selecting and controlling agents, conducting campaigns, and dealing with the challenges of governing compared to their
counterparts in pure parliamentary systems. To the extent that parties
maintain effective control over their agents who ascend to the top executive position, we can speak of parliamentarized parties. In contrast, to
the extent that parties delegate discretion in the electoral and governing
arenas to agents who may have been selected for characteristics unrelated to their faithfulness to the party itself and who cannot be recalled,
we can speak of presidentialized parties.

We are certainly aware that many noninstitutional factors figure into
party organization and behavior, including social-structural dynamics
and leaders' personalities. However, the configuration of formal political institutions restricts parties' movement along the continuum from
presidentialized to parliamentarized. Parliamentary parties can become
presidentialized in certain important ways, as we noted in Chapter 1.
Nonetheless, parties in parliamentary systems can never become presidentialized in the most important way, because party agents in parliamentary systems never enjoy separation of origin or survival. For the
same reason, although parties in presidential systems can resemble parliamentarized parties, they can never organize or behave as if they were
in a parliamentary *system*. To the extent that pursuit of the separately
elected president is important for the things that parties care about, then
parties will become presidentialized, no matter whether the system is
pure or semi-presidential.

We also recognize that parties everywhere resemble each other in
numerous and obvious ways. However, even scholars of the presidentialization of politics in parliamentary systems acknowledge that such a
dynamic will always be stronger in *actual* presidential systems (Poguntke
and Webb 2005b). Social-structural, historical, technological, and other
noninstitutional factors work everywhere to shape parties' structures
and behavior. Yet while parties can come to resemble each other struc-
turally and behaviorally across all political systems, the possibilities for
variation in structure and behavior increase as one moves away from
fused powers systems and toward the separation of powers. This does
not mean that all parties in separation of powers systems will always
look and behave completely differently from all parties in parliamentary systems. In fact, parties may resemble each other to a considerable extent. However, scholars have missed critical variation across
democratic regimes – variation that makes a difference for the key tasks
political parties undertake, such as choosing leaders, campaigning, and

selecting and implementing public policies. Far greater variance exists in party organization and behavior under separation of powers along these lines than under fused powers. Subsequent chapters explore these differences in greater depth.

APPENDIX 2A: COHABITATION IN SEMI-PRESIDENTIAL SYSTEMS – CASES AND DATA

Under semi-presidentialism, cohabitation occurs when two criteria are met: (1) the president and prime minister are from opposing parties and (2) the president's party is not represented in the cabinet. Here we discuss the operationalization of this concept in more detail and provide a list of cases.

It is important to the definition of cohabitation that the president and prime minister not merely come from *different* parties, but come from *opposing* parties. In most cases, identifying opposing parties is straightforward. However, in fluid multiparty systems or systems with two major opposing blocs rather than two major parties, it is sometimes difficult to identify parties that politically oppose each other. We counted the president and prime minister as opposed if they or their parties were the major competitors in the *final* round of popular voting for president, in either the election immediately preceding or immediately following their presence in the dual executive.

For instance, in cases like France, it makes no sense to count the Rally for the Republic (Gaullists) and the Union for French Democracy as opposing parties, even though they sometimes presented separate candidates in the *first* round of presidential elections. They have never competed against each other in a runoff. Thus when one party holds the presidency and the other the premiership, we do not see cohabitation (even ignoring the second element of our operationalization). Similar examples are found elsewhere (see Chapter 4). In any case, where a minor party (defined as an also-ran in the presidential race) obtained the premiership it was almost always in coalition with a larger party that won the presidency, and thus both parties would be in the cabinet, ruling out cohabitation according to the second criterion.

Cases in which presidents are "nonpartisan" also pose challenges in defining opposing parties. When a president has no party affiliation, he or she cannot literally come from a party that "opposes" the prime minister. Nonetheless, many nonpartisan presidents are closely identified with specific parties or with ideological tendencies that place them

closer to some parties than to others. In such cases we relied on secondary sources or contemporary news accounts to identify the president's de
facto partisan affiliation. When we could not resolve the ambiguity of a
president's partisan leanings, we ruled out the possibility of cohabitation
during that president's tenure.

A related challenge emerges when presidents come from parties that
are not major competitors in assembly elections or when one or both
major opposing parliamentary parties do not contest presidential elections. In such cases, we do not count cohabitation as having occurred.
(For these reasons, we count no cases of cohabitation in Ireland or
Slovakia.)

Having identified cases of opposing parties within the dual executive,
we turned our attention to the second criterion: determining whether the
party of the president – or parties identified as clear allies of a nonpartisan president – were represented in the cabinet. Only when the president's party had no such representation do we observe cohabitation. The
resulting cases are shown in Table 2.A.1, which groups the examples of
cohabitation by country and presidency, showing the name of the cohabiting prime minister(s) during each relevant presidency, and the parties
of each executive. The table also indicates the years in which cohabitation occurred and the percentage of the president's term that was taken
up by cohabitation. The final column indicates how cohabitation came
about, from one of the following three processes: through an assembly election that resulted in the appointment of a cohabitation cabinet;
through the election of a president opposed to the cabinet (but with no
change toward including the president's party in the cabinet); or through
an interelectoral cabinet change.

In preparing this list of cases, we relied on various sources. For electoral data, we consulted Mackie and Rose (1991); Rose, Munro, and
Mackie (1998); the PARLINE database on national parliaments maintained by the Inter-Parliamentary Union (http://www.ipu.org/parline-e/
parlinesearch.asp); *Psephos* – Adam Carr's Election Archive (http://
psephos.adam-carr.net/); and Electionworld (http://en.wikipedia.org/
wiki/User:Electionworld/Electionworld). For cabinet composition, we
referred to the PARLINE database. For postcommunist cases we also
relied on Blondel and Müller-Rommel (2001) and Sedelius (2006).
Another useful online database for presidents and prime ministers is
World Political Leaders, 1945–2008 (http://www.terra.es/personal2/
monolith/00index.htm). We also relied extensively on contemporary

TABLE 2.A.1. *Cases of Cohabitation*

Country and President(s)	Party	Cohabiting Prime Minister(s)	Party	Years	% of President's Term[*]	Election or Interelectoral?[**]
Bulgaria						
Zhelyu Zhelev	UDF	Zhan Videnov	BSP	1995–97	31	Assembly
Petar Stoyanov	UDF	Simeon Sakskoburggotski	NDSV	2001–02	11	Assembly
Georgi Parvanov	BSP	Simeon Sakskoburggotski	NDSV	2002–05	51	Presidential
Croatia						
Stjepan Mesić	HNS	Ivo Sanader	HDZ	2003–08	57[***]	Assembly
Finland						
Juho Paasikivi	KOK	Urho Kekkonen	ZE	1950–53, 1954–56	50	Interelectoral
Martti Ahtisaari	SDP	Esko Aho	ZE	1994–95	12	Presidential
Tarja Halonen	SDP	Matti Vanhanen	ZE	2003–08	19[***]	Interelectoral
France						
François Mitterrand	PS	Jacques Chirac	RPR	1986–88	30	Assembly
		Édouard Balladur	RPR	1993–95		Assembly

(*continued*)

57

TABLE 2.A.1 *(continued)*

Country and President(s)	Party	Cohabiting Prime Minister(s)	Party	Years	% of President's Term*	Election or Interelectoral?**
Jacques Chirac	UMP	Lionel Jospin	PS	1997–02	41	Assembly
Lithuania						
Algirdas Brazauskas	LDDP	Gediminas Vagnorius	Homeland Union	1996–98	25	Assembly
Rolandas Paksas	LDP	Algirdas Brazauskas	Social Democratic	2003–04	100	Interelectoral
Valdas Adamkus	Non-partisan conservative	Algirdas Brazauskas	Social Democratic	2004–06	42	Presidential
Macedonia						
Kiro Gligorov	SDSM	Ljubcho Georgievski	VMRO– DPMNE	1998–99	12	Assembly
Boris Trajkovski	VMRO– DPMNE	Branko Crvenkovski	SDSM	2002–04	31	Assembly
Branko Crvenkovski	SDSM	Nikola Gruevski	VMRO– DPMNE	2006–08	51***	Assembly
Mongolia						
Punsalmaagiyn Ochirbat	Democratic Union	Puntsagiyn Jasray	MPRP	1993–96	77	Presidential

President		Prime Minister		Years	No.	Type
Natsagiyn Bagabandi	MPRP	Mendsayhany Enkhsaikhan	Democratic Union	1997–98	38	Presidential
		Tsakhiagiyn Elbegdorj	Democratic Union	1998		Interelectoral
		Janlaviyn Narantsatsralt	Democratic Union	1998–99		Interelectoral
		Rinchinnyamiyn Amarjargal	Democratic Union	1999–2000		Interelectoral
Poland						
Lech Wałęsa	Solidarity	Jan Olszewski	PC	1991–92	55	Assembly
		Waldemar Pawlak I	PSL	1992		Interelectoral
		Waldemar Pawlak II	PSL	1993–95		Electoral
		Józef Oleksy	SdRP/SLD	1995		Interelectoral
Aleksander Kwaśniewski	SDRP/SLD	Jerzy Karol Buzek	AWS	1997–2001	40	Assembly
Portugal						
Mario Soares	PS	Aníbal Cavaco Silva	PSD	1986–95	96	Presidential
Jorge Sampaio	PS	José Durão Barroso	PSD	2002–04		Assembly
		Pedro Lopes	PSD	2004–05	29	Interelectoral

(continued)

TABLE 2.A.1 *(continued)*

Country and President(s)	Party	Cohabiting Prime Minister(s)	Party	Years	% of President's Term*	Election or Interelectoral?**
Aníbal Cavaco Silva	PSD	José Sócrates	PS	2006–08	100***	Assembly
Romania						
Traian Băsescu	PD	Călin Popescu-Tăriceanu	PNL	2007–08	43	Interelectoral
Slovenia						
Janez Drnovšek	LDS	Janez Janša	SDS	2004–07	62	Assembly
Sri Lanka						
Chandrika Kumaratunga	SLFP	Ranil Wickremasinghe	UNP	2001–04	21	Assembly

* Combined across all cohabiting prime ministers for any given president.

** Whether cohabitation resulted from an election or not, and if so, which type.

*** President still in office as of December 31, 2008.

news accounts, tracked through Lexis-Nexis online and Keesing's Record of World Events. For some individual countries, especially when there were ambiguities from the sources mentioned thus far, we relied on the following country-specific references, as follows.

- Finland: Nousiainen (2000), Strøm (1990)
- Lithuania: Krupavicius (2007), and personal communication with Erik Herron
- Mongolia: Fish (1998), Ginsburg (1998), Severinghaus (1996, 2000)
- Portugal: Amorim Neto and Costa Lobo (2009), Strøm (1990)
- Romania: Müller (2006)

3

Insiders and Outsiders

Madison's Dilemma and Leadership Selection

If we think of parties as teams of politicians who cooperate in elections and in government, then a critical question is, How do parties select their leaders? All organizations must cope with delegation problems, as principal-agent theory suggests. In this chapter, we consider how different democratic regimes shape the central issue parties face in terms of delegation: selection of those who seek the offices of president and prime minister.

As noted in Chapter 2, principals who hire agents face the inherent potential for agency losses, which occur when agents do not act faithfully in their principals' interest. In business or industry, disputes often emerge over the amount of effort the agents expend ("slacking"). In politics, by way of contrast, conflicts frequently emerge over the course of action agents pursue (Kiewiet and McCubbins 1991, 24).[1] Parties have good reason to fear such agency losses due to two problems: adverse selection and moral hazard.

Adverse selection is a danger because prospective agents have incentives to misrepresent their preferences, downplay their character flaws, and hide their lack of experience or skills – particularly if their true plans clash with the organization's preferences. When agents have misrepresented themselves, they can make Madison's worst nightmare come true if after selection to the leadership post they pursue their own interests, or pursue their own vision of what the party's goals *ought* to be – even if

---

[1] Agency losses almost always exist, no matter what the institutional context. As Lupia (2003, 35) notes, agency losses will equal zero only when an agent takes actions the principal would have taken given unlimited information and resources. Since such situations almost never arise, there is almost always some agency loss.

their personal interests or goals are *adverse* to the party's. In this chapter we focus on adverse selection problems; we turn to moral hazard problems in Chapter 4.

Like any organization, parties could reduce adverse selection problems that emerge once a contract has been signed if they could make optimal hiring decisions in the first place. Yet parties can never completely avoid adverse selection, simply because they lack perfect information about prospective agents' preferences, qualities, and qualifications. Still, given the danger of selecting an agent whose actions might adversely influence their interests, parties have powerful incentives to expend considerable resources screening and selecting candidates, looking for agents who send reliable signals.

Unfortunately, parties have few tools to encourage applicants to reveal their "true" preferences and goals, and they have no way to judge *ex ante* the likelihood that a potential leader will live up to his or her promise. This is a worrisome problem given the potential damage that a leader could do to a party's fortunes. Parties do not screen for suitable agents by posting "help wanted" ads and then selecting a short list of candidates to consider. Instead, they engage in an extended, implicit interview process that often lasts years, in which aspirants compete to send parties repeated signals about their usefulness and reliability. As in other professions, the most valuable signal a politician can send is previous experience. Parties therefore seek to minimize adverse selection problems by selecting candidates with certain kinds of experience.

The problem that all parties face is that the qualities that make a potential candidate useful for the party's collective goals may conflict with the qualities that suggest a candidate will reliably pursue those goals. Given our argument in Chapter 2, we expect parties will be less able to minimize adverse selection problems when at least part of the executive originates separately from the legislature. This is because the skills needed to win the prime minister's office in a parliamentary system are strongly correlated with the skills that make one a good party servant: an ability to embody the party's vision and to coordinate the party's bureaucracy and legislative contingent.

In contrast, the skills most useful for winning a presidential election include proven vote-drawing ability and an appealing, suprapartisan public image. These skills may only weakly correlate with the skills that make one a faithful executor of the party's will. Consequently, for any party that must nominate a candidate for a separately elected presidency – regardless of whether the group that decides that nomination is a party executive committee, a party convention, or the party's primary voters – the best potential agent from the party's organizational point of view may be incapable of satisfying the party from an electoral point of view, while the candidate most likely to win an election might be a less-faithful party agent.

Party organizations that confront this trade-off – typically portrayed as a choice between nominating an "insider" or an "outsider" – tend to be presidentialized, because they must select their de facto leader to prioritize winning the presidency. To the extent that we see evidence of different career trajectories of presidents and prime ministers across different democratic regimes, we have evidence of this trade-off in the real world. To be sure, leaders' different career trajectories are not the only source of evidence of contracting problems. In fact, candidate "type" represents an indirect form of evidence. Nevertheless, career trajectories do provide an important part of the picture, which we complete in later chapters.

The argument and evidence in this chapter extend beyond the long-standing conventional wisdom that suggests presidents and prime ministers tend to differ in background experience. This view is based only on differences between presidents and prime ministers in the "pure" democratic regimes, but unfortunately it offers no guidance about what to expect in semi-presidential hybrid regimes. Thus, after defining the continuum of party agents ranging from "insider" to "outsider," we leverage our principal-agent theoretical framework to derive hypotheses about expected career paths for presidents and prime ministers under all constitutional regimes. We subsequently explore executives' "types" through a global survey of presidents' and prime ministers' career trajectories since 1945.

Our findings both confirm and build upon the conventional contrast between parliamentary insiders and presidential outsiders. We confirm that presidents are indeed more likely than prime ministers to be outsiders – and show that this holds for all democratic regimes, including premier-presidential systems. However, we also find that prime ministers in both semi-presidential subtypes do not closely resemble their "insider" parliamentary cousins. Indeed, many prime ministers in semi-presidential systems are "outsiders," because – as we suggested in Chapter 2 – prime ministers in semi-presidential systems are at least partly agents of the president rather than the assembly majority.

Our findings also add nuance to the conventional distinction between insiders and outsiders. The key finding from our theoretical perspective is not so much that typical presidents arrive at the top position with little political experience per se, as the conventional view might suggest. Rather, the key point is that presidents *tend to reach the pinnacle of power with relatively weaker ties to their parties*. Presidents in all systems are relatively less likely to possess experience that signals reliability as a party agent. Our theoretical framework explains why this is so: in separate powers systems, parties "pre-select" candidates who will be the voters' direct agent, while in parliamentary systems parties select leaders who are direct agents of the party's legislative contingent.

Both this chapter and the next provide insights into the implications of this key difference in intraparty politics. In these chapters we provide evidence that the presidency's separate origin matters considerably for the types of politicians nominated and ultimately elected. The next chapter focuses on the implications of separate survival, which restricts parties' ability to discipline wayward agents once they are in office. Taken together, the separate origin and survival of the presidency guarantee weaker principal-agent links between a party and its president. By contrast, parliamentary government guarantees that the incumbent executive remains an agent of the legislative majority, and hence also of his or her own party in parliament.

DEFINING INSIDERS AND OUTSIDERS

Exploring whether executives are more or less likely to be insiders or outsiders across democratic systems – and thus confirming the extent to which adverse selection problems characterize intraparty politics across different democratic regimes – requires that we first define our terms. The notions of insiders and outsiders seem commonsensical, and in some ways this distinction echoes our continuum of presidentialized versus parliamentarized parties. In this light, US president Dwight Eisenhower (1953–60) might represent the archetypical outsider, having held no prior political office whatsoever before winning the presidency. At the other end of the spectrum we might hold up UK Prime Minister Winston Churchill (1940–45, 1951–55) as the archetypical insider. Churchill entered the House of Commons in 1900 and spent 37 of the next 40 years as a member of parliament before rising to the top spot – 7 of those as cabinet minister and 11 as Tory leader.

Readers may have in mind other examples of insiders or outsiders. Regardless, the question remains as to whether Eisenhower and Churchill are typical or exceptional. Despite the conventional wisdom, the extent to which presidents actually are outsiders remains an open empirical question, particularly when one considers *all* elected presidents, including those in hybrid systems. After all, as Mainwaring and Shugart (1997) noted in their evaluation of Linz's critique of presidentialism, many presidents qualify as insiders. Thus while Mexico's Vicente Fox (2000–06) or Brazil's Juscelino Kubitschek (1956–60) entered the presidency from the governor's office and never served as national legislator or as national party leader, Mexico's Felipe Calderón (2007–12) and Brazil's Lula da Silva (2003–10) are both consummate insiders. Is the conventional wisdom true, or just an appealing and convenient exaggeration that seems to fit with what we think *ought* to be true?[2]

The same question applies to the conventional wisdom about prime ministers. Churchill's path might be archetypal – but it could also be atypical. After all, as with insider presidents, we also know of outsider prime ministers. A prominent example is Italy's Silvio Berlusconi (1994–95, 2001–06, 2008–), who founded Forza Italia only two months before first winning the premiership. Other prime ministers who never led their party and never served in parliament include the Czech Republic's Jiří Paroubek (2005–06) and Hungary's Péter Medgyessy (2002–04). Examples such as these cast doubt on the conventional wisdom because they at least partly conform to Linz's (1994, 26) definition of an outsider as someone who rises to the top position "not identified with or supported by any political party, sometimes without any governmental or even political experience, on the basis of a populist appeal, [and] often based on hostility to parties and 'politicians.'" It thus remains possible that outsider prime ministers under parliamentarism are more common than the conventional wisdom implies. And of course, the conventional association of prime ministers with insiders and presidents with outsiders is not especially helpful in sorting out expectations about the occupants of these roles in semi-presidential systems.

---

[2] Among US presidents since World War II, only Eisenhower was a complete political novice. Ronald Reagan, Jimmy Carter, George W. Bush, and Bill Clinton had no prior national *legislative* experience but were hardly novices, all having served (at least) as state governors. Richard Nixon served 6 years in the national legislature and 8 as vice-president; Harry S. Truman served 10 years as senator and then as vice-president; John F. Kennedy spent 14 years in the legislature before his election; Lyndon Johnson spent 23 years in the legislature and then served as vice-president until Kennedy's assassination; and Barack Obama served 4 years in the US Senate after serving 7 years in the Illinois Senate. Still, it remains true that no American president has ever served in the cabinet or as de facto party leader prior to winning the White House. For discussions of selection of presidential "insiders" and "outsiders" in the United States, see Ceaser (1979), Busch (1997), and Cohen et al. (2008).

Our definition of the distinction between an insider and an outsider differs slightly from Linz's in that we lean more heavily on quantities that observers can concretely identify and measure. We dispense entirely with the question of the nature of a politician's appeals (i.e., whether "populist" or not) and do not consider whether or not a politician is temperamentally hostile to parties and/or the political establishment. Instead, building on comparative research on political ambition,[3] we suggest that one can learn a great deal about agents' true preferences, the strength of their ties to their principals, and thus about the nature of the contracting problems between principals and agents, through analysis of their career paths.[4]

What career path sends signals of agent reliability, and what suggests agent unreliability? The strongest indicator of "insiderness" is *the nature and extent of a prospective agent's links to a central party organization* – the organization that ultimately is responsible for nominating or "hiring" future national executives. Thus an ideal-type insider will not only be a member of a political party but will also have served as formal leader of the party, and for a relatively longer period of time than an outsider. Similarly, insiders are more likely to have served formally on the party's national executive committee, even if they did not rise to the position of party leader. Third, insider status is associated with service in the national legislature – and the longer one serves, the stronger the links between principal and potential agent. Fourth, principal-agent links will be stronger to the extent that a politician has served in the cabinet.

These four indicators define the core elements of the continuum distinguishing insiders from outsiders, and thus between parliamentarization (where executives are most closely tied to co-partisan legislators) and presidentialization (where the chief executive is the electorate's direct agent as well as – or even instead of – the party's). Three of these four

---

[3] Examples include Mayhew (1974); Smith (1979); Cain, Ferejohn, and Fiorina (1991); Carey (1996); Samuels (2003); Shugart, Valdini, and Suominen (2005); Siavelis and Morgenstern (eds.) (2008a).

[4] Parties in different democratic regimes likely attract different types of applicants for leadership positions, due to different payoffs to holding office. If presidencies are truly elected kingships, then perhaps the office attracts individuals with monarchical pretensions. Likewise, if a prime minister is merely first among equals, then perhaps prime ministers are far more likely to be party stalwarts. That is, it may be true that presidentialism selects for a certain type of person to compete for the highest office, and that those types of individuals are more likely to ignore organizational imperatives. However, we cannot directly measure personality type, nor can we measure how expected payoffs might influence such selection bias. Instead, we should look at behavior, rather than guess at the psychological predispositions of aspirants for higher office in different institutional contexts.

positions (leader, executive committee, and cabinet) are themselves positions as a party's direct agent. The more "agency experience" a potential national executive has, the greater the buildup of trust, information, and relevant organizational experience, and thus the more that internal party dynamics will resemble the ideal-type parliamentarized party.[5] By contrast, the less a potential national executive has built up these sorts of agency ties, the more the party is presidentialized.

Furthermore, following insights from comparative research on political ambition – and differing from Linz's definition to some degree – we suggest that evidence of insider or outsider status can be found throughout the entire arc of politicians' careers. That is, we can learn a great deal about politicians' relationships with their parties by considering what they do both *before* and *after* they have served as national executive. Parties do not merely confront *ex ante* problems of adverse selection. They also confront the problem of agents' *ex post* opportunism, known as moral hazard. To the extent that politicians continue working directly with their party after leaving national executive office, we can be fairly sure that they have not strayed *during* their term – that is, that moral hazard problems are relatively less important.

INSIDERS VERSUS OUTSIDERS: HYPOTHESES

In this section we derive our theoretical expectations. The conventional wisdom sets up what we call a "positional" hypothesis: *the position of prime minister or president per se determines where occupants of those positions tend to fall on the insider–outsider continuum.* This view suggests that parties in parliamentary democracies face minimal adverse selection problems because their pool of potential prime ministers tends to consist of existing high-ranking party personnel. Parties select leaders

---

[5] Not surprisingly, scholars have found a match between parties' *internal procedures*, which range from "closed" to "open," and the *types of candidates* selected, which range from "insiders" to "outsiders" (e.g. Kenig 2006; Freidenberg and Sánchez López 2001; and Siavelis and Morgenstern 2008b). The more closed the selection procedure, the more likely the selection of an insider will be, and vice versa. We ignore party selection criteria because theoretically, we have little reason to believe that such institutions matter much across democratic regimes. For example, the United States adopted primaries decades ago, but US presidential candidates were relative outsiders and remain relative outsiders in comparative perspective. Likewise, parties in presidential systems with "closed" candidate-selection mechanisms will still select relative outsiders compared to parties in parliamentary systems that employ relatively "open" candidate-selection mechanisms.

for their skills at managing the party organization and its parliamentary contingent; prior partisan experience gives parties the opportunity to vet their prime-ministerial candidates, and gives potential prime ministers the opportunity to signal over many years that they will uphold their party's values and pursue its goals (Strøm 2003, 70). Although parties are certain to consider their leader's popular appeal, the nature of parliamentarism does not *require* that they nominate prime-ministerial candidates who can win direct popular elections. Thus, we expect prime ministers in pure parliamentary systems to most resemble insiders.

The same conventional wisdom suggests that parties in pure presidential systems face an often-irresolvable tension over candidate selection and are more likely to select outsider candidates who lack relevant party and/or legislative experience and about whom parties know relatively less (Linz 1994, 26–28). In pure presidential systems, parties are not likely to select candidates for president for their skills at handling the party bureaucracy or managing the party's legislative contingent. Instead, because they must win an electoral contest separate from legislative elections, parties will select presidential candidates based on their outsider appeal, partly because the traits that appeal to voters may be only loosely correlated with the traits that send signals of reliability to party insiders. In making such choices, parties accept the possibility of adverse selection in order to enhance their chances of victory in the popular election for president. The conventional wisdom thus assumes a trade-off under pure presidentialism due to the incompatibility between being a good agent and being a good candidate. Given this, we expect executives in pure presidential systems to most resemble outsiders.

It remains unclear, however, whether the positional hypothesis also holds for semi-presidential regimes. If the positional hypothesis is true, it should hold regardless of the pure or hybrid nature of a regime: prime ministers in dual executive systems should closely resemble prime ministers in pure parliamentary systems, and presidents in semi-presidential systems should closely resemble presidents in pure presidential systems. As discussed in Chapter 2, early advocates of semi-presidentialism such as Max Weber argued that presidents in such systems would be above *all* the parties, in a nonpartisan sense. In practice, this notion is typically a fantasy. Indeed, some presidents in hybrid systems – as in some pure presidential systems – are only "above" parties in that they are able to reverse the principal-agent relationship and *dominate* their own party, not ignore it. This de facto reversal of the principal-agent relationship is one of the hallmarks of party presidentialization. Constitutional structure in semi-presidential regimes affects the balance of power between the president, the party, and the prime minister. It thus remains an open question whether, on average, presidents in hybrid systems should resemble outsiders while prime ministers in those regimes should resemble insiders.

To explain patterns along the insider-outsider continuum in all democratic regimes, as an alternative to the positional hypothesis we posit a "configurational" hypothesis. Under this perspective the key does not lie with the position of prime minister or president per se in each regime. Instead, *the configuration of constitutional authority in premier-presidential and president-parliamentary regimes tends to shape the career path its occupants tend to follow.* We derive this hypothesis from theoretical arguments recently developed in research on mixed electoral systems (e.g. Herron and Nishikawa 2001; Cox and Schioppa 2002; Moser and Scheiner 2004). That is, just as one element in a mixed electoral system is said to "contaminate" the other,[6] constitutions that mix parliamentary and presidential elements may feature contamination across the components of the hybrid. In theory, contamination in hybrid constitutions could run either way – from the presidential element to the parliamentary, or vice-versa. Yet because the presidency in hybrid systems is so crucial to parties' pursuit of their other goals, we have good theoretical reasons to expect most of the "contamination" to run from the presidential to the parliamentary component. This implies that career paths for *both* presidents and prime ministers in semi-presidential systems should tend toward the presidentialized end of the continuum, relative to prime ministers in pure parliamentary systems.

To understand the degree of presidential "contamination" of the parliamentary element of semi-presidential regimes, the configurational hypothesis focuses our attention on two key factors: the regime subtype (an institutional dimension) and cohabitation (a partisan dimension). As we discussed in Chapter 2, premier-presidential systems emphasize the parliamentary component of the hybrid design in one key respect: the prime minister and cabinet are formally accountable solely to the assembly majority. By contrast, in president-parliamentary systems the prime minister and cabinet are responsible simultaneously to the president and the assembly majority. A configurational hypothesis thus leads us to

---

[6] That is, the number of parties contesting single-seat districts decided by plurality rule might be greater than expected because of parties seeking proportional-representation seats and also presenting candidacies in the districts. Or the number of parties in the proportional-representation tier may be less than expected because of the focus of voters and other actors on the competition for seats via plurality.

expect that prime ministers in premier-presidential systems should resemble insiders more than their counterparts in president-parliamentary systems, though not as much as their counterparts in pure parliamentary regimes. In contrast, prime ministers in president-parliamentary systems should tend toward outsider status relative to their counterparts in pure parliamentary systems, because in this subtype the president's authority to appoint and dismiss the prime minister renders the latter an agent of the former, even though the prime minister remains dependent on parliamentary confidence as well.

Partisan compatibility between the president and prime minister provides the second source of "configurational" variation within semi-presidential systems. As we saw in Chapter 2, cohabitation occurs during just over one-fifth of the time in premier-presidential systems. As far as prime ministers' career paths are concerned, in cases of cohabitation the positional and configurational hypotheses converge: prime ministers under cohabitation should be insiders, insofar as the party that leads the assembly majority selects them to counterbalance the president. In other words, cohabitation is the "most parliamentarized" of situations under both semi-presidential subtypes. The infrequency of cohabitation under president-parliamentarism largely renders the point moot for that subtype. And under unified government, the configurational hypothesis leads us to expect prime ministers in president-parliamentary systems to be outsiders, to the extent that they are personal agents of the president rather than agents of the party. Prime ministers in premier-presidential systems should again resemble insiders more than their counterparts in president-parliamentary systems, though not as much as their counterparts in pure parliamentary regimes.

Yet what about presidents in dual-executive hybrids? Does the fact of assembly confidence contaminate the presidential half of the dual executive to some degree, making presidents in semi-presidential systems somewhat more likely to resemble insiders than those in pure presidential systems? Perhaps presidents in premier-presidential systems tend toward insider status for the simple reason that their parties in such regimes must groom leaders to win a popular presidential election – which predicts presidentialization of leadership recruitment – while simultaneously attempting to ensure the robustness of their parliamentary "branch." Without a parliamentary party capable of winning (alone or with partners) control of the assembly, a party may win the presidency only to face cohabitation. That is, prime-ministerial and cabinet responsibility to the assembly majority, coupled with the logic of popular presidential elections, implies that presidents should resemble insiders somewhat more so under premier-presidentialism than under pure presidentialism. However, this logic does not apply to president-parliamentary systems, due to their fundamental institutional logic that places the prime minister in a subordinate position to the president.

The positional and configurational hypotheses generate competing expectations regarding presidential and prime-ministerial "types" in dual-executive hybrid regimes. The positional hypothesis assumes no contamination from the presidential to the prime-ministerial branches of the dual executive, and implies simply that presidents and prime ministers in hybrid regimes should resemble their counterparts in the pure-type regimes. In contrast, the configurational hypothesis suggests that one side of the dual executive contaminates the other, partly as a function of the subtype's *institutional* configuration and partly as a result of *party-system* configurations. Next we confront these hypotheses with data on executives' career paths.

The strength of our argument depends on the breadth and consistency of the support we find for its empirical implications. At this point, it merits mention that we do not expect executives in pure presidential systems to have "zero" experience, nor do we expect every prime minister in pure parliamentary systems to have served as party leader for 5 years, for 10 years in the cabinet and 20 years in the legislature. Still, we expect career-path patterns to conform to our expectations: if parliamentarism minimizes parties' adverse selection problems while the separation of powers complicates such problems, we ought to see evidence of differences in the "types" of candidates who ultimately make it to the top spot in each democratic system.

CAREER PATHS OF INSIDERS AND OUTSIDERS

To compare insiders and outsiders across democratic regimes, we analyze the career paths of the universe of national executives – every president and prime minister in every democracy around the world between 1945 and 2007 (see Table 2.1). We gathered biographical information on all executives in these countries, provided the president was popularly elected and the prime minister was subject to the confidence of the assembly majority.[7]

---

[7] We excluded interim and caretaker administrations, and vice-presidents who took office following the death or resignation of a popularly elected president. For reasons

As a first cut toward testing the implications of our argument, we examine the positions politicians held immediately prior to assuming national executive office, across democratic regimes. This penultimate job provides a window into the pool of talent into which parties have promoted their executive candidates just before promoting them to the very top job. Table 3.1 presents this information. (The proportions may not add to 1.0 because politicians can hold multiple positions at once – for example, they can be party leader while also being a legislator.)

The first two rows include the two prior positions – national legislator and cabinet minister – that most typify the pool of party insiders. (We decided *not* to double-count these two positions, so a minister who was also a legislator – a very common combination in parliamentary systems – is counted only as the former.) These categories represent the jobs from which parliamentary parties would be expected to directly recruit their prime ministers, but from which presidents are less likely to emerge.

The findings in this table lend initial support for the positional hypothesis, simply because most of the proportions are higher for all prime ministers than for all presidents. For example, nearly 85% of prime ministers in pure parliamentary systems enter office from either the assembly (55%) or the cabinet (29%), while fewer than 40% of presidents in pure systems do so; 51% of all prime ministers across regimes jumped straight from the national legislature, while only 28% of all presidents made a similar move. Such differences are even starker for cabinet ministers: no more than 13% of presidents came straight out of the cabinet, while 28% of prime ministers did.[8] T-tests comparing all presidents against all prime ministers confirm a significant difference at p < .01 for both of these categories.

Although these findings suggest that the positional hypothesis may be on the right track, Table 3.1 also offers substantial support for the configurational hypothesis. Focusing on the first two rows, we see that presidents in premier-presidential systems are more likely than presidents in either pure presidential or president-parliamentary systems to

---

we explain below, we also excluded presidents and prime ministers from Austria as an extreme outlier case. This resulted in a sample of 852 national executives. Please consult Appendix 3A for information on how we constructed this dataset.

[8] The greater tendency of presidents to come from the legislature than from the cabinet is perhaps because the separation of legislative and executive institutions allows prominent opposition legislators to build the sort of independent reputation that is valued for a presidential campaign, whereas service in the cabinet may be antithetical to standing out and position-taking.

TABLE 3.1. *Immediate Pre-Executive Job (%)*

	Prime Ministers, Parliamentary (N = 403)	Premier-Presidential, Prime Ministers (N = 149)	President-Parliamentary, Prime Ministers (N = 76)	Premier-Presidential, Presidents (N = 50)	President-Parliamentary, Presidents (N = 23)	Presidents (N = 151)
National Legislator	.55	.50	.32	.35	.18	.27
Cabinet Minister	.29	.24	.34	.12	.18	.12
Party Leadership Position	.23	.22	.18	.16	.27	.19
Vice PM/Vice-President	.06	.03	.06	.02	.05	.09
Ex-Prime Minister	.04	.01	.01	.20	.23	.01
Ex-President or Presidential Candidate	.00	.01	.01	.04	.00	.13
Municipal/ Provincial Position	.02	.07	.06	.10	.09	.12
Other	.03	.02	.04	.02	.14	.14

come straight out of the legislature – and they are even more likely to do so than premiers in president-parliamentary regimes. This supports our expectation that presidents in premier-presidential systems should resemble insiders more than their presidential counterparts in other systems. Evidence in these two rows also supports the configurational hypothesis that we should see a stronger tendency toward outsider prime ministers in president-parliamentary systems, since those prime ministers are likely agents of the president rather than the party.

The proportion of executives coming from party leadership positions does not support the positional hypothesis. For example, presidents in president-parliamentary systems are somewhat more likely than other presidents to be party leader as they jump to the presidency. The proportion does not necessarily suggest that such presidents are always insiders (after all, .27 is not .77, for example) but it is notable that the highest proportion of the three groups of presidents emerges in this category, confounding the conventional distinction between "parliamentary insiders" and "presidential outsiders."

The next three rows concern former holders of the vice-premiership or vice-presidency, former prime ministers, and ex-presidents or former presidential candidates. What is notable is the relatively large proportion of presidents under semi-presidentialism who jump directly from the premiership.[9] We interpret this pattern as suggesting that for both dual-executive subtypes the premiership represents a position as "president-in-waiting." Parties use the premiership both to groom and to vet potential presidential candidates, an option that is obviously not available in pure presidential systems. Of course, to the extent that parties choose prime ministers because they might make suitable future presidents, we have evidence of contamination from the presidential to the parliamentary components of the hybrid regime – and of parties' acceptance of the trade-offs inherent in such presidentialization.

The last two rows of Table 3.1 indicate that a relatively higher proportion of presidents come from true outsider positions in subnational government or nonelective ("other") positions as diplomat, appointed bureaucrat, advisor to another politician, or as leader of a social movement. The configurational hypothesis gains additional support

---

[9] The one ex-prime minister in pure presidential systems came from Gambia, which switched to pure presidentialism from pure parliamentarism. Several prime ministers in pure parliamentary systems were heads of provisional governments prior to their country's independence, accounting for the relatively small proportion of ex-prime ministers in that regime type.

here: prime ministers in pure parliamentary systems are least likely to be outsiders, while prime ministers in hybrid systems are more likely to be plucked from outside the parliamentary party, most likely because presidents select them for their personal loyalty rather than their loyalty to the party.

In sum, our first piece of evidence – derived from the penultimate job prime ministers and presidents held before assuming the top spot – supports the configurational hypothesis over the positional hypothesis. Parties' adverse selection problems do vary across democratic regimes, but prime ministers per se are not insiders, while presidents are not always outsiders. Instead, the constitutional configuration of power affects the likelihood that parties will or will not select agents from inside their central organization. True insiders are found only among prime ministers in pure parliamentary regimes, while presidents in all regimes and prime ministers in hybrid regimes tend to depart from this ideal-type.

Let us now see whether this finding holds up to scrutiny of a longer arc of politicians' careers. Table 3.2 provides details about whether national executives have served at any time prior to assuming the top spot in four key political positions: party leader, other high-ranking party leadership positions, legislator, and cabinet minister.

The evidence strongly supports the configurational hypothesis. Consider service as party leader first: prime ministers in pure parliamentary systems should have the most party leadership experience of all, and they do. In contrast, prime ministers in both hybrid subtypes are far less likely to have led their parties.[10] Indeed, there is no substantial difference between prime ministers in premier-presidential systems (51%) and presidents in any system. Moreover, prime ministers in president-parliamentary systems are the *least* likely to have served as party leader (19%) before leaping to the top spot. In short, there is no support for the "positional" hypothesis here. From a party's point of view the premiership in president-parliamentary systems is a secondary position relative to presidency – just as we would expect it to be, given the configuration of institutional power in this subtype.

Let us now consider the proportion of executives who have served as legislators. The findings here also favor the configurational hypothesis.

---

[10] This may be partly because, whereas in pure presidential systems the only executive position available for party leaders to ascend to *is* the presidency, leaders in dual-executive systems can ascend to either position. As is clear in Table 3.1, there are on average about three prime ministers for every president in the semi-presidential systems, meaning that for many, being prime minister turns out to be the pinnacle of a career.

TABLE 3.2. *Positions Held at Any Point in a Career*

	Prime Ministers	Premier-Presidential, Prime Minister	President-Parliamentary, Prime Minister	Premier-Presidential, President	President-Parliamentary, President	Presidents
Lead Party (%)	.76	.51	.19	.56	.56	.50
# Years Lead Party	4.09	2.61	1.20	3.71	4.91	3.21
Other Party Leadership (%)	.42	.42	.34	.30	.33	.32
National Legislator (%)	.94	.80	.62	.70	.68	.58
# Years Legislator	9.40	6.80	5.04	6.10	3.91	5.34
Cabinet Minister (%)	.73	.60	.54	.46	.39	.47
# Years Cabinet	4.19	2.84	2.24	2.53	2.78	1.92

Nearly all prime ministers in pure parliamentary systems have served in the legislature at some point in their careers – and for over nine years, on average. In contrast, only 58% of presidents in pure presidential systems have done so – and for a much shorter period, on average. Also note that although approximately the same proportion of presidents in premier-presidential and president-parliamentary systems have served in the legislature (~70%), presidents in the latter subtype tend to serve for considerably less time – even though they are *more* likely to have served for any amount of time in the legislature than their prime ministers (68% vs. 62%)!

These patterns again support the idea that parties in premier-presidential systems tend to invest relatively more in bridging the legislative and executive branches of their party than parties in either president-parliamentary or pure presidential regimes. The combination of separate origin of the presidency with exclusive parliamentary responsibility of the cabinet to the assembly should encourage parties to recruit prime ministers more from both legislative and party-leadership ranks than parties in president-parliamentary systems – but less than in parliamentary systems – and also to recruit their presidents from "insider" positions relatively more than parties in pure presidential systems.

When we turn to service in the cabinet, some support exists for the positional hypothesis: 73% of prime ministers in pure parliamentary regimes served in the cabinet at some point in their career before assuming the top spot; the proportions are lower for prime ministers in hybrid regimes. The proportions are lower still for all presidents than for any group of prime ministers – and are the lowest for presidents in the president-parliamentary subtype. Finally, prime ministers in pure parliamentary regimes have served the longest on average in the cabinet, and presidents in pure presidential systems the least. However, differences also emerge "within" each position (prime minister or president), again casting doubt on the positional hypothesis.

Overall, the findings in Table 3.2 support the hypothesis that parties face different adverse selection problems in different democratic regimes. When parties control recruitment and select a single agent who is then responsible to the assembly majority, they tend to select insiders – leaders who have served as legislator, party leader, and cabinet minister. This is the ideal-type insider prime minister under parliamentarism. In contrast, when voters have a direct role in selecting national leaders, parties face a trade-off and are less likely to select insiders for either the presidency or the premiership. However, parties are somewhat more likely to select insiders in premier-presidential systems, the hybrid that leans most strongly toward parliamentarism.

This argument gains further support when we examine whether or not executives in different democratic systems had served in different *combinations* of positions prior to assuming office. We focus on combinations of the most important offices associated with insider status: legislator, cabinet minister, and party leader. If our argument holds water we should see stronger tendencies toward insider status for prime ministers in parliamentary systems and outsider status for presidents in pure presidential systems. In Table 3.3 we calculate the proportion of executives in our four regimes that held different combinations of political positions prior to assuming office.

The information in Table 3.3 strongly supports the configurational hypothesis. Prime ministers in pure parliamentary systems are far more likely to resemble insiders than those in other systems prior to assuming the top office, and presidents in premier-presidential systems show a slightly stronger tendency toward insider profiles than presidents in other regimes. Yet somewhat surprisingly, but following our configurational hypothesis, prime ministers in president-parliamentary systems are the most likely to resemble outsiders – in fact, they are more likely than any set of *presidents* to be outsiders!

As a final piece of evidence in support of our framework, consider what politicians do *after* they have served as national executive. As noted, principals do not merely confront *ex ante* problems of adverse selection – they also confront *ex post* problems of agents' opportunism, known as moral hazard. To the extent that politicians continue working with their party after leaving national office, we can be certain that they have not strayed *during* their term – that is, that moral hazard is less of a problem.

The conventional view of presidents as outsiders follows the stereotype of American presidents, who take their cue from George Washington. Washington was inspired by the story of the Roman general Cincinnatus, who defeated Rome's enemies only to retire immediately to his farm rather than grab the power that Roman elites handed to him on a platter. Indeed, American presidents have historically tended to abandon the hustle and bustle of party politics upon leaving the Oval Office. For example, at the end of his second presidential term, former general Dwight Eisenhower followed in Washington's footsteps and retired immediately to his farm near Gettysburg, Pennsylvania. The

TABLE 3.3. *Combinations of Pre-Executive Positions (%)*

	Prime Ministers	Premier-Presidential, Prime Minister	President-Parliamentary, Prime Minister	Premier-Presidential, President	President-Parliamentary, President	Presidents
Legislator + Minister	.69	.50	.29	.36	.27	.30
Legislator + Party Leader	.75	.50	.19	.44	.36	.33
Minister + Party Leader	.53	.31	.08	.30	.30	.27
Legislator + Minister + Party Leader	.52	.29	.07	.22	.23	.20

only US president to return to the legislature after his term was John Quincy Adams, who served in the House from 1831 to 1848. In recent decades ex-presidents have concentrated on writing their memoirs, giving speeches, and raising funds to construct their presidential libraries. Only Bill Clinton has remained active in party politics, at least partly to support Hillary Clinton's ambitions.

How frequently do ex-prime ministers and ex-presidents remain as leaders of their party, return to the legislature, or regain a spot in the cabinet, versus retiring completely from politics or being shunted into a less-important sinecure such as ambassador, diplomat, or representative to a regional parliament (e.g. the European or Central American Parliament)? This question returns to our theme of the differences in principal-agent relationships between parties and leaders. Differences in post-executive career opportunities represent different payoffs parties can offer potential leaders as forms of *ex post* compensation.

In parliamentary systems, former prime ministers frequently return to the national legislature. The most extreme historical example is Italian premier Amintore Fanfani, who remained in parliament for over 30 years after his first appointment as prime minister. He also served nine years in the cabinet after he first reached the premiership – and was returned to the prime minister's office four more times. Somewhat similarly, in pure presidential systems outside the United States it is common for presidents to continue in politics after leaving office. For example, Venezuelan presidents Caldera and Herrera Campins both had long post-presidential legislative careers – 28 and 20 years, respectively. (Caldera also returned to the presidency a second time.)

Table 3.4 shows that we cannot generalize from US experience: many ex-presidents do continue their political careers upon leaving office (see also Corrales 2008). These results hold up if US presidents are removed from the analysis. Indeed, the proportion of ex-presidents who continue to lead their party in both pure and hybrid systems is not insignificant, again warning against exaggerating the degree to which presidents are outsiders throughout their careers. For example, ex-presidents in president-parliamentary hybrids are twice as likely to remain at the head of their party than prime ministers in those systems.

Nevertheless, Table 3.4 also indicates that prime ministers in pure parliamentary regimes are the most likely to continue on the inside track, trailed closely by prime ministers in premier-presidential regimes, and then by prime ministers in president-parliamentary regimes. In contrast, presidents in all systems are less likely to reenter and remain in

TABLE 3.4. *Post-Executive Career Patterns*

	Prime Ministers	Premier-Presidential, Prime Minister	President-Parliamentary, Prime Minister	Premier-Presidential, President	President-Parliamentary, President	Presidents
Lead Party (%)	.46	.49	.26	.26	.50	.30
# Years Lead Party	2.48	2.65	1.10	1.52	2.17	1.88
Legislator (%)	.82	.69	.40	.16	.23	.20
# Years Legislator	7.18	5.33	1.69	0.87	2.00	1.20
Cabinet (%)	.26	.13	.05	.00	.00	.00
# Years Cabinet	1.15	0.38	0.13	0.00	0.00	0.00

the legislature than prime ministers. Furthermore, although fully one in four ex-prime ministers in pure parliamentary system regained a spot in the cabinet, as did smaller proportions of ex-prime ministers in hybrid systems, the corresponding percentage for ex-presidents in both pure and hybrid systems is *zero*.

Both the positional and configurational hypotheses gain support from the results in Table 3.4. On the one hand, presidents are less likely to hold to the insider career trajectory after leaving office and more likely instead to sever their ties with their parties, suggesting that the danger of moral hazard is highest in hybrid or pure presidential systems. On the other hand, presidents and prime ministers exhibit considerable variation in their career trajectories in different democratic regimes. In particular, premiers in president-parliamentary systems actually resemble outsiders, most likely because they served at the pleasure of the presidents in those systems rather than the party.

Overall, the evidence from politicians' career paths clearly supports the hypothesis that the configuration of institutional authority affects the "types" of politicians that parties select for the top spots. Presidents are more typically outsiders, but the degree of "outsider-ness" varies as a function of constitutional structure. Likewise, only prime ministers in pure parliamentary regimes fully embody the stereotypical insider. The constitutional structure of premier-presidential and especially president-parliamentary regimes tends to presidentialize politics to such a degree that prime ministers are less likely to be faithful party agents in those systems, relative to those in pure parliamentary systems. Instead, prime ministers often become agents of the president – especially in president-parliamentary regimes.

LIMITS OF PRESIDENTIALIZATION IN HYBRID REGIMES

Executives' career paths in semi-presidential regimes support the hypotheses that contamination occurs across the two components of the dual executive, and that most of this contamination runs from presidential to parliamentary component, as our theoretical framework expects. When parties must nominate a candidate for direct executive elections, they tend to presidentialize their organization and behavior. As a result, executives tend to have outsider profiles in semi-presidential systems, compared against insider prime ministers under parliamentarism.

Yet institutions are not destiny – and we should not be surprised if parties in semi-presidential systems sometimes overcome the formal configuration of authority and act more like fully parliamentarized parties. Parliamentarization of leadership selection means that parties would fully control recruitment to the top positions of president and prime minister, and select leaders who would not undermine the parliamentarized nature of the parties. In this section we discuss two factors that might support parliamentarization under semi-presidentialism. The first condition concerns the impact of cohabitation, while the second identifies the sources of parliamentarization in our most obvious outlier case – Austria, which is formally a president-parliamentary system.

The Impact of Cohabitation on Party Presidentialization

Recall from Chapter 2 that cohabitation occurs when the president and prime minister are from opposing parties and the president's party is not represented in the cabinet. These situations arise when the president's party cannot control an assembly majority, either alone or in cooperation with other parties. Given that presidents in semi-presidential systems typically have a constitutional role in the appointment of a prime minister, it remains to be seen whether presidents who face an opposition-controlled assembly tend to submit to the will of the assembly majority or negotiate over the selection of the prime minister and obtain an outcome more suited to their preferences.

We already saw in Chapter 2 that cohabitation occurs about 20% of the time in premier-presidential systems, but less than 1.5% of the time in president-parliamentary systems. Here we look more closely at the selection of prime ministers in cohabitation situations, as a means of testing the relative influence of presidents versus parliamentary majorities in cohabitation situations. We then consider whether presidents in some situations may be able to avert cohabitation by exercising leverage through their independent powers, despite facing an ostensibly unfavorable legislative situation.

To unpack this question, we examined the penultimate job of all prime ministers who were appointed to a cohabitation situation, to determine whether they were more often leaders of their party than prime ministers who served in situations of unified government. If so, we have evidence that under cohabitation semi-presidential systems oscillate toward parliamentarization, as Duverger predicted (1980; see also Lijphart 1999, 121–22). If cohabitation does produce parliamentarization, it should more frequently result in the appointment of a party leader as premier, because the opposition party will want to have its most powerful leader counterbalancing the president. The definition of "party leader" includes such roles as parliamentary leader of the party or leader of the (then) opposition, or the party's most recent presidential candidate.

Table 3.5 summarizes our findings, which should be compared to the proportions of party leaders appointed premier under all situations in semi-presidential systems reported in Table 3.1: 22% in premier-presidential systems and 18% in president-parliamentary systems. When we split the sample in Table 3.1 into cases of unified government and cohabitation, we see that prime ministers under cohabitation are about twice as likely to have most recently served as party leader, compared to prime ministers under unified government.[11] While the total number of prime ministers who are newly appointed under cohabitation is small (26 in premier-presidential systems and 1 in a president-parliamentary system), this difference is statistically significant. Moreover, the proportion – one-third – is even higher than the 23% of premiers who had been serving as party leaders in pure parliamentary systems reported in Table 3.1.

The evidence in Table 3.5 confirms that under semi-presidentialism, an incumbent president whose party (or alliance) loses a legislative election must frequently accept the opposition leader as head of his or her cabinet. Still, 33% means that in two-thirds of all cohabitation situations the main opposition party does *not* install its leader as prime minister. This raises two possibilities: that the opposition *chooses* not to install its leader as prime minister, or that the president influences *which member* of the opposition takes over the cabinet. The latter possibility implies that presidents can meddle in the affairs of parties that hold the assembly majority even when the constitution would seem to prevent their doing so. To illustrate that this is not merely a theoretical possibility and to shed light on the limits of parliamentarization even under cohabitation, we briefly discuss three examples of presidential interference with opposition majorities, in both semi-presidential subtypes.

Our first example comes from Mongolia, a premier-presidential system. In 1997 the Democratic Union Coalition held an assembly majority,

---

[11] The percentage of party leaders becoming prime minister in noncohabitation periods is slightly lowered by the fact that the president may be leading one of the parties. However, because our definition of party leader includes *assembly* leadership positions, nothing would preclude parties from promoting their assembly leader to the premiership when another of their leaders (or perhaps one of our "outsiders") has won the presidency. Such occurrences are evidently rare, and thus it is mainly in cohabitation situations – when neither the party itself nor an ally controls the presidency – that the leader is likely to become prime minister.

TABLE 3.5: *Party Leaders Becoming Prime Minister in Semi-Presidential Systems, Cohabitation vs. Unified Government*

	All Semi-Presidential PMs		Premier-Presidential PMs	
	Cohabitation (N = 29)	Unified Government (N = 197)	Cohabitation (N = 28)	Unified Government (N = 122)
Party Leader	.33	.15	.31	.16
Significance	$p = .01$		$p = .04$	

Note: Includes only those prime ministers who were newly appointed after a parliamentary election or between elections; that is, excludes three prime ministers who were already in power and remained in power when an opposing president was elected.

but the candidate of the Mongolian People's Revolutionary Party won the presidency. According to Severinghaus (2000) the remainder of the legislative term was volatile: there were three changes in prime minister, and during one contentious period in 1998–99, "the president vetoed one nominee for prime minister seven times in a row." Thus, while the legislative majority did control each of these cabinets, the president's insistence on determining which opposition leaders served in his cabinet severely limited parliamentarization.

A second example comes from Romania, another premier-presidential regime. As noted at the start of Chapter 1, the results of Romania's 2004 presidential runoff caused a realignment of the multiparty alliances that had just contested the assembly elections. In conceding defeat in the presidential runoff, incumbent prime minister and Social Democratic presidential candidate Adrian Năstase signaled that he expected a period of cohabitation with the winner of the presidential election, Traian Băsescu.[12] Năstase had good reason to expect to continue in the premier's job, because his party and its coalition partner the Humanist Party had won a strong plurality of seats and was close to achieving an assembly majority before the presidential runoff took place. However, after winning the runoff, Băsescu dismissed Năstase and nominated Călin Popescu-Tăriceanu of the National Liberal Party – an

---

[12] "Romania presidential candidate seeks cooperation with victorious rival," Radio Romania Actualitati, Bucharest, via *BBC Monitoring Europe*, December 13, 2004b.

ally of Băsescu's Democrats – as prime minister. Popescu-Tăriceanu then formed an assembly majority by enticing the Humanists to abandon their alliance with the Social Democrats.[13] Băsescu thereby avoided cohabitation simply by refusing to recommend as premier the leader of the alliance that had "won" the legislative election.[14]

Our final example is of presidential influence in a *potential* cohabitation situation in Taiwan, a president-parliamentary system. Given the constitutional configuration, in this case we expect even greater presidential influence than in Mongolia or Romania. In 2000, Taiwan's main opposition party, the Democratic Progressive Party (DPP), won the presidency from the long-ruling Kuomintang Party (KMT). However, the DPP held a minority of seats in Taiwan's assembly, and assembly elections were not scheduled for another year and a half. Taiwan's constitution contains no provision requiring the prime minister to resign upon the inauguration of a new president, but newly inaugurated president Chen Shui-bian dismissed the KMT premier and appointed another KMT official in his stead. However, he filled most of the rest of his cabinet with DPP officials. Note that this is *not* a cohabitation cabinet: even though the premier came from the opposition party, the KMT could not dictate the composition of the entire cabinet. In a situation that "should have" resulted in cohabitation, the president refused to accept the majority party's choice for premier – and also refused a cohabitation cabinet.

This mildly accommodative cabinet lasted just over four months, at which point the president simply appointed a DPP cabinet, ushering in a period of "divided government" in which the executive and legislative branches were led by different parties (Rigger 2002). This situation is obviously not cohabitation, because the president and the premier came from the same party. Instead, this situation resembled minority government under parliamentarism – and indeed, the premier always came

---

[13] "Premier-delegate announces Romanian Humanist Party joins government," Rompres news agency, Bucharest, via *BBC Monitoring Europe*, December 23, 2004a; and "Romania's ruling coalition signs governance agreement," Pro TV, Bucharest, via *BBC Monitoring Europe*, February 16, 2005.

[14] However, in March 2007 Popescu-Tăriceanu dismissed all the cabinet ministers from Băsescu's Democratic Party. This followed a lengthy period of conflict between the president and the premier, including a failed attempt to impeach the president. Thus although the 2004 events showed how a president can obtain an outcome in his favor despite a situation seemingly ripe for cohabitation, the 2007 events show the limits of that power. In the latter case, the premier decisively won the dispute with the president, resulting in cohabitation – a "parliamentarized" outcome. See "Romanian premier declares ruling alliance 'dead'," *BBC Monitoring Europe*, March 27, 2007.

from the DPP for the remainder of Chen's two four-year terms in office, even though his DPP and its ally, the Taiwan Solidarity Union, never managed to win a majority in the National Assembly. This period in Taiwan illustrates well the high degree of presidentialization we expect in president-parliamentary systems.

This brief exploration of opposing-majority situations in semi-presidential systems supports our expectations about how institutional configuration of power impacts prime-ministerial selection. When oppositions win an assembly majority in premier-presidential systems, the result is virtually always cohabitation. Moreover, in some cases – as in Mongolia – the president can still influence the assembly majority's choice for premier. In contrast, opposition majorities in president-parliamentary systems are extremely rare to begin with – we found only the Taiwanese case mentioned above and the single case of cohabitation in Sri Lanka[15] – and even in those situations, presidents can influence cabinet composition, as the Taiwanese case illustrates.

Parliamentarization in Austria

The president-parliamentary subtype grants the president so much formal authority over cabinet formation that parliamentarization of parties should be rare. However, rare does not mean never, as we illustrate by briefly exploring the case of Austria, which is the only obviously "parliamentarized" president-parliamentary regime in the world today. Our configurational hypothesis assumes that the presidency will be as important in reality as it is on constitutional parchment – which implies that prime ministers should always be subordinate to presidents in such systems. However, Austrian presidents have never played such a dominant role, despite the president's clear constitutional authority to determine the prime minister, dismiss cabinets that enjoy parliamentary confidence, and dissolve parliament.

Müller (1999) notes that Austria's informal "constitutional convention" requires that the president always appoint the leader of the largest party as *formateur*. In fact, the leader of the largest party has always formed the government. In addition, no postwar Austrian president has dismissed a government or dissolved parliament. Also, rather than

---

[15] Sri Lanka's cohabitation (2001–04) was "parliamentarized" in the sense that the leader of the assembly majority did become prime minister. Cohabitation ended when the president exercised his constitutional power to dissolve the assembly and call early elections, at which his party regained the majority.

nominating their most important leaders for president, parties tend to nominate elder statesmen. Campaign laws further inhibit presidentialization, as there is almost no public finance available for presidential candidates to campaign independently of their parties, in contrast to the generous subsidies available for all other elected offices (Müller 1999, 40). In short, unlike parties in other president-parliamentary regimes, Austria's parties have deliberately minimized the potential that they would become presidentialized.

Given these informal norms, Austrian politics does not follow the formal configuration of power its constitution outlines, and support for our configurational hypothesis in the analysis above declines when we include Austria. Austrian premiers are strong insiders, in contrast to prime ministers in all other president-parliamentary systems: 11 of 12 jumped to the premiership from the assembly or the cabinet, a far higher proportion than average for the regime subtype; all had also served at some point in parliament, 7 of 12 had served as party leader, and half had served in the cabinet.

Austria is clearly an outlier for our argument. The presidency's limited political relevance is partly a historical accident and partly a function of Austrian parties' conscious efforts. At the end of World War II, Austria re-declared its independence from Germany, which had annexed the country in 1938. To restore stability and the country's autonomy as rapidly as possible, Austrian political leaders decided to sidestep the often lengthy and contentious process of writing a new constitution. Instead, they agreed to simply revert to the country's constitution of 1920, which had been modeled on Weimar Germany's but had been amended in 1929 to give the president considerably greater autonomous powers. After the war, the two main parties – the socialist SPÖ and center-right ÖVP – entered into a governing coalition that lasted for two decades. During this time, the parties established an informal norm that the presidency would be largely ceremonial. The constitution has never been amended to formally reduce the presidents' powers, but presidents have rarely if ever taken advantage of their considerable formal authority.

In no other semi-presidential system do we see this degree of de facto political deviation from the de jure constitutional form. However, the Austrian experience suggests ways that parties – and thus the regime itself – may be parliamentarized even under institutions that tend to promote presidentialization. We expect such cases to be rare, and they evidently are. We have seen that cohabitation also tends to "parliamentarize" party politics – but only in premier-presidential regimes.

Finally, despite the Austrian case, parties tend to be highly presidential-ized in president-parliamentary regimes, as our theoretical framework predicts.

CONCLUSION

The dual executive of semi-presidentialism has become increasingly common around the world. This chapter provided the first comprehen-sive empirical exploration of differences in career paths between parlia-mentary and presidential executives, across all democratic regime-types. Principal-agent theory suggests that delegation involves risk of agency losses, which occur when the agent does not act faithfully in the princi-pal's interest. Political parties often have cause to worry that prospective agents will fail to pursue their promised course of action. To what extent does institutional context affect parties' ability to gauge the relative reli-ability of prospective agents? As in other professions, the most valuable signal politicians can send about their reliability is previous experience. To determine whether institutional context affects parties' ability to deal with potential problems of adverse selection, we explored the types of experience that leaders bring to the table under different institutional contexts.

We have good theoretical reason to believe that parties under the sep-aration of powers confront more difficult adverse selection contracting problems. This is because the qualities that make a potential candidate *useful* may or may not overlap with the qualities that make a candidate *reliable*. Parties always confront trade-offs between seeking votes and pursuing their policy goals (Strøm 1990); presidentialism exacerbates this problem by pushing parties to favor vote-seeking over policy-seeking (see Chapter 6). This incentive even exists under dual-executive hybrids, because the political importance of the presidency often leads parties to organize around pursuit of that office. Parties under any separation of powers system may be relatively more willing to sacrifice candidate reliability in order to be competitive in the presidential race. They may be willing to accept the risks of adverse selection because the potential payoffs of winning a direct executive election may exceed those of win-ning legislative seats.

To the extent that such a trade-off between partisan reliability and electoral utility exists, and to the extent that the separation of pow-ers exacerbates this trade-off, we expect parties to select different sorts of candidates. Scholars have long suggested that parties under pure presidential systems tend to select "outsider" candidates relative to parties in parliamentary systems. That is, scholars have long assumed that being a good *party agent* is incompatible with being a good *candidate* under the separation of powers. This chapter qualified this conventional wisdom by examining the career paths of all democratically elected executives around the world. On the one hand, it is clear that the conventional wisdom should not be exaggerated. Presidents are rarely total outsiders, and prime ministers are not always consummate insiders. National leaders in all political systems tend to have substantial political experience.

On the other hand, it is also clear that the *nature* of politicians' experience tends to differ across systems. In both pure and semi-presidential systems, parties emphasize the recruitment of executive personnel who are capable of winning a separate electoral contest, which implies less cumulative experience as a political insider. In addition, the institutional configuration of authority in dual-executive systems tends to "contaminate" the position of prime minister. Prime ministers in hybrid regimes do not closely resemble their insider parliamentary cousins. As one moves from the ideal-type parliamentary system to the ideal-type presidential system, politicians who make it to the top spot tend to have shorter legislative careers, are less likely to have served in the cabinet, and are less likely to have exercised a position of authority within their political party. These are the three most important methods by which parties acquire information about candidates' qualities and qualifications.

The separation of powers forces parties to make different sorts of leadership-selection choices. When a direct executive election exists, parties are willing to forgo rigorous screening and selecting mechanisms in their effort to find credible candidates. This suggests that under the separation of powers, parties have fewer tools at their disposal to encourage greater revelation of applicants' true incentives, and that there is relatively less that parties can do to judge *ex ante* the extent to which potential leaders will live up to their expectations. The potential losses for the organization are greater, but so are the potential gains.

APPENDIX 3A: CONSTRUCTING THE DATABASE ON LEADERS' CAREER PATHS

To create the database of national executives' career trajectories we first compiled a list of all leaders who qualified for analysis. We then generated a chronological biographical sketch of each prime minister/

president, and then converted that information into quantitative indicators. We searched for the following information: the incumbent's party at time of election; date of birth (and death if applicable); starting and ending dates of service as national executive; the year of the person's first obvious formal engagement with politics; whether (and for how many years) the person led the national party organization; whether (and for how long) the person served in the executive organ of the national party organization; the person's first political job or activity; the person's job or activity immediately prior to assuming national office; and whether and for how long the person had served as national executive previously and whether that experience had come in a nondemocratic situation.

We also sought information as to whether the person had served in one of the following jobs both before *and* after assuming national executive office: vice-president or deputy prime minister, legislator (and for how many years), institutional leaders within the legislature, cabinet member (and for how many years), appointed (not elected) president, diplomat, party founder, provincial executive (e.g. governor) or provincial executive candidate, provincial or local legislator (and for how many years), mayor or mayoral candidate, and how many times he or she had run and lost previously for national executive candidacies.

We obtained nearly all of our information from online sources. On average, each biography derived information from two to three sources. General online sources included Lexis-Nexis Academic, ProQuest Newsstand, Factiva, the Biography Reference Bank, the Hutchinson Encyclopedia of Biography, Chambers' Biographical Dictionary, Oxford University Press's Dictionary of Political Biography and Dictionary of Contemporary World History, and the *New York Times* online archive. We also utilized the online collection of detailed political biographies provided by the Centro de Investigación de Relaciones Internacionales y Desarrollo (http://www.cidob.org/es/documentacion/biografias_lideres_politicos).

Numerous other resources proved helpful. Many contemporary politicians have their own websites – for example, Argentine president Carlos Menem's can be found at www.carlosmemen.com; Danish premier Anders Fogh Rasmussen provides biographical information at www.andersfogh.dk; and Italian prime minister Romano Prodi provides a biography at www.romanoprodi.it. Likewise, many academic institutions and national historical organizations provide online biographies of important leaders. For example, we discovered extensive information about Italian premier Alcide de Gasperi at www.degasperi.net;

the Philippine Presidency Project provides biographies of that country's presidents at http://www.pangulo.ph/index.php; the Balkan Political Club has extensive biographical information on many former leaders of countries in that region (http://www.balkanpoliticalclub.net/en/fm.php). Furthermore, any former prime minister who is or was ever a member of the European Parliament or the Council of Europe has an online biography (see www.europarl.europa.eu or http://assembly.coe.int).

Many countries' government websites also make available biographical information about past national leaders, in the native language as well as in English. For example, information about Albanian presidents can be found at http://www.president.al/english/pub/presidentet.asp; information about Australian prime ministers can be found at www.primeministers.naa.gov.au/meetpm.asp; information about British premiers can be found at www.number10.gov.uk. Some countries' parliaments' websites include information about former and/or current prime ministers. Thus, information on Einars Repse, Latvian prime minister between 2002 and 2004, can be found (in English) on the site of Latvia's parliament (www.saeima.lv), where he was serving at the time we constructed this database (summer 2007). Finally, political parties often provide biographical sketches about former leaders who served as national executive. For example, information about Armenian premier Serzh Sargysyan can be found at the website of the Armenian Republican Party, http://www.hhk.am/eng/index.php?page=history_hhk.

4

Constitutional Design and Intraparty Leadership Accountability

In Chapter 3 we showed that careful selection of agents – the power to hire – can mitigate adverse selection problems. Yet perhaps the most important *ex ante* sanction that a principal can write into an implicit contract about an agent's *ex post* behavior is the power to *dismiss* that agent – the power to fire that agent if he or she does not perform up to certain standards. Principals who possess dismissal power can keep an agent in line and minimize the problem of moral hazard, which occurs when an agent violates the spirit of a contract after it has been signed. In contrast, principals who lack the ability to rid themselves of a wayward agent have good reason to fear the problem of moral hazard.

All democracies possess ways to remove and replace national leaders against their will. However, important differences exist across democratic regimes in terms of *parties*' ability to remove and replace their leaders against their will while those leaders are serving as incumbent heads of government. For example, once in office, parliamentary prime ministers remain subject to ongoing partisan as well as legislative confidence. This sets a relatively low bar for their removal. And indeed, as we detail below, parties in parliamentary systems regularly remove their own prime ministers between elections. Direct partisan control over the premiership minimizes the danger of moral hazard.

In semi-presidential systems, parties also regularly remove their own prime ministers between elections. However, semi-presidentialism complicates parties' ability to control prime ministers' fates, because hybrid constitutions typically afford presidents some influence over prime-ministerial deselection – and presidents frequently take advantage of this authority. This means that under many conditions, prime ministers in semi-presidential systems are relatively less accountable to their party than are prime ministers in parliamentary systems, precisely because they are instead accountable to the president.

The problem that parties in both pure and semi-presidential systems face is that they cannot fire their own sitting president. The separation of survival limits parties' ability to hold their agents accountable, thereby weakening parties' ability to act as citizens' agents in government. Indeed, the very notion of a powerful executive whom citizens directly elect for a fixed term is anathema to the notion of "responsible party government." Our approach points toward a tension in democratic theory: even though scholars equate modern democracy with party government, the separation of survival dramatically alters the quality of democracy because it weakens parties' control over their agents.

The contrast between presidents' separate survival and prime ministers' fused survival forms the basis of this chapter's focus on executive deselection. The implications of variation in parties' ability to fire their agents-in-government complement the findings in Chapter 3, which showed that adverse selection problems are minimized under parliamentarism. This chapter reveals that parliamentarism also minimizes the danger of moral hazard. Arguably, this chapter's findings are more substantively important than those of Chapter 3 because control over deselection is more important for generating incentive compatibility between principals and agents, and is thus more important for explaining political outcomes of interest. We therefore first describe the relatively high degree of control parties exert over their agents in parliamentary systems. Then we discuss how semi-presidential systems complicate parties' ability to hold their prime-ministerial agents to accounts. Finally, we expose parties' inability to control their directly elected presidential agents.

FIRING PARTY AGENTS UNDER PARLIAMENTARISM

In parliamentary systems the composition of the executive branch can change for a number of reasons, including electoral loss or the collapse of a multiparty coalition. Yet what is distinct about parliamentarism is the degree to which *intra*party politics determines control over the executive branch. Scholars of parliamentarism have certainly noted the relevance of intraparty politics for government turnover,[1] but party scholars have

---

[1] See e.g. Warwick (1994); Kenig (2006); Maravall (2008); and Tegos (2007).

yet to consider the extent to which intraparty control over the executive branch varies across democratic regimes.

Using the same database employed in Chapter 3, we counted a total of 374 changes of prime minister in 39 pure parliamentary systems since 1945. This census does not include changes to or from caretaker or interim prime ministers and does not include incumbent prime ministers at the time the dataset was constructed (summer 2007). By exploring published biographies, Lexis-Nexis, the *New York Times* online historical archives, and a variety of other sources, we uncovered the specific reason each prime minister left office. Of these 374 changes, 16 resulted from an incumbent's death or physical incapacitation, leaving 358 cases. We were unable to find information on 4 cases, leaving 354. Of these, 113 prime ministers (31.9%) left office due to election losses, and 115 changes (32.4%) resulted from *inter*party conflict such as coalition collapse.

We attributed 19 cases (5.4%) to "other" reasons, including dismissal by a monarch, governor-general, or unelected president; a military coup or threatened coup; or the incumbent's indirect election or appointment as president. This leaves 107 cases, 30.2% of the total, in which a change of prime minister resulted from *intra*party politics. This percentage serves as a baseline for cross-regime comparison and also illustrates parties' *organizational* hold on executive power in pure parliamentary regimes. In 89 of these cases, the party of the prime minister did not change – but this means that in 18 cases the incumbent party sacrificed control over the premiership to fire its own leader! Clearly, parties can and do revoke their agents' contracts frequently under pure parliamentarism, without serious internal or external repercussions.

When intraparty politics forces an incumbent prime minister from office, a key question is "was he pushed or did he jump?" It is sometimes difficult to tell, but one can usually distinguish a more-or-less voluntary resignation from an actual defenestration. In slightly more than half of the intraparty cases (58 of 107) the incumbent resigned voluntarily and his or her party simply emplaced someone else. Most of these changes occurred due to an incumbent's age or exhaustion, as in the retirements of the UK's Winston Churchill in 1955, Sweden's Tage Erlander in 1969, or New Zealand's Keith Holyoake in 1972. In a few cases the incumbent prime minister resigned to take a different job – as was the case when the Greek parliament elected Prime Minister Konstantinos Karamanlis as the country's president in 1980. His New Democracy Party simply replaced him with George Rallis. Similarly, Norwegian prime minister

Gro Harlem Brundtland resigned in 1996 to head the World Health Organization, and her Labor Party replaced her with Thorbjørn Jagland. Regardless of the reason, in all of these cases the prime minister's party handled the transfer of executive authority as an internal affair, without taking other parties' or voters' preferences into account.

Not all prime ministers resign willingly: intraparty pressure forced incumbent prime ministers from office in 49 of 107 cases. Sometimes prime ministers perceive rising internal opposition and resign prior to being ousted, thereby saving what little is left of their reputation and dignity. In such cases, parties do not have to initiate a formal deselection procedure, but the incumbent nonetheless cannot independently determine the date of his or her departure from office. In other cases, incumbent prime ministers actually lose their colleagues' support and are pushed out. For example, British prime minister Anthony Eden famously resigned under pressure from his Conservative Party colleagues in the humiliating aftermath of the Suez Crisis in 1957.[2] In other cases prime ministers depart because their performance disappoints their copartisans. For example, the New Zealand Labour Party forced incumbent prime minister David Lange to resign in 1989 because the party's popularity was sagging. Geoffrey Palmer took over, but intraparty pressure also forced him out for similar reasons, after less than a year. Parties have forced their own prime ministers from office at least once in 21 pure parliamentary systems.[3]

Sometimes parties even formally remove their own premier. In a few cases, party discipline has collapsed and premiers find themselves out of a job because elements of their own party voted with the opposition. For example, defections on a confidence vote cost the Belgian Socialist Party's prime minister his job in 1946; likewise, in 1966 the Dutch premier quit after a co-partisan introduced a motion to defeat a government proposal. Similar episodes have occurred in Germany, Greece, Israel, Italy, and Japan. In other cases incumbent prime ministers are tossed from office via partisan no-confidence votes or leadership challenges. For example, leadership challenges in both major Australian parties can occur at any time via a motion in the party's legislative caucus (Davis 1998, 167).

---

[2] Like Eden, several prime ministers claimed to resign for health reasons, but such explanations usually provide public cover for serious intraparty dissension.

[3] A few parties in parliamentary systems have adopted "fixed terms" for their leaders, but a fixed term as *party leader* is irrelevant if the prime minister loses the support of the majority of his or her parliamentary co-partisans, simply because *prime ministers* do not sit for fixed terms.

Such rules have made life difficult for several Australian prime ministers (Kenig 2006). In 1991, Paul Keating successfully challenged incumbent prime minister Bob Hawke for leadership of the Australian Labor Party, even though Hawke had just led Labor to its fourth consecutive election victory. Hawke immediately resigned. In 1971, the Australian Liberal Party deposed its sitting prime minister John Gorton in similar fashion (Davis 1998, 174).

Perhaps the most famous example of this sort is the ouster of the UK's Margaret Thatcher, as noted in Chapter 1. An internal rule requires that the leader of the British Conservative Party stand for reelection annually, regardless of whether the party is in opposition or in government (Davis 1998, 78). Thatcher used this procedure to pry open the door to power in 1975, when she defeated Edward Heath for the party's leadership. At that time the Conservatives were in opposition. Yet despite leading the party to three consecutive election victories, Thatcher lost her own job under the same rule in 1990, after which John Major was selected as party leader. Party rules did not require Thatcher to resign as prime minister, but in losing the party leadership she lost the authority to lead the government, and she quickly resigned. Simply by winning the party's internal election, Major became prime minister.

Parliamentary parties' internal governance mechanisms clearly serve to keep prime ministers from growing too comfortable in their positions. Prime ministers do not sit for fixed terms of office; parliamentary parties can swap leaders without input from voters or from other parties. The fact that this process is common has not gone unnoticed, but its frequency has not been placed in comparative perspective – nor have scholars considered its importance for understanding party politics across democratic regimes. For any political party, parliamentarism limits the danger of moral hazard because executives do not sit for fixed terms. Prime ministers are not only responsible to the assembly majority, but also to their party. This means that intraparty politics has a substantial impact over who runs the government as well as how those people run the government. As we begin to detail in the next section, other democratic regimes weaken parties' direct control over their agents and heighten the danger of moral hazard.

FIRING PRIME MINISTERS UNDER SEMI-PRESIDENTIALISM

In parliamentary systems, accountability follows a single chain of delegation from voters to parties to the party leader. In dual-executive hybrids, the chain of delegation is more complex. The key source of variation is that party organizations do not have sole authority to deselect the prime minister – except, as we shall see, under situations of cohabitation. Instead, presidents enter the picture. Even in the premier-presidential subtype, presidents often deselect the prime minister, a fact that is puzzling given their lack of constitutional authority to do so. In this section we first compare the sources of prime-ministerial turnover under semi-presidentialism with our findings for parliamentary systems. We then explain how presidents' formal and informal influence limits parties' hold over their prime-ministerial agents in the assembly. Finally, we describe how cohabitation offers parties the opportunity to retain greater control over their prime ministers.

Sources of Prime-Ministerial Turnover in Semi-Presidential Systems

As in parliamentary systems, control over the office of prime minister in semi-presidential systems can change because of an election loss or because of *inter*party conflict, either within the governing coalition or between the government and the opposition. And just as in parliamentary systems, *intra*party politics can also drive prime-ministerial turnover in hybrid systems. However, semi-presidentialism also introduces a different intraparty dynamic to the question of prime-ministerial turnover, because both presidents *and* the party's parliamentary caucus can influence prime-ministerial turnover.

As discussed in Chapter 2, different configurations of constitutional authority should influence presidents' relative influence over prime-ministerial deselection. In premier-presidential systems, the assembly majority possesses exclusive formal authority to dismiss the prime minister and cabinet. Yet in president-parliamentary systems the president also has the authority to dismiss the prime minister, regardless of the preferences of the party or parties that comprise the assembly majority. This suggests that presidents should have relatively greater influence over prime-ministerial deselection in president-parliamentary regimes.

In what follows, we distinguish "parliamentary" from "presidential" sources of prime-ministerial turnover in semi-presidential systems. "Parliamentary" sources of turnover resemble the dynamics we observed above in pure parliamentary systems: that is, prime ministers can be forced from office due to elections, or due to inter- or intraparty conflict between elections. "Presidential" sources, however, are unique to semi-presidential systems: prime ministers can be forced from office as a function of *presidential* elections, and also as a function of inter- or intraparty *presidential* pressure between elections.

Presidential elections that cause a change in prime minister clearly indicate party presidentialization, because to the extent that a president can influence cabinet composition immediately after winning election (or reelection), the prime minister has become the president's agent rather than the agent of the party's assembly contingent. Given the formal distribution of power, we expect prime-ministerial turnover following *assembly* elections to occur relatively more frequently in premier-presidential regimes, while turnovers following *presidential* elections should be relatively more frequent in president-parliamentary regimes.

Very few premier-presidential constitutions require the incumbent prime minister to submit his or her resignation upon the inauguration of a new president: only Armenia's and Lithuania's among our cases contains such a provision.[4] Precisely because such provisions are so rare, if we observe prime-ministerial turnover following a presidential election in premier-presidential systems, it must be a function of informal political norms and practices. As we describe below, the most important informal source of presidential authority in premier-presidential systems is *partisan* – presidents' influence within their own party. That is, when the president's party (or a coalition of allied parties) forms the assembly majority, parties become informally presidentialized because the prime minister tends to be the president's political subordinate – even in premier-presidential systems, the subtype with "weaker" presidents.

Table 4.1 provides a breakdown of the reasons prime ministers leave office, by subtype of semi-presidential regime.[5] As expected, prime ministers are far more likely to depart because they have lost an assembly election in premier-presidential systems than in president-parliamentary regimes. The proportion of prime ministers who leave office because of the result of assembly elections echoes the proportion we found in pure parliamentary systems, supporting our point that this subtype leans

---

[4] Although such a provision does not technically give a president "dismissal" power, if the resignation of the incumbent prime minister allows the newly inaugurated president to install a different premier, he or she clearly has exerted influence over the cabinet independent of the will of the assembly majority.

[5] As with the analysis in Chapter 3, we exclude Austria. And as with our analysis of pure parliamentary systems, these figures exclude prime ministers who died in office (three in president-parliamentary regimes) and those for whom we found no information (three in president-parliamentary regimes), and also excludes caretakers, interim prime ministers, and incumbents at the time the dataset was constructed.

TABLE 4.1. *Reasons for Prime Minister Termination in Semi-Presidential Regimes*

Reason for Termination		Premier-Presidential Prime Ministers (%)	President-Parliamentary Prime Ministers (%)
Parliamentary	Lost Election	33.1	9.5
	Interparty Conflict	22.8	7.9
	Intraparty Conflict	19.9	25.4
Presidential	Ran for/Elected President	6.6	9.5
	Interparty Conflict	6.6	12.7
	Intraparty Conflict	10.2	27.0
Other		0.7	7.9
(N)		136	63

toward parliamentarism. Also as expected, the impact of intra- or inter-party conflict within the assembly is relatively more important in premier-presidential systems, accounting for about 43% of all cases as opposed to about 33% of all cases in president-parliamentary systems. It is worth recalling that the proportion of prime ministers under pure parliamentarism who left office because of intra- or interparty conflict was 63%.

Overall, nearly 76% of all cases of prime-ministerial turnover in premier-presidential regimes are due to factors specific to parliamentary politics – assembly elections or intra- or interparty conflict in the assembly. In contrast, the same parliamentary factors account for only about 43% of all cases of prime-ministerial turnover in president-parliamentary regimes. Rather obviously, the reason that parliamentary factors are more important in premier-presidential regimes is because "presidential" factors are relatively more important in president-parliamentary regimes. Even so, presidential influence accounts for a sizable proportion of prime-ministerial turnover in both hybrid subtypes. First, we can see that in both regimes a number of prime ministers depart office because they decide to run for president.[6] This sort of ambition is impossible

---

[6] This number may be puzzling given the data in Chapter 3, which showed that a relatively large proportion of presidents had previously been prime minister. This is because

under parliamentarism and confronts parties in semi-presidential systems with the adverse selection problem highlighted in Chapter 3.

Table 4.1 also reveals that presidents have both intra- *and* interpartisan influence over prime ministers' fates, in both regime subtypes. As should be expected, such influence is far more important in president-parliamentary regimes (where constitutions give presidents formal authority to dismiss the premier) than it is in premier-presidential systems (40% of all cases vs. 17%). Yet even the relatively lower percentage for premier-presidential systems represents a puzzle, because the formal rules of that subtype imply that presidents should have no influence at all. Evidently, presidents in premier-presidential systems possess informal authority to deselect the premier – the result of party presidentialization rather than the formal rules.

As we argued in Chapter 2, when the presidency is an important political prize, parties will organize to win that office. Despite the potential benefits of winning the presidency, this imperative also entails potential agency losses. To the extent that presidents gain influence over prime-ministerial selection and/or deselection, parties have relinquished the most important source of political power that exists in a premier-presidential system. The figures in Table 4.2 indicate that presidents do influence prime ministers' fates in many premier-presidential systems. This means that despite the formal constitutional balance of power, parties have permitted a de facto reversal of the principal-agent relationship, as presidents use their partisan authority to shape and reshape their party in their own image.[7] Somewhat surprisingly, this authority even crosses party lines, as 6.6% of our cases represent instances of presidential influence in the dismissal of a premier from a *different* party.

Presidents' Informal Influence in Premier-Presidential Systems

The information in Table 4.1 reveals that presidents frequently drive prime ministers from office in both types of semi-presidential systems. In president-parliamentary regimes, presidents' partisan influence is well understood. Yet in premier-presidential systems, presidents' influence

there are many more prime ministers than presidents. Only a few prime ministers get to be president, but a fair number of presidents were prime ministers.

[7] Here we have in mind a distinction between "constitutional" and "partisan" powers that is similar to that developed by Mainwaring and Shugart (1997) for Latin American presidential systems.

represents something of a puzzle. Examples help us illustrate the sources of such authority.

Let us first consider how presidential elections sometimes result in the prime minister's dismissal, even if the incumbent prime minister and the president come from the same party – and even if the incumbent prime minister enjoys the confidence of the assembly majority. For example, newly elected Finnish presidents have twice fired the incumbent premier. Similarly, of the six directly elected presidents thus far in the French 5th Republic, five assumed office with a prime minister of their own party already leading the Assembly – but four of these presidents dismissed the incumbent premier.[8] This happened after both the 2002 and 2007 presidential elections, even though assembly elections were just a month away: rather than wait for the outcome of the legislative election, both presidents essentially asked the voters to ratify their personal choices.

These examples suggest that prime ministers in premier-presidential systems must have the *personal* confidence of the president as well as the *institutional* confidence of the assembly majority. Such cases reveal the nature of the implicit contract under which parties hire presidential candidates in premier-presidential systems: the candidate becomes the head of the party and is essentially delegated the right, upon winning the presidency, to change premiers. This alters the principal-agent relationship written into the constitution, which gives the assembly majority exclusive authority to deselect the premier. Parties are particularly unlikely to challenge this informal authority if the president had long coattails in a recent legislative race or is expected to help his or her party in an upcoming legislative election. Such informal partisan influence – above and beyond any formal constitutional powers, and without any formal presidential accountability to the party – marks the very essence of a presidentialized party.

Let us now explore examples of presidential influence between elections. To understand presidents' informal influence more fully, consider the key provisions in the French constitution – the model for this hybrid subtype. The French constitution states that the president "terminates the appointment" of the prime minister *"when [the prime minister] tenders the resignation of the government,"*[9] but it says nothing more

---

[8] De Gaulle in 1965 is the only exception, but he had been serving as the appointed president prior to 1965 and had appointed the incumbent prime minister himself.

[9] Article 8. Source: http://www.assemblee-nationale.fr/english/8ab.asp#TITLE%20III, August 9, 2008. Italics added for emphasis.

about prime-ministerial responsibility to the president. (However, it goes into considerable detail about the prime minister's responsibility to the *assembly*.) This phrasing implies that presenting a resignation letter to the president is merely a formality required after an election loss or a no-confidence vote, for example.

Nonetheless, under unified government, French presidents have long had their way with their own parties' premiers. For example, Socialist president François Mitterrand dismissed three different premiers from his party between elections in efforts to improve his party's stature – and by extension, his own chances at reelection. President de Gaulle even dismissed one premier for "completing his mission" – leading their party to an election victory – which suggests that the premier was an excellent party agent, but that for some reason he displeased his real boss, the president.[10] Overall, of the 18 changes in prime minister since the advent of the 5th Republic, 5 followed assembly election losses and 12 resulted from presidential influence; only one has been a function of interparty conflict in the assembly. This contrasts with the dominant dynamic in the pure parliamentary 4th Republic, in which each of the 21 prime ministers resigned due to interparty conflict in the National Assembly.

French presidents are not alone in possessing informal authority to dismiss the prime minister, despite the lack of formal constitutional authority to do so. For example, in 1999 Romania's president Emil Constantinescu fired his party's premier, Radu Vasile. Given the formal constitutional chain of delegation, Vasile considered challenging the president's action in court, but he backed down and resigned (Dow Jones 1999). And in 1977, Finnish president Urho Kekkonen publicly "requested" that Premier Martti Miettunen resign. Both Kekkonen and Miettunen were members of the Center Party. However, Kekkonen wanted to replace Miettunen's minority government with a broad coalition that would control over 75% of the parliamentary seats but would be headed by the Social Democratic Party instead of the Center Party (even though it would still include ministers from the Center Party).[11] We know of no functionally equivalent case like this under pure parliamentarism, in which a party heading a minority government fires its own premier, "voluntarily" relinquishes the premiership to another party, and reenters the cabinet in a subordinate position.

---

[10] "Pompidou named French premier," *New York Times*, April 15, 1962, p. 3.
[11] "Helsinki cabinet quits; Majority coalition due," *New York Times*, May 12, 1977, p. 16.

Under unified government, presidents in premier-presidential systems have even been able to dismiss premiers who were not their co-partisans. As noted in Table 4.1, such influence accounts for 6.6% of all cases of prime minister turnover. One such case occurred in Lithuania in 1992, when independent president Valdas Adamkus forced out premier Gediminas Vagnorius. The president and prime minister had squabbled publicly for some time, and eventually Adamkus went on national TV to demand Vagnorius's resignation. In response, Vagnorius accused Adamkus of violating the separation of powers; the premier's party and an allied party then passed a resolution supporting the incumbent government. However, by "going public," the president leveraged his popularity against the prime minister's unpopularity – and Vagnorius was compelled to resign a week later (*East European Constitutional Review* 1999).

Presidents' ability to remove another party's premier is even more puzzling than any informal intraparty influence they might acquire. Any case of interparty presidential influence is a clear violation of the notion of exclusive cabinet responsibility to the assembly under premier-presidentialism. Nevertheless, the nontrivial number of cases of interparty presidential influence over prime-ministerial deselection suggests that presidents' influence in premier-presidential systems is systemic and not limited to their own party. Our findings suggest that presidents' authority to dismiss another party's agent can be a function of alliance-formation: in multiparty systems, parties sometimes form coalitions in which one party gets the presidency while another gets the premiership. When entering such alliances, parties apparently accept a deal in which the president determines how long the premier and the cabinet stay in office.

In sum, presidents' formal authority in president-parliamentary regimes gives them substantial influence over prime-ministerial deselection. Yet we also find that presidents frequently possess considerable informal influence over prime-ministerial deselection in premier-presidential regimes, even if they lack the requisite formal institutional authority. Such informal influence typically derives from presidents' position as de facto party leader, although sometimes this power even extends to the interparty dimension of politics, leaving parties allied with incumbent presidents also vulnerable to presidential influence. This is precisely what we mean by party presidentialization: given presidents' separation of survival, presidents' influence over prime ministers presents parties with potentially quite severe adverse selection and moral hazard problems.

Cohabitation: How to Avoid Party Presidentialization

The examples above reveal the extent to which presidents influence their own and allied parties, even in premier-presidential systems. However, all of these examples came from situations of unified government. Cohabitation, by contrast, places limits on presidents' partisan influence. Recall that we defined cohabitation as situations in semi-presidential systems when the prime minister is from a party opposed to the president, and the latter's party is not in the cabinet. These should be the most "parliamentarized" phases of semi-presidential systems. Recall also that in Chapter 3 we noted that parties are relatively more likely to select their leaders as premier under cohabitation than under unified government. Here we ask how premiers lose their jobs in cohabitation situations. If cohabitation embodies a particularly "parliamentarized" phase of semi-presidential governance, then it should end through processes that typify parliamentarism. That is, cohabitation should end either due to election results or due to intra- or interpartisan disputes in parliament, and not due to presidential influence.

Table 4.2 confirms this hypothesis, showing that election results are the most common way to end a period of cohabitation. In about 40% of the cases, cohabitation ended because the incumbent prime minister's party lost an assembly election, resulting in a new cabinet that included the sitting president's party. Another 30% of cohabitation periods end through interparty conflict in parliament. In these cases an opposition-controlled coalition collapses and a new government forms that includes the president's party. And in a few cases, intraparty conflict forces a prime minister from office, and the president's party enters the new government.

Thus in about 78% of our cases of cohabitation, "parliamentary" factors ended a prime minister's tenure. In contrast, "presidential" factors ended cohabitation in only 22% of the cases. And what is notable here is that in all of these cases, cohabitation ended because of the results of a presidential election. (For example, because the incumbent president's party lost to the incumbent prime minister's party, resulting in unified government for the former assembly opposition.)[12] In none of our cases did a president push a prime minister from office under cohabitation. (Of course, we cannot rule out the possibility that the incumbent

---

[12] In one case, cohabitation ended because the premier sought and lost the presidency: Lionel Jospin in France in 2002. Jospin resigned the premiership immediately upon Jacques Chirac's reelection as president, and his Socialist Party also lost the assembly election a month later.

TABLE 4.2. *Reasons for Termination of Cohabitation in Semi-Presidential Regimes**

		Cohabitation PMs (%)
Parliamentary	Election Resulted in Unified Government	40.7
	Interparty Conflict	29.6
	Intraparty Conflict	7.4
Presidential	Presidential Election Resulted in Unified Government	11.1
	Premier Ran for/Elected President	11.1
	Interparty, Presidential Influence	0.0
	Intraparty, Presidential Influence	0.0
	(N)	27**

* Does not necessarily mean termination of the prime minister, but rather the reason the prime minister ceased to be in a cohabitation situation; this includes the one case of cohabitation under president-parliamentary system, which ended via an assembly election.
** Total number of completed cohabitation periods (this excludes five prime ministers still in office under cohabitation at the end of 2008).

president maneuvered behind the scenes.) This finding is striking: presidents in premier-presidential systems can clearly change the prime minister when their allies control the assembly majority, but they cannot do so when they face a majority opposition. This is exactly what we should expect theoretically, if cohabitation represents a "parliamentary" phase, as Duverger (1980) predicted, even before the first cohabitation had occurred in France, and as Lijphart (1999, 121–22) has argued.[13]

[13] It is also notable how much less frequently intraparty conflict within parliament ends cohabitation relative to its importance overall for ending prime ministers' tenures, whether in premier-presidential or pure parliamentary systems. Intraparty conflict within the assembly represents more than a fifth of all prime minister terminations under premier-presidentialism and close to a third under parliamentarism. Yet only 2 of 27 cohabitation premiers ended their terms this way. Parties logically – and quite sensibly – may be more careful to avoid internal conflict that might jeopardize their hold on the cabinet when they face an opposing president, whose influence would likely peak precisely when it came time to bargain over replacing the prime minister.

Cohabitation periods under premier-presidentialism are important inasmuch as they reveal the conditions under which presidents are politically sidelined in such systems. However, it would be a mistake to assume that cohabitation returns parties to a fully "parliamentarized" state. After all, under cohabitation, the party that holds the premiership but not the presidency will understand the need to have a leader able to win the next presidential election. Indeed, the sitting premier is likely to be a future presidential candidate – as was the case in two periods of cohabitation in France, for example: Jacques Chirac, premier from 1986 to 1988, ran for the presidency and lost in 1988 but won in 1995; and Lionel Jospin, premier from 1997 to 2002, ran for the presidency and lost in 2002, when Chirac was reelected.

This section's analysis of the sources of prime-ministerial deselection in semi-presidential systems reveals that party presidentialization is greater in president-parliamentary systems than in premier-presidential systems, just as the constitutional structure of authority in these subtypes would lead one to suspect. However, prime-ministerial deselection – and thus intraparty politics generally considered – is presidentialized in both subtypes, except under periods of cohabitation. This is because presidents – agents who cannot be fired – employ both formal constitutional and informal partisan powers to shape cabinet composition. For this reason, moral hazard is a greater danger under hybrid constitutions than under pure parliamentarism. Regardless of the constitutional configuration of authority, political parties tend to be highly presidentialized under both subtypes of semi-presidentialism.

FIRING A DIRECTLY ELECTED PRESIDENT

This chapter emphasizes the notion that the separation of survival enhances presidents' influence over their parties relative to prime ministers, and limits parties' ability to hold their leaders-as-presidents to account. As shown above, in both parliamentary and semi-presidential systems, parties can and frequently do replace prime ministers who have grown unpopular or who have strayed from the party line. However, parties cannot deselect presidents. Parties possess few tools besides legislative obstruction to use against directly elected presidents who decide to go their own way. To be sure, a party that obstructs its own president is sending a loud signal. Yet no matter how loud, such a signal is not, in the final analysis, equal to a party's power to cast its agent aside – nor, in semi-presidential regimes, is such a signal equivalent to a president's ability to fire his or her prime minister.

In theory, legislative parties do possess one mechanism to deselect presidents: impeachment (Baumgartner and Kada, eds. 2003; Hochstetler 2006b; Pérez-Liñán 2007). Legislators threaten presidents with impeachment with some frequency, and sometimes these threats do force presidents to resign. The modern presidents who have resigned under pressure include US President Richard Nixon in 1974, Ecuadoran Presidents Abdalá Bucaram in 1997 and Jamil Mahuad in 2000, Paraguayan President Raúl Cubas Grau in 1999, and Venezuelan President Carlos Andrés Pérez in 1993. Successful impeachments carried to their (partial or full) conclusion include the cases of Brazilian President Fernando Collor in 1992, Malagasy President Albert Zafy in 1996, Philippines President Joseph Estrada in 2001, and Lithuanian President Rolandas Paksas in 2004. In addition, in 2005 Ecuador's Congress declared that President Lucio Gutiérrez had "abandoned his duties" and deposed him from office. Nineteen other presidents (one twice) have survived formal impeachment threats or trials.[14]

Intraparty prime-ministerial deselection in parliamentary and semi-presidential regimes can expose an internal leadership crisis within the incumbent party, or – in semi-presidential regimes – it can reveal presidents' efforts to shape the cabinet independently of the assembly majority's preferences. Whatever the reason, such events are fairly common, and they proceed fairly rapidly. In contrast, impeachments are extraordinary constitutional procedures that involve a detailed and public legislative investigation, a media feeding frenzy, recourse to the judicial branch of government (depending on the constitutional procedure), and the mudslinging of a potentially lengthy public trial. As such, they are never purely intraparty political disputes, and they never represent a "normal" method for swapping out the national executive.

---

[14] We counted 31 cases of formal impeachment threats against directly elected presidents in our set of presidential and semi-presidential democracies (those listed in Chapter 2): the 6 completed plus the 5 threatened impeachments that forced presidents to resign listed in this paragraph, plus 20 other formal impeachment motions in Belarus (1996), Colombia (1996), Ecuador (1987), Malawi (2005), Paraguay (1997), Nicaragua (2002), Peru (1991 and 2005; different presidents), the Philippines (2005), Romania (1995 and 2007; different presidents), Russia (1998), South Korea (2004), Sri Lanka (1991 and 2002; different presidents), Taiwan (2000 and 2006; the same president, once in each of his terms), Ukraine (2004), the United States (1998), and Zambia (2001 and 2003; different presidents). This list only includes democracies after 1945; it therefore excludes cases in Panama in 1955, Nigeria in 2002, Peru in 2000, and the United States in 1868. It also does not include informal, extra-legislative "challenges" to presidents (Hochstetler 2006), even if such challenges result in a president's ouster (as, for example, in Argentina in 2001 or Bolivia in 2003), and it does not include impeachments of indirectly elected presidents such as Indonesia's Wahid in 2001 or Paraguay's González Macchi in 2002.

In addition, impeaching or forcing a president to resign suggests that the incumbent party nominated not merely an incompetent but a criminal to lead the party and the nation. This represents a shameful turn of events for that party as well as for the citizens who voted for that candidate. Given this, legislators in a president's party are rarely in a position to benefit from dragging their own leader through the mud, accusing him or her of criminal acts and/or treason, and deepening a political crisis of their own making. In contrast, legislators in parliamentary systems never confront such profound existential dilemmas because if their leader refuses to resign they can initiate no-confidence proceedings (either within the party or in the parliament) or force the prime minister to call new elections as a referendum on public confidence in the administration. Thus, to put it bluntly, impeachment is not a viable intraparty accountability mechanism. There is a universe of difference between a party that dismisses its prime minister and a party that attempts to send its own leader to prison.

Given this, a party in a separation of powers system must be confronted with an imminent threat to its own survival before it will encourage its own president to resign. The case of Richard Nixon illustrates this point well. The break-in at Democratic Party headquarters at the Watergate Hotel occurred in June 1972, seven months before Nixon's second inauguration. As a result of the scandal following the cover-up of the break-in, Nixon resigned – over two years later, on August 8, 1974. Yet just two weeks prior to that date, despite mounting evidence of a criminal conspiracy at the highest levels of government, 10 of the 17 Republicans on the House Judiciary committee voted *against* all three articles of impeachment that Democratic committee leaders had drawn up.[15]

Republican support for Nixon finally evaporated only after the Supreme Court ordered the president to release recordings of conversations that revealed he had lied about his knowledge of the break-in and that he had ordered the Federal Bureau of Investigation to end its investigation into the case. Only after witnessing the public outcry following these revelations did Republican congressional leaders press Nixon to resign because they feared the electoral consequences of a drawn-out Senate trial. Such fears were warranted, and Nixon had even addressed them in a press conference months earlier. When asked in February of 1974 if he would consider resigning if it became clear that his party

[15] Source: www.watergate.info. N.d. "Analysis of the Impeachment Votes of the Committee on the Judiciary of the House of Representatives." http://www.watergate.info/impeachment/impeachment-articles-analysis.shtml, accessed May 24, 2007.

would suffer a disastrous result in the November midterm legislative elections, Nixon said:

No, I want my party to succeed, but more importantly, I want the presidency to survive. And it is vitally important in this nation that the presidency of the United States not be hostage to what happens to the popularity of a president at one time or another. (Nixon 1974)

Nixon could not have expressed our main point better: the separation of survival reverses the principal-agent relationship, by making the party hostage to the president. Nixon's resignation may have prevented things from getting even worse for the Republicans, but they still lost 49 House seats in 1974, and would not win a majority in the House for another two decades.

The implications of this sequence of events are the following: in contrast to the relative frequency with which prime ministers are induced to resign when their parties view their continued presence in office as a political liability, a president, by virtue of the legitimacy a direct election confers and because of the separation of survival, is unlikely to step aside in a similar situation. Moreover, while a party can relatively easily dump its own prime minister, impeaching one's own president risks collective political suicide. Given this, parties almost never seek to use impeachment as an internal accountability mechanism.

Between 1946 and 2007, our 53 democracies directly elected 223 different individuals as president. (Several served more than one consecutive term, and a few served more than one nonconsecutive term.) Ten of these presidents died in office, three were victims of military coups,[16] and two engineered self-coups and remained in office in nondemocratic settings.[17] This leaves 208 presidents. Six of these were removed from office through impeachment or other constitutional procedures, and eleven others resigned under pressure. However, intraparty politics forced a president from office early in only *one* of these cases, or about 0.5% of the total.[18]

---

[16] Several presidents deposed by militaries did not enter our dataset for technical reasons. For example, Juan Perón was not technically the candidate elected in 1973 in Argentina. He assumed office extra-constitutionally, and was deposed extra-constitutionally as well. Likewise, Brazilian president João Goulart assumed office from the vice-presidency after the incumbent resigned, and was deposed in 1964.

[17] Alberto Fujimori of Peru in 1992 and Ferdinand Marcos of the Philippines in 1972.

[18] This calculation includes administrations that were complete by 2007. One additional potential case exists, the impeachment of President Joseph Estrada of the Philippines in 2001. Estrada was elected in 1998 on the *Laban ng Makabayang Masang Pilipino* (LAMMP) ticket. In 2000 he was accused of corruption, and in October of that year the Philippine House of Representatives voted to impeach him. Several of Estrada's

By way of comparison, recall that intraparty politics accounted for 30% of the cases of prime-ministerial turnover in pure parliamentary systems.

This simple fact reveals that it is wrong to call the increased frequency of presidential challenges and resignations around the world a "de facto parliamentarization" of presidential regimes (Marsteintredet and Berntzen 2008), because true parliamentarization would necessarily let legislatures remove presidents via simple majority rule and would also let president's parties swap out the nation's chief executive via a simple intraparty mechanism. Rather obviously, this is not the case. What we are seeing in separate-powers systems around the world is manipulation of constitutional rules for political purposes by both presidents and opposition majorities, not "parliamentarization."[19]

To illustrate the moral hazard problems that presidential parties confront, we searched for examples of parties that attempted to impeach their own president. We found only five cases in which elements of a president's party supported an impeachment effort. A majority in the president's party supported impeachment in only two of these cases, and only one effort succeeded. By examining these five cases we can learn a great deal about problems that presidentialized parties confront in terms of holding the de facto leaders to account.

Members of the Sri Lankan UNP Fail to Fire Their President

The effort to dismiss Sri Lankan president Ranasinghe Premadasa (1989–93) reveals just how counterproductive impeachment can be as a mechanism of intraparty accountability. In 1991, 120 of the 225 members of the Sri Lankan parliament, including 47 of 125 members from Premadasa's United National Party (UNP), brought charges of "corruption, nepotism, and subverting the constitution" against the president. Although most who signed the impeachment motion came from the opposition, two dissident UNP faction leaders and several dozen of their followers also signed (Burger 1992, 744–45). Thus in this case a minority of legislators in the president's party initially supported impeachment.

co-partisans voted with the prosecution, raising the question of whether LAMMP sought to remove its own leader. However, Kasuya (2004) notes that many LAMMP members who voted against Estrada had only joined the party immediately prior to the 1998 elections. Because parties in the Philippines are typically ephemeral and fluid, this case remains unclear.

[19] To be sure, the line between "attempted abuse" and "normal politics" is unclear, but that does not change the point that such cases are not "parliamentarization."

However, nearly all of the UNP members of parliament who initially supported impeachment soon retracted their signatures and publicly pledged their loyalty to the president (Samath 1991a, 1991b) because they were threatened with expulsion from the UNP. In fact, the UNP did expel the few holdouts who refused to sign the loyalty oath. According to the Sri Lankan constitution, the seat of a member of parliament who changes party affiliation – whether through defection or expulsion – is declared vacant (*Straits Times* 1991). The constitution also gives the president the power to nominate the member's successor and to decide whether to simply seat the replacement or to hold a special by-election. The dissident UNP members of parliament challenged the constitutionality of their expulsion, but the country's Supreme Court found that the party was within its rights (Agence France-Presse 1991). Quite obviously, a country's impeachment provisions are irrelevant if the president has sufficient support within his own party to expel dissidents from the party and to even expel party-switchers from the legislature.[20] After nearly all of the original signatories of the impeachment motion recanted, the Speaker of the Sri Lankan Parliament declared that the motion lacked the required number of signatures to proceed. Thus by the end of this episode Premadasa had *gained* power within his own party.

Ethnic caste and economic class distinctions rather than policy differences were at issue in this case of intraparty conflict: Premadasa came from a middle caste, while the two dissident UNP factional leaders came from wealthy high-caste families that had long dominated Sri Lankan politics. These leaders believed the president had served the party well by winning the 1988 election, but that he had overstayed his welcome. They feared that his success would threaten long-established cultural and social norms (*Economist* 1991). Such a dynamic illustrates our point that presidentialized parties face trade-offs between electoral and governing considerations. Premadasa's opponents failed to realize that in nominating a candidate who could win the election, they would have to stomach his domination of the party for the duration of his term. When these elites grew weary of Premadasa's influence, they sought to remove him from office by the only mechanism available: impeachment.

---

[20] This constitutional context gives presidents extraordinary coercive power if they want it: Burger (1992, 744n) reports that immediately after assuming office, Sri Lankan president J. R. Jayewardene (1978–89) obtained a written, undated resignation letter from every UNP member of parliament!

This strategy backfired badly, as the president used his constitutional authority to stop the impeachment process in its tracks and turn the UNP machinery on his tormentors. The separation of survival and Sri Lanka's constitutional rules allowed Premadasa to reverse the principal-agent relationship and "fire" rebellious members of his own party. (Had he lived to see the day, James Madison would have been horrified.) In the end, the UNP's factional leaders' unwillingness to accept the inherent trade-offs of a separately elected president seriously damaged the party's fortunes. The party's deep rift – as well as Premadasa's mysterious 1993 assassination – caused it to lose the next presidential race as well as 31 of its 125 seats in the following year's assembly elections.

South Korea's Millennium Democratic Party Tears Up the Contract and Pays the Price

A second example similarly illustrates how repudiating one's own president can be politically suicidal. In December of 2002 Roh Moo-hyun won South Korea's presidential election. The opposition Grand National Party (GNP) retained a majority in Korea's unicameral legislature, while Roh's Millennium Democratic Party (MDP) was split between his supporters and supporters of previous president Kim Dae-jung. After Roh's inauguration, the GNP presented a "different reason to impeach Roh every month" (Lee 2005, 9n). Roh's party failed to unite in his defense, and so in September 2003 Roh and his supporters split from the MDP and formed the Uri Party. The rump MDP members then joined the GNP in the opposition. Together these two parties held over two-thirds of the seats, meaning they could override presidential vetoes, propose constitutional amendments to be put before voters in national referenda, and impeach the president.

In March 2004 the legislature voted 193–2 to impeach Roh on various charges, even though public opinion polls showed that 70% of South Koreans opposed the move. All 47 Uri party members boycotted the vote. Impeachment then became the driving issue of the April 2004 midterm elections, at which the Uri party tripled its seats, gaining an assembly majority. The GNP lost 28 of its 149 seats, but the president's enemies in his former party paid the worst price: the MDP lost all but nine of its 63 seats (Lee 2005, 11). As in Sri Lanka, in South Korea the president's enemies badly misread public opinion and paid a heavy price. (The Korean Supreme Court reinstated Roh in May 2004, and he served out his term.)[21]

Nicaragua's President Tears Up the Contract, and His Party Cannot Respond

Nicaraguans elected Enrique Bolaños as president in 2002. The previous president, Arnoldo Alemán, had handpicked Bolaños to be his successor. In fact, Alemán believed he and his Constitutionalist Liberal Party (PLC) could control Bolaños from the legislature and thus return Alemán to power five years later, as permitted by the Nicaraguan constitution (Muñoz 2002). (Nicaragua's constitution provided Alemán with a seat in the assembly automatically upon finishing his term.) However, immediately after assuming office Bolaños began investigating corruption in Alemán's administration. The former president was stripped of his parliamentary immunity, convicted of numerous crimes, and sent to prison for several years.

For assiduously prosecuting his mentor, the PLC expelled Bolaños. Bolaños then formed a new party, the Alliance for the Republic (APRE). In October 2004, the PLC, which the jailed Alemán still dominated, joined with the opposition Sandinista Party (FSLN) to bring impeachment proceedings against Bolaños for alleged campaign finance violations during the 2001 campaign. Together the PLC and the FSLN controlled over two-thirds of the 91 seats in the Nicaraguan Assembly (LatinNews Daily 2005). However, under intense pressure from the US State Department and the Organization of American States (OAS), the impeachment effort did not advance.[22] For the PLC, the repercussions of this effort were grave: in the 2006 presidential elections the PLC candidate finished third, behind the APRE candidate and the FSLN's winning candidate, former revolutionary and ex-president Daniel Ortega.

Bolaños tore up the implicit contract he had signed with his party and his former boss and struck out on his own, with only minority support within his own party. In a parliamentary system, his party would thus

---

[21] However, his popularity foundered, and he left the Uri party in early 2007 (Onishi 2007).

[22] See LAWR (2004); Joynes (2005); EFE News Service (2005); Global Insight Daily Archives (2005); BBC (2005); Briones (2002); and Sandoval (2004). This story has historical precedent in Nicaragua: in 1947 the country's legislature removed President Leonardo Argüello for daring to act independently of the country's de facto ruler, Anastacio Somoza García.

have replaced him one way or another. Yet even supposing that the OAS and US government had *not* pressured the PLC and FSLN to back off, the PLC could not have treated its dispute with Bolaños as merely an internal party matter: given the requirement of a supermajority vote to impeach Bolaños, Alemán and his followers needed the help of the PLC's main electoral and ideological rival, the FSLN.

As for Ortega, ending Bolaños's presidency quickly was actually not in his interest. He sought to divide PLC forces for as long as possible, because doing so was the only way he could win a free and fair presidential election under Nicaragua's qualified plurality rules.[23] Moreover, in an era of strengthened international democratic norms, impeachment required the blessing of the international community. This is intriguing, not because the impeachment would have succeeded if not for the intervention of the OAS and the United States (surely it might have), but because one cannot imagine an internal party leadership dispute in a parliamentary system (no matter how cynically motivated) becoming a matter requiring international mediation. Under the separation of powers intraparty leadership disputes are not merely politicized but are constitutionalized, which in today's world means that international actors can legitimately pressure domestic actors to stick to the letter of their country's constitution – and which means that parties have a far harder time holding their leaders to accounts.

How to Defenestrate Your Party's President: Paraguay 1999

Our fourth case is historically unique in that it is the only example of a majority within a governing party initiating a successful effort to remove its own president: the resignation of Paraguayan President Raúl Cubas Grau of the *Asociación Nacional Republicana* (ANR, or Colorado Party) in 1999. Cubas was politically weak from the get-go: he was able to obtain his party's nomination only because the Paraguayan Supreme Court disqualified the ANR's desired nominee, General Lino Oviedo, for participating in a coup attempt in 1996. Prior to the 1998 election Oviedo was imprisoned. However, early in his presidency Cubas thumbed his nose at the Paraguayan Supreme Court and freed his pal Oviedo.

---

[23] The constitution had been changed, under FSLN urging, to permit the election of the presidential candidate with a plurality of only 35% of the vote as long as there was a 5-percentage point margin over the runner up. (Ortega would go on to win, 38%–29%.)

This act also defied the will of the majority faction within Cubas's own Colorado Party, led by Vice-President Luis Argaña. Argaña's supporters wanted Oviedo to remain in prison and out of politics. Thus, Argaña's allies in Paraguay's legislature declared that Cubas "did not represent the Colorado Party" and initiated impeachment proceedings. After all, as Vice-President, Argaña would assume the presidency if Cubas were forced from office (Pérez-Liñán 2007). A period of political chaos followed, which culminated when pro-Oviedo thugs assassinated Argaña on the streets of Asunción. This denouement cost Cubas his remaining political support and forced him to resign and flee into exile.

To our knowledge, this is the only case in which a party *could* resolve its internal leadership disputes on its own, without needing to reach out to other parties. The Colorado Party had ruled Paraguay continuously for over six decades, in both authoritarian and democratic periods. Given this, the Argañistas – who controlled the Colorado organization after Oviedo's imprisonment – had good reason to believe that they could contain the negative political repercussions of an impeachment, and therefore that they could use impeachment as a method of leadership replacement.

Political conditions in Paraguay at the time thus reveal the conditions that enable a party to remove its own leader through impeachment: *a presumption that the incumbent party can control all the levers of power in the present and in the future.* This means that the incumbent party must single-handedly control all branches of government, from a supermajority position. Such conditions are extremely rare, even in single-party governments. And even though the ANR remained in power until 2008, it has paid a price for its internecine warfare. From democratization in 1989 through the 1998 elections, the party held the presidency as well as a single-party majority in both chambers of Paraguay's legislature. Yet in 2003 its presidential candidate won only a plurality of 37% of the votes, and the party lost its majority in both legislative chambers. By 2008, it had also lost control over the presidency.[24]

Venezuela's Acción Democrática Fails to Support Its President

Our final case illustrates what a party stands to lose if it does not defend its president from impeachment charges: the resignation of Venezuelan President Carlos Andrés Pérez of Acción Democrática (AD) in 1993. In

---

[24] Political Database of the Americas, http://pdba.georgetown.edu/Elecdata/Para/para.html, accessed 6/4/08.

this case an opposition legislator initiated impeachment proceedings, but members of the president's party did not vigorously oppose the charges, partly because a majority of AD legislators opposed Pérez's key policy initiatives. Acción Democrática's tepid defense severely discredited the president and contributed indirectly to his downfall. For our purposes, this case clearly exposes the sorts of accountability problems presidentialized parties confront that parliamentarized parties do not. Conventional wisdom holds that AD was one of the most highly parliamentarized parties in the history of modern Latin American democratic politics (Martz 1966; Coppedge 1994; Mainwaring and Scully 1995). Given this, if any presidentialized party could hold its leader to account, it should have been AD – and to the extent that AD could not hold its leaders to account, no party in any pure presidential system truly can.

Pérez took office (for the second time) in 1989 as leader of a minority government. He had won AD's October 1987 internal primary by a three-to-one margin (Coppedge 1994, 128), but his rivals retained control over the party machine, determining the agenda of the party executive committee meetings, publicly opposing Pérez's nomination, and proclaiming their opposition to Pérez's economic policy proposals.[25] (Pérez won the internal primary with support from the rank and file and state and municipal party bosses.) Given the animosity emanating from within his own party, after winning the election Pérez appointed nonpartisan technocrats to economic ministries and engaged in what Corrales (2002) has called a "party-neglecting" governance strategy.

Acción Democrática's leaders *attempted* to hold Pérez to the party line. In particular, they tried to keep Pérez from implementing neoliberal economic reforms. To do so AD acted as a "virtual opposition force" by relaxing party discipline, which in this instance means allowing legislators to defy presidential initiatives, contrary to the party's usual practice of giving their party's president nearly universal support (Pérez-Liñán 2007, 222). As a result, Pérez never imposed his will on AD leadership or legislators (Coppedge 1994, 103). For example, in October 1991 the party's president publicly demanded the resignation of economic ministers from the president's cabinet (Pérez-Liñán 2007, 29, 223). However, despite these efforts, Pérez ignored his party and undertook one of the "policy switches" that swept Latin America in the 1980s and 1990s (Stokes 2001).

---

[25] Personal communication, Professor Michael Coppedge, University of Notre Dame, 5/28/07.

When Venezuela's economic and political situation began to deteriorate in the early 1990s, partly as a consequence of Pérez's reforms, antigovernment protests erupted across the country. Police and military repression of those protests only engendered greater enmity against Pérez and his government. In February 1992, disgusted with corruption, impunity, and the downward spiral of political chaos, army colonel Hugo Chávez led an attempted coup; other military officers attempted a second coup later that year. Given the minority government situation, any parliamentary system would have forced Pérez from office via a no-confidence vote by this time. Yet given the separation of survival, AD was stuck with a president whom its leadership – and much of the Venezuelan population – had angrily repudiated.

In November 1992, an opposition politician accused Pérez of appropriating US$17 million in public funds for personal gain. The case was filed with the country's Prosecutor General, who then requested that the Supreme Court weigh in. The Supreme Court decided to proceed with a trial. The Venezuelan Senate subsequently voted unanimously – including AD senators – to suspend Pérez's mandate, forcing him from office temporarily. According to Kada (2003, 126), Pérez claims that he urged AD senators to support the Supreme Court's decision, because he mistakenly believed he would quickly be absolved. Yet once a contrary decision came out, repudiating the Court was politically infeasible. The Venezuelan constitution permits presidents to take a 90-day leave of absence. After that time, Congress must decide whether to declare the position permanently vacant, and if it does so, it must nominate a replacement. Because Pérez's trial was only getting started after 90 days, Congress was forced to vote on Pérez's status. The decision required only a majority vote – and because AD controlled only a minority of seats, it lost and Pérez was removed from office (Kada 2003, 127).

In failing to support its own president from the outset and by indirectly aiding the opposition's efforts to bring him down, AD committed political suicide, which contributed to the collapse of Venezuela's stable if elitist party system. Pérez had won the presidential election and AD won the largest bloc of legislative seats in 1988. Yet it finished a distant third in the 1993 elections and did not even run its own presidential candidate in 1998.[26] By 2000 Hugo Chávez had swept aside the

---

[26] Election Results Archive, http://www.binghamton.edu/cdp/era/, accessed May 28, 2007.

remnants of Venezuela's party system and was consolidating his new "5th Republic."

If AD had existed in a parliamentary system, it would probably never have nominated Pérez in the first place. Yet because the party needed an "electable" candidate, Pérez won the nomination without support from a majority in the party's central organization. Then, despite AD's vaunted centralization, cohesiveness, and organizational strength, the party organization could not hold its own president to the party platform, nor could it dismiss Pérez once his policies had proven enormously unpopular. AD was forced to swallow a bitter pill, and to deal with a situation a parliamentary party would never have confronted. Violent protests and two attempted coups certainly undermined Pérez's government – but the opposition's successful effort to unseat Pérez capitalized on the weak support Pérez received from his own party. AD's efforts to undermine its own president proved self-defeating, and illustrate why such actions are so rare: a party that turns on its own leader but cannot remove that leader from office runs the risk of self-destruction.

CONCLUSION

At the start of this chapter we noted that while careful *ex ante* selection of agents can mitigate adverse selection problems, the ability to sanction an agent *ex post* – in particular to *dismiss* an agent – is far more consequential for principals' ability to realize their goals. All democracies possess mechanisms to remove and replace national leaders against their will. However, not all *parties* in all democracies have equal ability to fire their agents who hold executive office. Substantial variation in the internal balance of power between party principals and party agents exists under different democratic constitutions, suggesting that the danger of moral hazard – the likelihood that a party's agent will depart from the party's preferred position on any number of important issues – is highly correlated with regime-type.

In pure parliamentary systems, about three in ten changes in prime minister result from purely *intra*party politics. Parliamentary constitutions offer parties comparatively simple and easy mechanisms of intraparty accountability, including leadership review and deselection. Because the executive emerges from the parliamentary majority, intraparty politics directly determines *who* runs the government as well as *how* those people run the government. The frequency and relative ease with which parties swap out their agents under this regime-type suggest that moral hazard is minimized in parliamentarized parties.

In semi-presidential regimes, parties possess a similar hold over their prime-ministerial agents. However, such systems also give presidents – a less-faithful party agent – influence over prime-ministerial selection and deselection. Presidents' place in the line of accountability between parties and prime ministers complicates parties' ability to hold *either* their prime ministers *or* their presidents to account. That is, presidential "contamination" of the relationship between the party and the prime minister under semi-presidentialism attenuates parties' organizational control over the composition and direction of government.

It is worth remembering from Chapter 2 that the founders of semi-presidentialism desired this result. And in fact, the president-parliamentary subtype almost completely eliminates parliamentary parties' influence over the composition and direction of government. As for premier-presidential systems, presidents also frequently swap out premiers, despite their lack of formal authority to do so. Presidents' influence derives from their informal, de facto position as party leader. In such regimes we therefore only see limits on presidents' influence under cohabitation. In contrast, when presidents' parties and/or allies control the assembly majority, intraparty politics becomes highly presidentialized and we see a reversal of the party-leader principal-agent relationship: the prime minister becomes the *president's* agent, rather than the party's.

In both pure and semi-presidential regimes, parties cannot credibly threaten presidents with removal – whether for ineffectiveness or something worse. Thus, parties' direct influence over the occupant of the executive in systems with direct presidential elections typically ends at the nomination stage of the electoral process. After that, intraparty politics almost never determines between-election presidential leadership changes. Presidents are sometimes forced from office between elections, but parties almost never take the initiative to remove their own president. The rarity of such efforts suggests that politicians understand how damaging impeachments can be for the incumbent party – and the frequency of attempts to impeach *another* party's president tends to support this point. Politicians are usually loath to accuse their own party's president of ineptitude or corruption – much less an offense against the constitution. Pursuing such a course of action is costly because impeachment proceedings focus the media spotlight on the incumbent party's shortcomings, not just the president's. In contrast, parliamentary parties can and frequently do remove an unpopular, incompetent, or even corrupt prime minister before the party must face the voters.

The evidence in this chapter clearly shows that parties lack mechanisms of *ex post* accountability to keep their presidential agents in line. They cannot deselect presidents who stray too far from the party line, underperform, are corrupt, or turn out to be incompetent or a fool. While the threat of deselection pervades party politics in parliamentary systems, deselection via impeachment cannot be considered part of a hypothetical contract between the party as principal and a candidate for president as its agent. Presidents' comparatively greater insulation from intraparty deselection relative to prime ministers means that there is greater danger of a de facto reversal of the principal-agent relationship in separate power systems, in which presidents come to control their parties for their own purposes.

5

Electoral Separation of Purpose within Political Parties

Chapters 3 and 4 considered differences in parties' ability to select and deselect leaders across democratic regimes. In this chapter we explore the implications of our theoretical argument further, by moving into the electoral arena. In political systems where voters cast separate ballots – often at separate times – for a party's executive and legislative candidates, those candidates can seek support from different elements of society and can even campaign on different bases. Seen through the lens of principal-agent theory, under both pure and semi-presidentialism, the separation of origin forces parties to confront a problem in the electoral arena that they do not face under pure parliamentarism: how to minimize the likelihood that their agent will develop a support base that does not fully overlap with the party's.

In this chapter we explore the degree to which parties' candidates for executive and legislative office derive support from and respond to different sets of voters, a phenomenon we call *electoral separation of purpose*. Conceptually, electoral separation of purpose measures the degree to which the electoral process generates misalignment of the political incentives between a party's executive candidate and its median legislative candidate. A continuum exists, with complete "fusion" of electoral purpose at one end, and complete "separation" of electoral purpose at the other end.

By definition, electoral separation of purpose cannot exist in parliamentary parties. In all parliamentary parties a prime minister's vote is necessarily perfectly aligned with the votes his or her party received, simply because there is no way for a citizen to vote for a party's prime-ministerial candidate without also endorsing the party's legislative candidate or slate. In parliamentary elections a party's legislators and candidate for executive office share precisely the same vote base, collectively decide the content of their platform, and respond to the same national policy demands (Samuels and Shugart 2003). In government, this generates similar political incentives for a party's executive and legislative branches, meaning that under parliamentarism it is relatively unproblematic to think of the party as the principal and the candidate as the agent. Of course, intraparty tension can still arise in parliamentary parties, but such incentive incompatibility cannot derive from the voting process itself, due to the fusion of origin of the executive and legislative branches of government.

No parties ever occupy the opposite end of our continuum; "complete" electoral separation of purpose is theoretically possible but practically impossible. It would require *all* voters to split their tickets – that is, for every voter to cast a vote for one party for president and another party for the legislature. However, as we will show, considerable electoral separation of purpose is possible, and even typical. As one moves away from total fusion of electoral purpose, a party's candidates for executive and legislative office tend to share the same vote base less and less. This is because candidates for the two offices may campaign on different grounds and respond to distinct policy demands. Such a situation generates substantial incentive incompatibility between a party's executive and legislative branches, and suggests that we should not assume that the president is a perfect agent of his or her party.

Such misalignment of political incentives has a source that is unique to pure and semi-presidential systems: the existence of the separation of electoral origin of the executive and legislative branches of government. Holding constant other institutional factors such as the electoral cycle, separation of origin can generate electoral separation of purpose in two ways. First, even assuming citizens vote for presidents and legislators on national policy issues, the relatively greater incentives for vote-seeking in the executive race means that presidential candidates have incentives to adopt *broader* policy positions than their parties. Second, voters might not vote for presidents and legislators on the same national policy issues. Instead, voters might evaluate presidential and legislative candidates from the same party on entirely *different* bases. For example, voters might cast their vote for president based on candidates' national policy positions but evaluate legislative candidates based on their success at "bringing home the bacon" (Samuels and Shugart 2003). To the extent that different "branches" of a single political party derive electoral support from different voters or for different reasons – whether because presidents have adopted different policies from those of their parties or because citizens vote for presidents based on policies and legislators based on constituency service – presidents and legislators from a single political party can have very different political incentives. Such incentive incompatibility is the essence of electoral separation of purpose within a political party.

Thus at one end of our continuum, both the prospective candidate for executive office and the median member of the party's legislative contingent advocate precisely the same policies and are elected by precisely the same constituency. In such cases the party's voters are likely to believe that the candidate embodies the party's platform, and vice versa. These situations of complete fusion of purpose should reduce *ex post* moral hazard problems in the governing arena. Toward the other end of the continuum, candidates for executive office and the median member of the party's legislative contingent might respond to different constituencies and advocate different policies. Such a situation involves considerable ticket splitting, which tends to generate incentive incompatibility between presidents and their parties. Thus under high electoral separation of purpose, a party that wins an election is more likely to confront challenges managing the principal-agent relationship with its president. And to the extent that we can observe electoral separation of purpose, we have evidence that presidents and their parties are not unitary agents of their voters.

We did not invent the concept of separation of purpose – it originates in the *Federalist Papers*, if not in Montesquieu or even earlier. In *Federalist #51* Madison urged that "ambition be set against ambition." That is, he believed the key to preventing tyranny lay with deliberately generating incentive incompatibility between the president and Congress. Scholars have explored the implications of Madison's argument for *interbranch* relations, but have largely ignored the key fact that in democracies with separate origin and/or survival, *interbranch* relations are first and foremost *intraparty* relations, whether under unified or divided government. That is, one cannot meaningfully consider the potential clash of incentives across separate branches of government without first considering the potential clash of incentives across branches of political parties. In saying this we are not merely critiquing our colleagues (such as Cox and McCubbins 2001) but also engaging in self-critique of our own work that ignored this point (e.g. Shugart and Haggard 2001; Samuels and Shugart 2003).

To understand executive-legislative relations, one must first understand intraparty relations. And in separation of powers systems, the electoral separation of origin implies the possibility of electoral separation of purpose – incentive incompatibility between branches of a single party that arises as a result of the electoral process. This result is impossible in pure parliamentary systems. Parties in systems with separately elected executives face unique challenges: how to accommodate the potentially conflicting demands of those who voted for the executive branch of the party but not the legislative branch (and vice versa), and how to bridge the institutional gap between the executive and legislative branches of government. Some parties address these dilemmas fairly well, but others do not. Regardless, parties confront such dilemmas only when executives and legislators are elected separately.

In this chapter we quantify the extent of electoral separation of purpose in the world's pure and semi-presidential regimes. In the next section we discuss the relationship between separation of purpose and two other well-known political science concepts, the personal vote and presidential coattails. We then assess the potential institutional sources of electoral separation of purpose, describe how we measure the phenomenon, and then present our findings.

ELECTORAL SEPARATION OF PURPOSE: THE PHYSICAL SEPARATION OF VOTES

Separate election of the executive and legislative branches of government makes electoral separation of purpose likely, but not inevitable, across both countries and parties. Before we discuss the factors that contribute to separation of purpose, we first note a conceptual analogy between the impact of separation of origin on intraparty tension and the manner in which certain electoral systems challenge legislative party cohesion. Then we relate electoral separation of purpose to the concept of presidential coattail effects. These discussions clarify the extent to which separation of purpose is a function of systems in which the executive and legislative branches exhibit electoral separation of origin.

Separation of Origin and Incentives to Cultivate a Personal Vote

The impact of separate electoral origin of both branches of government on intraparty politics is analogous to the impact of electoral-system variation on the "personal vote" in legislative elections (Carey and Shugart

1995). Some legislative electoral systems do not allow voters to cast a ballot for a particular candidate, only for a party's list of candidates. Such closed-list systems make it impossible for a voter to favor one candidate without accepting or rejecting the party as a whole. In contrast, other electoral systems allow for intraparty competition, allowing candidates from a single party to earn their votes on different bases from each other, even within the same constituency. Systems that enhance the personal vote either fragment parties or force parties to adopt mechanisms that connect legislators with disparate constituencies and incentives to common party goals (Cox 1987; Cox and McCubbins 1993).

Separate origin of the executive and legislative branches has an analogous impact on political parties because it encourages parties to present candidates for the presidency who can cultivate a personal vote above and beyond that of their party. Evidence in Chapter 3 confirmed this effect – presidents are more likely to be "outsiders" – which suggests that the attributes that attract votes in a direct presidential election may be only loosely correlated with the attributes of a good party servant. The data we present in this chapter show that whether presidents are insiders *or* outsiders, they frequently diverge from their parties in the electoral arena. Because parties in systems with separation of origin seek to field presidential candidates who can attract a broad swath of voters, presidential candidates often fish for votes in different ponds from their co-partisans who are running for legislative office. Thus both the separation of origin and certain personal-vote electoral systems generate intraparty incentive incompatibility that party organizations must attempt to overcome.

Separation of Origin and Presidential Coattail Effects

A discussion of the relationship between presidential and legislative candidates from the same party should also address the concept of presidential coattails. To the extent that coattail effects are present, parties are presidentialized because the executive election rather than factors specific to legislative elections drive legislative party success. Comparativists have only begun to explore presidential coattail effects, but their likely presence in separation of powers systems beyond the United States points to an important party-system difference across democratic regimes.

Empirically, the degree of separation of purpose equals the extent to which the electorates of branches of the same party do not overlap. Operationally, the data used to measure separation of purpose are the same as those used to measure presidential coattails: constituency-level aggregate vote returns for executive and legislative candidates, or individual-level survey data on vote choices. However, there is no necessary correlation between separation of purpose and presidential coattail effects. Indeed, a party could benefit from presidential coattails even if the constituencies of its presidential and legislative candidates only partly overlapped. Consider a case in which a presidential candidate is very popular and helps elect his co-partisans to the legislature. Upon examining the data, we might discover that the presence of that particular presidential candidate provided a boost of 5% of the vote to the candidates in every legislative constituency. However, it is also possible that the presidential candidate received 55% of the vote in every legislative district, but the legislative candidates received only 30% in every district. The correlation between vote shares would be perfect, but the actual constituencies of the president and his or her party would differ considerably – in this case, almost half of the president's voters chose to vote for another party in the legislative race.

This example suggests that we can see relatively high separation of purpose even when we also see relatively high presidential coattails. Conversely, we might also see low separation of purpose along with low presidential coattails. In this case, a presidential candidate would neither help nor hurt his or her party's legislative candidates – but both branches of the party could still have overlapping constituencies. In short, presidential coattails and separation of purpose are conceptually related, but only orthogonally so. Separation of purpose focuses on the extent to which the constituencies of the presidential and legislative candidates overlap. Low separation of purpose is *likely* for parties that benefit from high presidential coattails effects, but not *necessary*.

SOURCES OF VARIATION IN ELECTORAL SEPARATION OF PURPOSE

Under parliamentarism, there is always complete fusion of electoral purpose: the party and its leader share precisely the same electoral base. Parties in pure or semi-presidential systems will not necessarily exhibit substantial electoral separation of purpose. Indeed, parties that engineer sufficient fusion of purpose can minimize the agency problems that the separation of origin tends to encourage (even though they can still be troubled by the agency problems the separation of *survival* generates). The factors that divide the party's executive and legislative "branches" in the electoral arena derive from the political institutions peculiar to pure presidential and hybrid constitutional formats, and from internal party politics.

Scholars have identified several political institutions that tend to separate or unify the electorates of the president and the median legislator – that is, that enhance or curtail separation of purpose across branches of government. These include the relative "personalization" of legislative electoral rules, varying possibilities for reelection of president and legislators, and the extent of legislative malapportionment (Carey and Shugart 1995; Cox and McCubbins 2001; Shugart and Haggard 2001; Samuels and Shugart 2003; Samuels and Snyder 2001).[1] The same logic also holds within political parties: institutions can separate or unify the electorates of a party's executive and legislative "branches."

The two key institutional sources of intraparty separation of purpose are ballot format and the electoral cycle. The existence of a fused ballot or not is perhaps the most important institutional source of fusion or separation of purpose. When voters' ballots are fused, electoral separation of purpose cannot vary – it is minimized. In theory, complete fusion of purpose – total overlap between the president's and the party's constituency – is possible if voters can split their tickets, but it is unlikely. Even in systems with highly "party-centric" electoral institutions (Carey and Shugart 1995), if voters can split their tickets the constituencies of the executive and legislative branches of the same party are likely to diverge to some degree. In contrast, with a fused ballot, the president's constituency necessarily perfectly corresponds to the party's constituency.

By electoral cycle, we mean whether elections for the executive and legislative branches are temporally separated or not. Elections for the two institutions may be concurrent, in which case they are held on the same day, or they may be nonconcurrent, by which we mean held on different days. (In concurrent elections, the ballot may be fused or not. Perhaps obviously, nonconcurrent elections require separate ballots. In most presidential systems, even if elections are held concurrently, voters cast separate ballots: voting for executive and legislature requires separate marks or pulls of a lever.) Concurrent elections encourage – but by no means require – voters to think of presidential and legislative candidates as members of the same team, and thus to vote accordingly (Shugart 1995; Samuels 2004). When executive and legislative elections are held

---

[1] Separation of purpose is orthogonal to the relative power of each branch and cannot be merely "added" to it. See Samuels and Shugart (2003).

nonconcurrently, the opposite is more likely the case, and not simply because the time between elections makes voters forget who is playing for which team. Instead, nonconcurrence allows presidential and legislative candidates to campaign on entirely different appeals. Presidents could campaign on foreign-policy or economic-management experience while legislators might focus on their local connections and ability to benefit the local constituency. We thus expect far greater fusion of purpose in concurrent elections.

Separation of purpose can also derive from parties' varying ability to internally resolve adverse selection problems arising from selection of a presidential candidate – and, when the incumbent is eligible for re-election, from failure or success in resolving moral hazard problems of holding an incumbent president to account while in office. As suggested by the career-path data in Chapter 3, internal party institutions cannot consistently resolve parties' adverse selection problems when parties must nominate a candidate for a direct presidential election. Even strong parties may only sometimes nominate a faithful guardian of the party line – and in any case, unless a fused ballot is employed, direct presidential elections can completely neutralize parties' efforts to keep their agent close at hand on the campaign trail. By implication, this means that separation of purpose can vary substantially within the same party over time – which further implies that neither intraparty mechanisms *nor* national political institutions can fully predict the degree of electoral separation of purpose. Electoral separation of purpose can vary from party to party within a country, and even from election to election within a party.

MEASURING ELECTORAL SEPARATION OF PURPOSE

Observable measures of separation of purpose might include evidence that the president and his or her party campaign on different issues or themes; receive votes from different groups of voters; or advocate different policies in the legislature. Such evidence would illustrate the extent to which presidents and parties go their own ways. In what follows we explore a simple measure of electoral separation of purpose: the average difference across all constituencies between a party's executive and legislative vote in each constituency. To the extent that this average approaches zero, electoral separation of purpose is minimized. As the average difference in executive and legislative vote across constituencies increases, separation of purpose increases.

To obtain this measure of the extent to which a party's executive and legislative constituencies overlap, one needs electoral data for both legislative and presidential elections at the level of the legislative constituency. Such data have been widely employed in the study of US politics – particularly in the study of presidential coattail effects – but have rarely been used in comparative politics. This has partly been due to the relative difficulty of obtaining district-level electoral data for both presidential and legislative elections in many presidential democracies. However, in recent years such data have become more widely available.

We sought constituency-level electoral data for every democracy in the world that has direct presidential elections. As in previous chapters, this includes the 53 countries that score 5 or higher for more than five years consecutively on the Polity IV score between 1946 and 2007. We matched results in legislative elections against concurrent presidential elections and against nonconcurrent presidential elections held up to five years prior to the legislative elections.[2] We compared results only when the presidential election was contested and excluded all independent presidential candidates because they cannot be compared against any party.[3] We also excluded nonconcurrent "founding" legislative elections, which lack a prior democratic presidential election against which to compare. We sought data for any candidate or party that obtained at least 10% of the vote in either the presidential or assembly election.

These 53 countries held 297 elections eligible for inclusion in our study; these are listed in Appendix 5A; we list data sources in Appendix 5B. Of these 297 elections we dropped 32 because the presidential race was uncontested, the presidential candidates were nonpartisan, or because parties ran candidates in one race and not the other.[4] We were able to find data for at least one party (typically the winning party if data for only one party were available) in 38 countries, in 181 of the remaining

---

[2] Exceptions to this rule were made when the legislative election occurred within three months of an upcoming presidential election. In such cases we matched the legislative election with the *subsequent* presidential election. Eliminating these few cases would not change our main finding that that nonconcurrent elections manifest substantially lower electoral separation of purpose than concurrent elections.

[3] This explains certain obvious gaps in our list of included elections, such as the seven Irish parliamentary elections held between 1973 and 1989.

[4] A few elections (e.g. Mexico in 1997 and the United States in 1962, 1982, and 2002) were also excluded because of redistricting between the previous presidential election and the legislative election, which made comparison of results in the two elections one against the other impossible. The 1966 US election was also excluded because of redistricting due to the *Baker v. Carr* decision on malapportionment.

265 elections (68%), for a total of 417 party-election cases. Our data-base has gaps, but this is without question the largest collection of cross-national district-level electoral data ever assembled that includes both presidential and assembly elections.

Once we had gathered the data, we simply took the absolute value of the difference between a party's percentage of valid votes in the executive race and its percentage of valid votes in the legislative race, and then took the average of these values across all constituencies in the country. This gives us a figure we will call ESP, for Electoral Separation of Purpose. Unlike in parliamentary systems, where only one value of ESP is possible, parties in presidential and semi-presidential systems can theoretically obtain ESP values anywhere from 0 to 100. To obtain a value of zero, the percentages a party's presidential and legislative candidates obtain in every constituency must be precisely the same. Such an outcome occurs when a fused ballot is employed, but it is unlikely in other situations. To obtain a value of 100, a presidential candidate would have to receive 100% of the vote in every constituency, while that candidate's co-partisans in the legislative race receive 0% in every constituency – theoretically possible but highly improbable.

ILLUSTRATIVE EXAMPLES OF ELECTORAL SEPARATION OF PURPOSE

To illustrate the concept of Electoral Separation of Purpose and to provide some idea of how much the measure can vary both within and across countries, we first provide several examples. Figures 5.1 and 5.2 provide contrasting cases from the United States. Figure 5.1 charts the proportion of votes the 1980 Republican presidential candidate (Ronald Reagan) received in each congressional district against the proportion of valid votes the Republican House candidate in those districts received. The 45-degree line indicates where the vote for president and House candidates would fall if both received equal proportions of the vote in a constituency. Such proportions could vary *across* constituencies (resulting in little circles up and down the 45-degree line) as a function of variation in party support across constituencies. However, for our purposes the important question is the degree to which the vote for a party's presidential and legislative candidates varies *within* constituencies, taking all constituencies into account.

To reiterate, ESP is the average of the absolute value of the differences, in percentage terms, between a party's valid vote in the presidential and

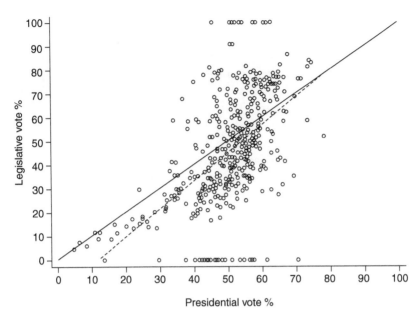

FIGURE 5.1. Constituency-Level Results, US Republicans 1980.

legislative elections. In this election ESP = 25.81, the second-highest value for any US election in our dataset.[5] That is, on average Reagan's proportion of the two-party vote differed from the Republican House candidate's by about 26%, which means that the base of the Republican "presidential party" did not correspond well with the base of the Republican "congressional party." As the circles indicate, in some districts Reagan outperformed his party's House candidate while in others he underperformed. Although several factors contribute to this divergence at the constituency level – including whether an incumbent was running in the House election – the key reason Reagan's vote diverged from his party's is because that year many moderate Democrats split their ticket, voting for Reagan instead of Jimmy Carter, while still casting a vote for the Democratic candidate for the House. Reagan won the election with 50.7% of the vote to Carter's 41%, even though the Democrats retained control of the House by a margin of 277–158.

An ESP figure of 25.81 indicates that in many districts there is wide divergence in the proportion of votes going to the Republican candidates

---

[5] There are 42 US party-election combinations in our data; the highest score is for the Democrats in 1980: 25.88.

for different "branches" of their party – including those districts where the Republican House candidate faced no opposition at all.[6] This fact is well known to observers of American political history in the post–civil rights era, when white Southern Democrats and Midwesterners in particular often split their tickets between a Republican for president and a Democrat for the House. This case illustrates our point that when electoral separation of purpose is high, it remains unclear who "the party's" voters are in a presidential system – those who voted for the party's presidential candidate, or those who voted for the party's legislative candidates. Of course, the answer is "both," which implies that the party is split into executive and legislative branches, which can be at odds with each other.

Figure 5.2 comes from the 2004 election between Republican George W. Bush and Democrat John Kerry, again showing the Republicans' results. By 2004 most of the "Reagan Democrats" who had split their tickets in 1980 were now either fully in the Republican fold, voting for that party in both the presidential and the congressional elections, or they had gone back to voting for Democrats in both the presidential and legislative races. Observers have chronicled the increasing cohesiveness of both parties' congressional delegations and the concomitant decline in split-ticket voting over recent decades (e.g. Kimball and Gross 2007). As a result, here the ESP score is 10.98, the second-lowest in our dataset for the United States. This number confirms a well-understood long-term shift of white southerners into the Republican fold, and suggests that by the 2000s the executive and legislative branches of the Republican Party overlapped to a much greater degree relative to 1980. Of course, 10.98 is still not "0.00," meaning that many American voters continued to split their tickets.

The examples from the United States illustrate our point that electoral separation of purpose, as measured by the degree to which the electorates of a party's legislative and executive candidates overlap, can vary within parties over time independently of the institutional context.[7] The electoral system did not change in the United States between 1980 and 2004, and both of those years saw concurrent presidential and congressional

---

[6] Uncontested House constituencies are included, as they should be. The whole point of this exercise is to compare the extent to which the "presidential" and "legislative" parties match each other across geographic space.

[7] In a two-party system, if electoral separation of purpose is relatively high for one of the large parties it will be high for the other party. However, this correspondence may or may not decline as the number of parties in the system increases.

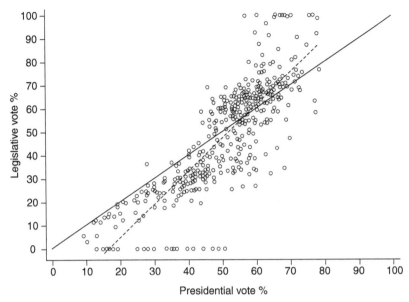

FIGURE 5.2. Constituency-Level Results, US Republicans 2004.

elections. Nonetheless, the dynamics of inter- and intraparty politics changed considerably over that time period. The existence of the separation of origin cannot explain variation in the degree of electoral separation of purpose. Instead, intraparty politics from one election to the next can change the relationship between a party's "executive" and "legislative" branches.

Results from French elections between 1995 and 2002 bolster these points and provide additional insight. What is especially helpful for purposes of comparison is that the same three individuals dominated these elections: Jacques Chirac of the conservative RPR, Lionel Jospin of the Socialist Party, and Jean-Marie Le Pen of the far-right National Front. The presence of these three men in every party/year case except one (Jospin resigned his position as Socialist leader just before the 2002 Assembly elections) largely controls for the possibility that voters abandoned a party or candidate they had previously supported because that party changed its leader.

We also gain leverage on the question of the sources of electoral separation of purpose by noting that all three of these men are party insiders. Le Pen founded the National Front and has been active in politics since the 1950s. Chirac led his party for two decades, was elected mayor of

TABLE 5.1. *Electoral Separation of Purpose (Average %
Difference), France*

	National Front	Socialists	Rally for the Republic
1997	1.50	6.51	14.55
2002	5.59	13.74	16.45

Paris, and served two stints as prime minister. Similarly, Jospin led his party for several years and also served in the cabinet and the Assembly. All else equal, given our argument in Chapter 3, we should expect a close alignment between all three men and their parties.

In the presidential election of 1995, Le Pen finished a distant fourth in the first round, and Chirac defeated Jospin in the second round. Despite Jospin's loss, he won reelection as Socialist leader – even though he held no parliamentary seat. Two years later, Chirac called early Assembly elections. At that election Jospin not only won a seat but also led the Socialists and their leftist allies to a resounding victory, and thus became prime minister in a cohabitation situation. In the 2002 presidential election, Chirac ran for reelection and Jospin again ran against him. This time Jospin suffered a humiliating defeat in which Le Pen bested him in the first round. Jospin immediately resigned as prime minister. (This is the reason Jospin was not the Socialist leader at the Assembly elections held one month later.)

Table 5.1 presents the ESP scores for each candidate and party, comparing the vote in the first round of presidential elections (1995 and 2002) against party votes in the subsequent legislative election (1997 and 2002). Three things merit note. First, the results indicate that – as in the United States – separation of purpose can vary over time for each party. Second, the results also reveal that concurrence is not everything. All elections in France are nonconcurrent, and the 1997 Assembly election was two years after the presidential election. However, the National Front had *lower* ESP in 1997 than in 2002, when the legislative election was held just a month after the presidential election. In fact, the ESP scores in both elections for Le Pen and candidates from his National Front are below average for all parties in nonconcurrent semi-presidential elections (11.70). Likewise, ESP for the RPR (Rally for the Republic) was virtually identical in 1997 and 2002, despite the considerable difference in the "degree" of nonconcurrence of the two legislative elections. Finally,

Table 5.1 shows that separation of purpose can vary *by party* at each election – which implies both that the institutional context is not determinative and that separation of purpose in one party does not necessarily determine the degree of separation of purpose in the other parties.

Examples from Brazil and Mexico, two pure presidential systems with very different electoral institutions for both branches, help flesh out our understanding of the sources and extent of electoral separation of purpose. Figures 5.3 and 5.4 chart the degree of electoral separation of purpose for Brazil's two most important parties, the Partido da Social Democracia Brasileira or Party of Brazilian Social Democracy (PSDB) and the Partido dos Trabalhadores or Workers' Party (PT) between 1994 and 2006. The PSDB's leader Fernando Henrique Cardoso won the presidency in 1994 and was reelected in 1998, while PT leader Luiz Inácio Lula da Silva won the presidency in 2002 and was reelected in 2006. Like France, Brazil uses a two-round majoritarian system for its presidential elections, although the elections went to a second round only in 2002 and 2006. The Chamber of Deputies is elected concurrently with the first round of the presidential election. There are 27 legislative districts, corresponding to each of Brazil's 26 states plus its capital territory, using open-list proportional representation with district magnitudes that range from 8 to 70. This combination of rules, along with the country's famously high party-system fragmentation, creates the potential for a high degree of separation of purpose between legislative parties and their presidential candidates.

Figures 5.3 and 5.4 pool all the information over four elections. Scholars have long known of the problematic relationship between parties' executive and legislative branches in Brazil (Figueiredo 1994; Samuels 2000); our examination of recent election returns confirms that separation of purpose for Brazil's two most important parties is quite substantial. (In fact, the 1994 value for the PSDB is the highest ESP score in our dataset.) Note the nearly horizontal slopes of the interpolated regression lines, which indicate an extremely weak relationship between the presidential vote and the party vote for both of these parties.

Table 5.2 provides the ESP scores for these two parties for these four elections. Even for the PT, which is Brazil's most cohesive party (Mainwaring 1999) and has the strongest base of partisan identifiers in the electorate (Samuels 2006), substantial divergence exists between the legislative party's base and the presidential candidate's base. Some of this electoral separation of purpose in the PT reflects Lula's increasing vote share, from 27% in 1994 to 32% in 1998 and finally to 46% in the first

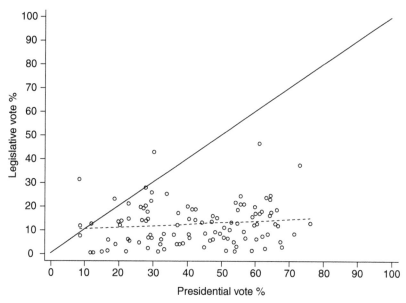

FIGURE 5.3. Constituency-Level Results, Brazilian PSDB 1994–2006.

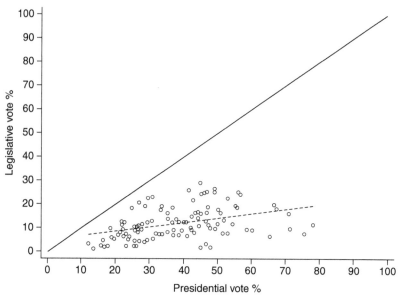

FIGURE 5.4. Constituency-Level Results, Brazilian PT 1994–2006.

TABLE 5.2. *Electoral Separation of Purpose (Average %
Difference), Brazil*

	PT	PSDB
1994	16.44	46.64
1998	18.18	38.27
2002	30.33	11.39
2006	39.98	26.52

PT = Brazilian Workers' Party; PSDB = Party of Brazilian Social
Democracy.

round in 2002. To win, Lula had to appeal far beyond his party's base
because the PT's supporters – as measured by those who voted for its legislative candidates – comprised a relatively small slice of Brazil's electorate.
The PT barely obtained 18% of the vote in the legislative race and had
always been in opposition to previous governments. Given this, it could
never have been the dominant party in a governing coalition under parliamentarism. Only the strong "personal vote" of its presidential candidate
provided the PT the opportunity to gain control of the government.

The PT's ESP score in 2006, when Lula won reelection, is the fifth-
highest score out of 417 in our dataset. As described at the start of Chapter
1, electoral separation of purpose was so bad that the correlation between
executive and legislative votes for Lula and the PT that year was negative. Let us reiterate this, to be as clear as possible about what happened
that year within the PT: *in 2006, in constituencies where the PT's presidential candidate did well, its legislative candidates did poorly, and vice
versa.* Such an outcome is utterly inconceivable under parliamentarism –
but occurred in 5% of our cases in pure and semi-presidential systems.[8]
A party in a parliamentary system facing a situation in which its likely
performance in an upcoming election was negatively correlated with the
popularity of its leader would replace that leader. Yet in systems with separate origin, legislative parties frequently find themselves dealing with a
president who derives support from a very different electoral base.

As a contrast to Brazil's experience, let us now consider Mexico's main
parties. Here presidents are elected by plurality rule, and concurrent and

---

[8] Many other cases saw low but positive correlations between presidential and legislative
vote totals; the average correlation for party results in pure and semi-presidential elections, including the elections that used fused ballots, is .69.

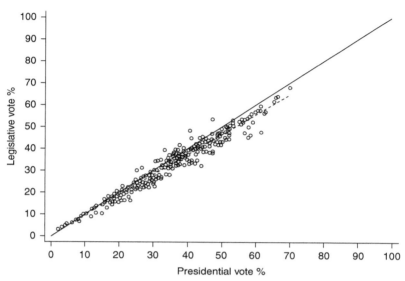

FIGURE 5.5. Constituency-Level Results, Mexican PAN 2006.

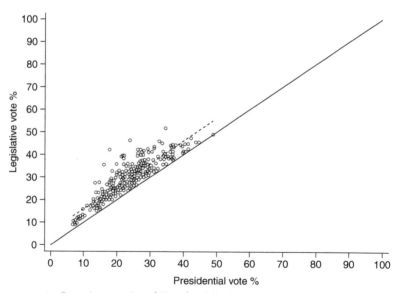

FIGURE 5.6. Constituency-Level Results, Mexican PRI 2006.

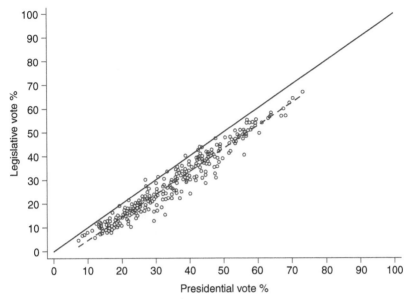

FIGURE 5.7. Constituency-Level Results, Mexican PRD 2006.

midterm legislative elections alternate every three years. Legislators are elected by a mixed-member system in which, unlike in Brazil, candidates of the same party do not compete with one another; moreover, in contrast to many other mixed-member systems, voters do not cast separate legislative party and candidate votes. In addition, legislators are ineligible for immediate reelection.

Few electoral systems promote such a low personal vote – and not surprisingly, research shows that the three main parties are indeed highly cohesive in legislative voting (Nacif 2002; Carey 2009). This set of institutions ought to provide a good environment for low ESP. Figures 5.5 through 5.7 thus plot the 2006 presidential and legislative election results for the center-right National Action Party (PAN), the centrist Institutional Revolutionary Party (PRI), and the leftist Party of the Democratic Revolution (PRD). Clearly, for each party the relationship between the presidential and legislative vote in each of Mexico's 300 single-member districts is much higher than what we saw in the United States or Brazil. The circles bunch tightly around the interpolated line for each party, and the interpolated line falls very close to the 45-degree line, especially for the winning party in 2006, the PAN.

TABLE 5.3. *Electoral Separation of Purpose (Average % Difference), Mexico*

	PRD	PRI	PAN
2000	2.94	2.57	4.80
2003	6.63	6.33	12.58
2006	6.39	5.91	2.95

PRD = Party of the Democratic Revolution; PRI = Institutional Revolutionary Party; PAN = National Action Party.

Even within this environment, it is worth noting that ESP has fluctuated somewhat over time, as Table 5.3 indicates. Still, the low ESP scores in Mexico (only the midterm result for the governing PAN in 2003 exceeds 7.0) contrast with the Brazilian and US cases. Strikingly, ESP is lower in the Mexican three-party system than in the American two-party system, implying no direct correlation between the number of parties in the system and greater ESP.[9]

These examples from the United States, France, Brazil, and Mexico confirm this chapter's main points: separation of purpose can vary within parties over time, across parties at a given election, and across countries. Given this, cross-national analysis that relied on variation in institutional context would provide at best a partial picture of the sources of electoral separation of purpose. To understand the sources of ESP we must consider institutional factors – as we do in the remainder of this chapter – as well as the intrapartisan political context for each party at each election – which we do in Chapters 6 and 7.

THE GLOBAL EXTENT OF ELECTORAL SEPARATION OF PURPOSE

The figures presented in the previous section provide snapshots of electoral separation of purpose for a few parties. In some cases the electoral constituencies of the executive and legislative branches of the same party overlap nearly completely. In such cases ESP approaches zero. Yet

---

[9] Electoral separation of purpose (ESP) may be a function of the presidential electoral rules – one or two rounds – in combination with the legislative electoral rules, as well as concurrence (see later in the chapter).

in others, considerable divergence exists, causing ESP to increase. The question remains as to the degree of variation in electoral separation of purpose across all pure and semi-presidential systems. In this section we first present the aggregate evidence, and then compare the sources of separation of purpose in pure versus semi-presidential systems.

Electoral Separation of Purpose: The Global Evidence

Pooling our data results in 417 party-election combinations in 38 countries. In the entire sample, ESP ranges from 0.00 to 46.64; the overall mean is 9.70 (median 7.33). This means that on average in all pure and semi-presidential systems, in every constituency the vote for a presidential candidate and his or her legislative co-partisans differs by about 10%. In many cases, the difference is much larger: 17 countries had at least one party with ESP in the top 10% of all scores, 20.43 or higher. As these summaries of the data indicate, the distribution exhibits a clear skew toward the lower end, nearer to zero. This skew in the distribution – coupled with the fact that there is no case as high as 50, the theoretical midpoint if the full range of possible separation were observed – indicates that most parties have only small to moderate electoral separation of purpose. We discuss implications of the shape of the data distribution further below, but it is important throughout to keep in mind that any deviation from ESP = 0 is *impossible* in parliamentary systems. Thus, even a rather moderate ESP value indicates potential challenges to parties in presidential and semi-presidential systems that parties in parliamentary systems simply do not face.

Tables 5.4 and 5.5 provide descriptive statistics for all countries for which we have five or more party-cases: the minimum, maximum, and mean ESP values, separated by pure and semi-presidential systems. The difference in ESP scores between these regime-types at the aggregate level is small (mean 9.36 for pure presidential and 10.74 for semi-presidential);[10] below we will explore in some detail how regime-type affects electoral separation of purpose. For now, we focus on ballot structure and electoral cycle, which are factors that vary much more across pure presidential regimes than semi-presidential systems.[11]

[10] Note that we did not separate ESP scores in premier-presidential and president-parliamentary systems. There are only 32 observations from president-parliamentary systems, too few to generalize from.
[11] Very few semi-presidential systems have concurrent elections (only 18 party-year observations), and none uses a fused ballot.

TABLE 5.4. *Electoral Separation of Purpose, Pure Presidential Systems*

Country	Minimum	Maximum	Mean	N
Argentina	1.13	21.20	8.35	22
Bolivia*	0.00	9.80	2.83	18
Brazil	6.66	46.64	24.79	14
Chile	6.36	36.90	17.56	18
Colombia	1.13	22.05	11.36	17
Costa Rica	0.83	25.78	6.46	29
Dominican Republic	4.65	15.08	9.59	5
Ecuador	2.21	27.21	8.69	24
El Salvador	3.37	35.71	16.10	10
Honduras*	0.00	5.22	2.05	10
Malawi	5.08	30.70	14.86	5
Mexico	2.57	12.58	5.68	9
Nicaragua	0.32	6.43	2.12	9
Panama	4.86	9.43	7.19	7
Paraguay	1.57	8.05	2.98	8
Uruguay*	0.00	0.00	0.00	23
United States	8.79	25.88	15.86	42
Venezuela	0.33	20.03	5.02	28
Zambia	2.76	11.35	6.01	7

* Some elections had a fused presidential–legislative ballot.

TABLE 5.5. *Electoral Separation of Purpose, Semi-Presidential Systems*

Country	Minimum	Maximum	Mean	N
Bulgaria	5.53	25.71	15.13	10
Finland	1.94	15.86	8.09	9
France	1.50	16.45	10.45	7
Ireland	5.45	14.64	9.67	10
Peru	1.35	14.62	6.70	10
Poland	3.46	12.87	7.78	6
Portugal	4.92	44.12	16.32	12
Romania	2.70	10.44	5.64	6
Slovenia	1.96	33.54	14.48	5
Sri Lanka	8.36	13.30	11.14	9
Taiwan	5.04	10.30	8.16	8

Earlier we hypothesized that both ballot structure and the electoral cycle would impact the degree of ESP. Within our sample, 93 elections were held concurrently and 40 nonconcurrently, resulting in 241 party-election cases with ESP scores in concurrent elections and 176 in non-concurrent elections. Overall, the mean ESP in concurrent elections is 7.20, while the mean in nonconcurrent elections is 13.11. Of course, fused ballots are used only in concurrent elections, and once we exclude the 34 party-election cases with fused ballots (leaving 207 cases) the mean value of ESP in concurrent elections increases to 8.38.

Electoral separation of purpose values in the sample of concurrent elections that do not employ a fused ballot range from 0.32 to 46.64, while those for nonconcurrent elections range from 1.5 to 44.12. Assuming our sample is not biased in any particular way due to missingness, the relatively small difference when fused elections are excluded from the calculation of the mean for concurrent elections suggests that "forcing" low electoral separation of purpose through ballot structure only minimally reduces ESP. In contrast, nonconcurrence has a larger impact on ESP, creating a substantially greater physical separation between the executive and legislative votes than merely not having a fused ballot in concurrent elections.

Table 5.6 confirms these institutional effects, showing that the difference in ESP scores between concurrent and nonconcurrent elections is statistically significant in a difference-of-means test. The second column confirms that this difference holds up if we include only those countries that employ a mixed electoral cycle – that is, those where any given presidential cycle includes both a concurrent legislative election and at least one that is nonconcurrent, such as in Argentina, Mexico, the United States, and formerly Ecuador.[12] Because it is possible that the observed difference in column one is a function of other factors that happen to correlate with the electoral cycle, we leverage the existence of

---

[12] Several countries with different term lengths for president and assembly allow the elections to be concurrent when they fall in the same year. For example, El Salvador had concurrent elections in 1994, but normally they are nonconcurrent. Cases of this sort are not considered "mixed" although the individual elections enter into the data in the first column of Table 5.6 according to the timing of each election. We also do not include as mixed those cases that have shifted from nonconcurrent to concurrent (as in Brazil), or vice versa (as in the Dominican Republic) due to a constitutional change in term lengths or election timing. Ecuador, where various constitutional changes have led to some presidents having legislative elections at their midterm, while others have not, is considered mixed only for those presidents who have experienced a midterm election.

TABLE 5.6. *Electoral Separation of Purpose by Electoral Cycle*

Electoral Cycle	All Elections	Elections in Mixed-Cycle Cases	Elections in Mixed-Cycle Cases, Excluding United States
Concurrent, Excluding Fused Ballots	8.38 (7.26–9.50) N = 207	10.96 (9.06–12.86) N = 48	5.23 (3.81– 6.66) N = 22
Nonconcurrent	13.11 (11.91–14.33) N = 176	13.03 (11.21–14.86) N = 36	10.71 (7.91–13.52) N = 20
Pr(T < t)	0.000	0.063	0.000

95% confidence intervals in parentheses. Excludes fused elections.

these mixed-cycle cases to see if the results hold at the within-country and within-presidency levels of analysis.

The second column in Table 5.6 shows that the means for concurrent and nonconcurrent elections do converge to some extent when we isolate the effect in the mixed-cycle subsample. However, the third column reveals that the US case is driving this convergence. When we exclude cases from the United States, the difference between the concurrent and nonconcurrent elections is actually greater than it is with those cases included. This means that ESP tends to be relatively high in the United States regardless of whether the election is concurrent or at the presidential midterm. However, in the other mixed-cycle cases we still see a strong difference in the impact of the electoral cycle on ESP. As scholars have shown for other contexts (Shugart 1995; Samuels 2004), we can therefore be confident that nonconcurrence has important effects on electoral politics – in this case, tending to increase electoral separation between branches of the same party.

Exploring Institutional Configurations: Regime-Type and Electoral Cycle

Earlier, we noted that the difference at the aggregate level between pure and semi-presidential systems is not large. However, we have just seen that the difference between concurrent and nonconcurrent elections is substantial. In this section, we explore the combined impact of regime-type and the electoral cycle.

While ESP scores tend to be higher under nonconcurrent elections, there is a certain ambiguity in interpreting why that might be the case. Greater electoral separation of purpose could emerge when elections are on different dates because voters want different things from their executive and legislative votes (Samuels and Shugart 2003). Alternatively, greater ESP could arise from variations in voters' partisan preferences over time, within a president's term. That is, nonconcurrent elections may increase ESP by minimizing the extent to which the presidential race "contaminates" the legislative race, or they may increase ESP because they reflect the ebbs and flows of voter opinion about the incumbent president or about the parties themselves.

Thus under one plausible scenario, if a party's candidate won a presidential election at time *t*, but then governed incompetently, voters might punish that president's party at the next (nonconcurrent) legislative election. In this case voters are not voting for the legislative and executive candidates of a single party for different reasons. Instead, the president has simply lost support – and voters are taking it out on the president's party, which might even lose hold of the premiership as a result. (Of course, it remains the case that if voters abandon a legislative party because of the actions of an unaccountable president's performance, then the party is presidentialized.) Whether elections are concurrent or not, the separation of origin opens up a possibility that simply does not exist in parliamentary systems: an executive entering *and* remaining in office despite lacking a supportive electoral coalition in the legislative election.

It is possible that some of the difference between *wanting different (same) things* and *voting against (for) the president* might vary with institutional context. Here we explore whether different ways of combining regime-type and electoral cycle have distinct ESP profiles. We will employ kernel-density analysis so that the distributions of ESP scores can be seen at a glance under different institutional combinations. We will compare three different combinations: (1) pure presidential, concurrent elections; (2) semi-presidential, nonconcurrent elections; and (3) pure presidential, nonconcurrent elections. (Unfortunately, concurrent elections are too rare in semi-presidential systems for us to compare the impact of concurrent versus nonconcurrent elections in those regimes.)

How might we expect these three configurations to differ in terms of the extent of ESP? As the discussion above implied, when elections are concurrent we can expect voters to see the executive and legislative branches of a party as members of the same team. That is, they should be most likely to vote for both the executive and legislative wings of the party, and for the same reasons. While ESP is rarely as low in separate-powers systems (absent a fused ballot) as it is in parliamentary systems, we should expect a pronounced peak in the occurrence of ESP close to the zero end of the scale when elections are concurrent in pure presidential systems.

In contrast, we expect nonconcurrent elections in semi-presidential systems to peak further away from zero than concurrent elections in pure presidential systems. The reason is that in semi-presidential systems, nonconcurrent legislative elections can always give the opposition party control over part of the executive, if the election results in cohabitation. That is, this regime-type may encourage voters to see legislative elections as an opportunity to expel the president's party from the cabinet. By implication, voters are casting ballots in the presidential and subsequent nonconcurrent legislative elections for the "same reason" – perception of the president's and his or her party's performance on national policy questions.

For nonconcurrent elections in pure presidential systems, we expect the occurrence of ESP to peak ever further away from zero than in nonconcurrent semi-presidential systems. In these elections, voters can always "send a message" to the president by voting against his or her party's legislators, but they cannot punish the president by giving the opposition party control over part of the executive branch. Thus, as scholars have argued, nonconcurrent elections in pure presidential systems offer legislators the opportunity to campaign on entirely different bases than during concurrent elections. Indeed, nonconcurrent elections are precisely the times when legislative candidates are most likely to turn their campaigns away from national conditions and toward an emphasis on their ability to provide constituency service. As a result, ESP may increase even further than in nonconcurrent elections in semi-presidential systems.

We now turn to the distributions of ESP scores to explore these possible effects of regime-cycle configurations, by means of the kernel-density functions depicted in Figure 5.8. The comparison of the three configurations appears exactly as we described above. The highest peak near ESP = 0 is for concurrent elections in pure presidential systems. The peak for nonconcurrent elections in semi-presidential systems is both lower and farther from the zero end of the scale, while the peak for nonconcurrent elections in pure presidential systems is lower and less pronounced than the other two.

The differences of means between each of these configurations are significant, but what a simple comparison of means cannot reveal is the

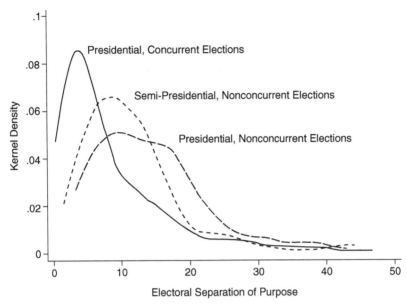

FIGURE 5.8. Effect of Regime-type and Electoral Cycle on Electoral Separation of Purpose – Kernel Density Estimates.

possibility of either a second mode or a long tail in one or more of the distributions. Note that the kernel-density estimate for nonconcurrent elections in pure presidential systems shows a peak that is at about the same value on the horizontal axis as that for nonconcurrent elections in semi-presidential systems, yet the distribution of the former does not fall nearly as rapidly as that of the latter. This is precisely the pattern we should see if there is a greater tendency of voters to vote *against* the president's party, whether to send a message or to indicate a preference for the parochial favors offered by a candidate of a different party.[13]

Evidence shown earlier confirmed that electoral separation of purpose can vary within countries at a given election, and within and across parties over time in a given country. The evidence in this section confirms that the electoral cycle and regime-type, more so than ballot structure, tends to separate the electoral bases of the executive and legislative

[13] The argument about the impact of a nonconcurrent election on control of the executive branch under semi-presidentialism clearly applies more to the premier-presidential subtype than to president-parliamentarism. There are not enough observations for us to test the latter subtype separately; however, a plot (not shown) like the one in Figure 6.8, but with only the premier-presidential cases included in the semi-presidential estimate, is almost identical to that shown.

branches of any given party. The findings suggest that the electoral fates of the executive and legislative wings of a given party are more closely tied together when elections are concurrent – as they often are in pure presidential systems, but only rarely in semi-presidential systems.

The findings also confirm that nonconcurrence has different effects on electoral separation of purpose in different regime-types. Nonconcurrence generates higher electoral separation of purpose in pure presidential systems, where such elections do not affect who heads the cabinet. This means that both regime-type and the electoral cycle matter for producing electoral separation of purpose. Of course, it is worth remembering that *all* systems with separation of electoral origin differ from pure parliamentary systems, where ESP is always zero due to the fusion of origin.

CONCLUSION

Governance in separate powers systems depends a great deal on a president's relationship with his or her party. This relationship, in turn, is a function of the extent to which the policy preferences and goals of the president and his or her party coincide or diverge. The fusion of origin in pure parliamentarism means that co-partisans who seek to occupy the executive and legislative branches share the same electoral base. Given this, similar political incentives motivate the two branches of the same political party. In contrast, the separation of origin under pure and semi-presidentialism opens up the possibility of separation of purpose – the possibility that presidents and their parties might go their own way in the electoral arena.

To the extent that presidents and parties diverge in the electoral arena, once in office they must bridge their divide internally, even if they hold a single-party majority. Such division is unthinkable in pure parliamentary systems. And of course, where such preference divergence exists, the separation of survival means that the dynamics and outcomes of inter-branch bargaining will differ from what occurs under parliamentarism – and not simply across branches of government but within the party that controls the executive branch, across that party's own internal executive and legislative branches.

High separation of purpose does not condemn parties to constant, intense intraparty warfare. As we noted above and saw in Tables 5.4 and 5.5, Brazil, the United States, and Portugal are countries in which parties sometimes have high levels of electoral separation of purpose. Yet high separation of purpose in these countries does not mean that presidents are never able to work with their parties. After all, a party can also have overlapping executive and legislative constituencies and still have conflictual intraparty relations. Our argument only suggests that *the higher the electoral separation of purpose, the more likely is intraparty conflict.* If presidents and their parties have similar vote bases, then intraparty politics should be relatively less fraught with tension. Electoral and legislative coalition building should be easier, cabinet nominations and the distribution of politically valuable resources should proceed with little controversy, and fewer disputes should arise over the content of policy proposals.

High electoral separation of purpose is not necessarily always bad for a party. Party leaders who wish to compete for control of the executive branch may recognize the trade-off that separation of origin implies, accepting the need to nominate a relative outsider to broaden the party's appeal in the presidential election or even tolerating an insider who nonetheless builds a suprapartisan campaign organization. We shall see examples of these phenomena in Chapter 7. In some cases, tolerating such electoral separation of purpose may be the party's only ticket to executive power – and presumably it is better for the party's collective interests to elect its leader to the executive branch, even with a sharply different vote base than that of its legislators, than it is to be in permanent opposition under the leadership of an executive candidate who is unable to attract a broader electorate.

Such separation is simply one way in which parties may be presidentialized: as we noted in defining this term in Chapter 1, a hallmark of presidentialization is the greater delegation to the party leader of the power to shape his or her campaign for the top office. Nonetheless, parties that promote or tolerate such separated purpose as a means to win executive elections are inevitably increasing their dangers of both adverse selection and moral hazard: once ensconced in a fixed-term office thanks to a suprapartisan appeal, presidents may come into conflict with their parties on a range of policy issues.

In sum, in both the electoral and governing arenas, *separation of origin can result in separation of purpose* – something that is not possible in parliamentary systems. This chapter provided a broadly comparative portrait of this important yet ignored aspect of electoral party politics in pure and semi-presidential systems. The possibility that presidents and legislators from the same party can go their own ways in the electoral arena has important theoretical and empirical implications. For example, unlike prime ministers, presidents can and do differ considerably from their own parties in terms of placement on the left-right ideological spectrum (Bruhn

2006; Wiesehomeier and Benoit 2007). To the extent that presidents differ from their parties and cannot be dismissed by their parties, presidents are decidedly not agents of their parties' median voter or median legislator, as we normally assume for a parliamentary party. Such divergence and autonomy between branches of a single political party is impossible under parliamentarism. The evidence in this chapter thus reveals the utility of our principal-agent framework for understanding intraparty politics. To the extent that the president and the party have different bases in the electorate, voters have two distinct agents within a single political party, both of which must transact with each other to get anything done.

APPENDIX 5A: SOURCES FOR DISTRICT-LEVEL ELECTORAL DATA

In 1999, Samuels and Mark Jones of Rice University received funding from the National Science Foundation to gather district-level data from presidential systems around the world (SES 99–11136). They subcontracted with experts from several countries to gather the data and prepare explanatory reports. The reports, and the data which are used in this project, are on file with and can be obtained from Samuels. Samuels personally updated the files; sources are listed below.

Argentina:

- Dirección Nacional Electoral. 1983–2003. "Escrutinios definitivos" ("Definitive Results"). On file with the authors.

Austria:

- www.electoralgeography.com "Austria," http://www.electoralgeography.com/en/countries/a/austria/. Accessed June 20, 2007.

Bolivia:

- 1985–97: Grace Ivana Deheza. 2001. "District-Level Elections Database Project: Bolivia." Report and Data files. Unpublished. On file with the author.
- 2002: Bolivia. Corte Nacional Electoral. 2002. "Acta de Computo Nacional, Elecciones Generales 2002." La Paz: Corte Nacional Electoral. Download from www.cne.org.bo. Accessed December 12, 2006.
- 2005: Corte Nacional Electoral. 2007. "Resultados Elecciones 2005." Microsoft Excel Spreadsheet. Obtained via email from the CNE, April 4, 2007, on file with the authors.

Brazil:

- 1945: Brazil. Tribunal Superior Eleitoral. 1945. *Dados Estatísticos: Eleições Federais, Estaduais, e Municipais.* Volume 1. Rio de Janeiro: Departamento de Imprensa Nacional.
- 1989–2002: Jairo Nicolau, "Banco de Dados Eleitorais do Brasil." On-line database at http://jaironicolau.iuperj.br/database/deb/port/index.htm. Last accessed December 26, 1006.
- 2006: Universo On-Line. 2006. "UOL Eleições 2006." http://placar.eleicoes.uol.com.br/2006/1turno/index.jhtm. Last accessed December 29, 2006.

Bulgaria:

- Department of Government, University of Essex. 2002. "Political Transformation and the Electoral Process in Post-Communist Europe." Online databank at http://www.essex.ac.uk/elections/. Last accessed December 28, 2006.
- "Bulgaria," http://www.electoralgeography.com/en/countries/b/bulgaria/. Accessed last December 28, 2006.

Chile:

- 1937–73: Urzúa, Germán. 1986. *Historia Política Electoral de Chile (1931–73).* Santiago: Tamarcos-Van.
- 1989–2001: Patricio Navia. 2001. "District-Level Elections Database Project: Chile." Report and data files. Unpublished. On file with the authors.
- 2005: Chile. Ministerio del Interior. "Sitio Histórico Electoral." Online database. www.elecciones.gov.cl. Last accessed December 28, 2006.

Colombia:

- 1974–90: Lijphart Elections Archive, http://dodgson.ucsd.edu/lij/southamerica/colombia/. Last accessed March 20, 2007.
- 1991–2006: Registraduria Nacional de Elecciones, www.registraduria.gov.co. Last accessed December 24, 2006.
- Maria Escobar-Lemmon, 2001. "District-Level Elections Database Project: Colombia." Data files. Unpublished. On file with the authors.

Costa Rica:

- 1953–98: Michelle Taylor-Robinson, 2001. "District-Level Elections Database Project: Costa Rica." Report and data files. Unpublished. On file with the authors.

- 2002–06: www.electoralgeography.com, data from www.tse.go.cr. Last accessed December 28, 2006.

Dominican Republic:

- Junta Central Electoral, www.jce.do/app/do/Resultados.aspx. Last accessed December 28, 2006.

Ecuador:

- 1979–98: Andrés Mejía-Acosta. 2000. "District-Level Elections Database Project: Ecuador." Report and data files. Unpublished. On file with the authors.
- 2006: Ecuador, Tribunal Supremo Electoral. "Resultados Elecciones 2006, 1a Vuelta." www.tse.gov.ec/resultadosparciales2006. Last accessed December 28, 2006.

El Salvador:

- 1994: http://pdba.georgetown.edu/Elecdata/ElSal/pres94.html.
- 2003: http://psephos.adam-carr.net/countries/e/elsalvador/elsalvador-2003.txt.
- 2006: http://www.elsalvador.com/especiales/2006/elecciones/home/index.asp.

Finland:

- All data obtained from Statistics Finland website, http://www.stat.fi/tk/he/vaalit/index_En.html. Last accessed December 28, 2006.

France:

- "Elections Presidentielles 1965–2002" (Microsoft Excel data file). Centre de Donneés Socio-Politiques (www.cdsp.sciences-po.fr).
- "Elections Legislatives 1997" (Microsoft Excel data file). Centre de Donneés Socio-Politiques (www.cdsp.sciences-po.fr).
- "Elections Legislatives 2002" (Microsoft Excel data file). Centre de Donneés Socio-Politiques (www.cdsp.sciences-po.fr).

Ghana:

- Charles Wiafe-Akenten, 2001. "District-Level Elections Database Project: Ghana." Report and data files. Unpublished. On file with the authors.

Guatemala:

- Fabrice Lehoucq, 2001. "District-Level Elections Database Project: Guatemala." Report and data files. Unpublished. On file with the authors.

Honduras:

- 1989–93: Honduras used a fused ballot.
- Michelle M. Taylor-Robinson, 2001. "District-Level Elections Database Project: Honduras." Report and data files. Unpublished. On file with the authors.
- 2005: http://www.tse.hn/files/common/Diputados%202005.pdf. Accessed March 20, 2007.

Indonesia:

- Electoralgeography.com, http://www.electoralgeography.com/en/countries/i/indonesia/. Accessed March 20, 2006. Original Source: Indonesia National Elections Commission, http://www.kpu.go.id/.

Ireland:

- Presidential Elections: Department of the Environment, Heritage and Local Government, Republic of Ireland. http://www.environ.ie/DOEI/DOEIPol.nsf/0/7b0f5af65995bd3980256f0f003bc80e/$FILE/presidentialelectionresults.doc. Accessed June 28, 2007.
- 2002 Parliamentary Election: http://electionsireland.org/. Accessed June 27, 2007.
- All other parliamentary elections: Daniele Caramani. 2000. CD-ROM supplement to *The Societies of Europe: Elections in Western Europe since 1815 – Electoral Results by Constituencies*. London: Macmillan Reference Ltd.

Korea:

- Jongin Jo. 2001. "The Korean Electoral System." Report and Data files. Unpublished. On file with the authors.
- 2002 Presidential Election: Chosun Ilbo newspaper website, http://english.chosun.com/, and "Psephos," Adam Carr's Election Archive, http://psephos.adam-carr.net. Last accessed December 29, 2006.

- 2004 Legislative Election: Korean National Election Commission www.nec.go.kr, from Adam Carr's Election Archive, http://psephos. adam-carr.net. Last accessed December 29, 2006.

Madagascar:

- 2001 and 2002 results: "Psephos," Adam Carr's website, http://psephos.adam-carr.net/countries/m/madagascar/madagascar20021.txt. Accessed March 20, 2007. Original source: Republic of Madagascar, Ministry of the Interior and Administrative Reform, http://www.mira.gov.mg/.

Malawi:

- 1999: Kimberly Butler, 2001. "District-Level Elections Database Project: Malawi." Report and data files. Unpublished. On file with the authors.
- 2004: Malawi SNDP, "2004 Malawi Presidential and Parliamentary Elections." http://www.sdnp.org.mw/~solomon/mec/index.htm. Last accessed March 20, 2007.

Mexico:

- All data obtained from Mexico's Instituto Federal Electoral website, www.ife.org.mx. Last accessed December 22, 2006.

Mozambique:

- "Psephos," Adam Carr's election website, http://psephos.adam-carr. net/countries/m/mozambique/mozambique2.txt.

Nicaragua:

- 1990–2001: Political Database of the Americas, http://pdba. georgetown.edu/. Last accessed December 29, 2006.
- 2006: Consejo Supremo Electoral, www.cse.gob.ni/index.php?s=1. Last accessed December 29, 2006.

Panama:

- Carlos Guevara-Mann. 2001. "District-Level Elections Database Project: Panamá." Report and data files. Unpublished. On file with the authors.

Paraguay:

- All data obtained from Paraguay's Tribunal Superior de Justicia Electoral, http://www.tsje.gov.py. Accessed December 23, 2006.

Peru:

- 1980–85: Gregory Schmidt, 2001. "District-Level Elections Database Project: Perú." Report and data files. Unpublished. On file with the authors.
- 2001–06: Oficina Nacional de Procesos Electorales, www.onpe.gob. pe. Accessed December 23, 2006.

Poland:

- All data obtained from www.electoralgeography.com. Last accessed December 29, 2006. Original source: Central Electoral Committee of Poland, http://www.pkw.gov.pl.

Portugal:

- All results obtained from the Portuguese National Elections Commission, http://eleicoes.cne.pt/cne2005/sel_Eleicoes.cfm?m= raster. Last accessed December 15, 2006.

Romania:

- All data obtained from Romanian Central Election Bureau, http://www.kappa.ro/guv/bec/ceb96.html. Last accessed December 22, 2006.

Slovakia:

- All data obtained from Slovakian Statistics Bureau, http://www.statistics.sk/. Last accessed December 24, 2006.

Slovenia:

- All data obtained from www.electoralgeography.com. Original source: Republic of Slovenia Elections and Referenda, http://volitve. gov.si/en/index.html. Last accessed March 17, 2007.

Sri Lanka:

- All data obtained from the following websites: http://www. slelections.gov.lk/, http://www.lanka.net/slelections/, and http:// www.srilankanelections.com/. Accessed December 26, 2006.

Taiwan:

- Tse-Min Lin. 2001. "District-Level Elections Database Project: Taiwan." Report and data files. Unpublished. On file with the authors.

Tanzania:

- United Republic of Tanzania, National Electoral Commission. 2000. "General Election 2000: Presidential Election Results," and United Republic of Tanzania, National Electoral Commission. 2000. "General Election 2000: Parliamentary Election Results." Dar Es Salaam: National Electoral Commission.

Ukraine:

- http://www.electoralgeography.com/en/countries/u/ukraine/.   Last accessed March 17, 2007.
- Original results from Central Elections Commission of Ukraine, http://www.cvk.gov.ua/.

United States:

- Presidential election results from 1956–96 by congressional district were provided by Professor Gary Jacobson, University of California, San Diego.
- Presidential election results for 2000–04 by congressional district were obtained at Polidata, http://www.polidata.org/. Last accessed March 20, 2007.
- All House results were obtained at the Clerk of the U.S. House of Representatives website, http://clerk.house.gov/members/electionInfo/elections.html. Last accessed March 20, 2007.

Uruguay:

- Uruguay uses a fused ballot.

Venezuela:

- 1958–93: Brian Crisp, 2001. "District-Level Elections Database Project: Venezuela." Data files. Unpublished. On file with the authors.
- 1998–2000: Consejo Nacional Electoral, http://www.cne.gov.ve/. Last accessed December 29, 2006.

Zambia:

- All data obtained from the Electoral Commission of Zambia, http://www.elections.org.zm/. Last accessed December 29, 2006.

APPENDIX 5B: COUNTRIES AND ELECTIONS INCLUDED

We sought district-level data for both executive and legislative elections from every pure and semi-presidential system in the world. In Table 5.B.1 we list every legislative election in all democracies that directly elect their national executive since 1946. Elections for which we obtained constituency-level party election returns for both the presidential and matching legislative election are in bold italics.

TABLE 5.B.1

Country	Legislative Elections Qualifying for Inclusion
Argentina	*1983, 1985, 1987, 1989, 1991, 1993, 1995, 1997, 1999, 2001*, 2003, 2005
Armenia	1998, 2003
Benin	1991, 1995, 1999, 2003
Bolivia	*1985, 1989, 1993, 1997, 2002, 2005*
Brazil	*1945*, 1950, 1954, 1958, 1962, *1990, 1994, 1998, 2002, 2006*
Bulgaria	*1994, 1997, 2001, 2005*
Chile	*1965, 1969, 1973, 1989, 1993, 1997, 2001, 2005*
Colombia	1958, 1962, 1966, 1970, *1974, 1978, 1982, 1986, 1990*, 1991, 1994, *1998, 2002, 2006*
Costa Rica	*1953, 1958, 1962, 1966, 1970, 1974, 1978, 1982, 1986, 1990, 1994, 1998, 2002, 2006*
Croatia	2000, 2003
Cyprus	1981, 1985, 1991, 1996, 2001, 2006
Dominican Republic	1978, 1982, 1986, 1990, *1998*, 2002, *2006*
Ecuador	*1979, 1984, 1988, 1992, 1994, 1996, 1998, 2002, 2006*
El Salvador	1985, 1988, 1991, *1994, 1997, 2000, 2003, 2006*
Finland	1951, 1954, 1958, 1962, 1966, 1970, 1972, 1975, 1979, 1983, 1987, 1991, *1995, 1999, 2003*

(*continued*)

TABLE 5.B.1 *(continued)*

Country	Legislative Elections Qualifying for Inclusion
France	1973, 1978, 1981, 1986, 1988, 1993, *1997, 2002*
Gambia	1982, 1987, 1992
Georgia	2003, 2004
Ghana	2004
Guatemala	*1999*, 2003
Honduras	*1985, 1989, 1993, 1997, 2002*
Indonesia	*2004*
Ireland	*1948, 1951, 1961, 1965, 1969, 1992, 1997, 2002*
Korea	1988, 1992, 1996, 2000, *2004*
Lithuania	1996, 2000, 2004
Macedonia	1994, 1998, 2002, 2006
Madagascar	1993, 1998, *2002*
Malawi	1994, *1999, 2004*
Mali	2002
Mexico	*2000, 2003, 2006*
Moldova	1991, 1996
Mongolia	1996, 2000, 2004
Mozambique	1994, *1999*, 2004
Namibia	1994, 1999, 2004
Nicaragua	*1990, 1996, 2001, 2006*
Panama	1989, *1994, 1999*, 2004
Paraguay	*1993, 1998, 2003*
Peru	*1980, 1985*, 1990, *2001, 2006*
Philippines	1953, 1957, 1961, 1965, 1969, 1987, 1992, 1995, 1998, 2001, 2004
Poland	*1991, 1993, 1997, 2001*, 2005
Portugal	1976, 1979, 1980, 1983, 1985, *1987, 1991, 1995, 1999, 2002, 2005*
Romania	*1996, 2000, 2004*
Russia	1995, 1999, 2003
Senegal	2001
Slovakia	2002, *2006*
Slovenia	*2000, 2004*
Sri Lanka	*1989, 1994, 2000, 2001, 2004*
Taiwan	*1996, 1998, 2001*

Country	Legislative Elections Qualifying for Inclusion
Ukraine	1998, 2002, 2006
United States	1948, 1950, 1952, 1954, *1956, 1958, 1960, 1964, 1968, 1970,* 1972, *1974, 1978, 1980, 1984, 1986, 1988, 1990, 1992, 1994, 1996, 1998, 2000, 2004, 2006*
Uruguay	*1954, 1958, 1962, 1966, 1971, 1989, 1994, 1999, 2004*
Venezuela	*1958, 1963, 1968, 1973, 1978, 1983, 1988, 1993, 1998, 2000,* 2005
Zambia	*1991, 2001, 2006*

6

The Impact of Constitutional Change on Party Organization and Behavior

As we argued in Chapter 2, all parties face collective action problems – and all parties confront the dilemmas raised by delegating power and resources to a single leader who will stand as the party's candidate for national office. The question we seek to answer is precisely how differences in the relationship between voters and the executive and legislative branches of government shape parties' ability to address these challenges.

Under parliamentarism's fusion of executive and legislative authority, parties organize to win legislative seats, and retain maximum accountability over their prime-ministerial agents. Yet under the separation of origin and/or survival, parties face different organizational and behavioral incentives. As shown in Chapters 3 and 4, when voters have two agents – the legislative party and a president – parties face more complex intraparty delegation and accountability problems. Moreover, when winning the executive branch directly – rather than winning legislative seats – becomes parties' driving goal, parties must favor "vote-seeking" incentives in election campaigns. Chapter 5 provided evidence that parties' executive and legislative vote bases can diverge quite widely in separation of powers systems. In short, parties that concentrate on winning executive elections will develop different organizational forms, nominate different sorts of leaders, and adopt different electoral strategies than they would under parliamentarism.

To test the hypothesis that parties organize and behave differently under different democratic constitutional regimes, we would ideally compare parties in countries that shifted from purely fused powers to purely separated, or vice versa. A change from parliamentarism to presidentialism in a stable and competitive democracy would allow a "before" and "after" comparison. Unfortunately for political science research, changes of this nature are extremely rare. In fact, since World War II we know of only one shift from a pure-type regime to another under democratic auspices: The Gambia in 1982. However, despite the case's theoretical potential, The Gambia changed its constitution under a single hegemonic party and subsequently experienced no change in party leadership. Moreover, a 1994 military coup suspended Gambian democracy.

We must therefore look for stable democracies that made less-extensive changes in the fusion or separation of executive authority that also had a relatively high degree of interparty competition both before and after changing constitutional formats. Two cases fit this bill: France in 1958–65 and Israel in 1992 and again in 2001. In 1958, France amended its parliamentary constitution to enhance the powers of its indirectly elected president, and a 1962 referendum adopted direct presidential elections starting in 1965. As for Israel, in 1992 the country changed its (unwritten) parliamentary constitution by adopting direct prime-ministerial elections starting in 1996, but – partly because the reform rapidly and dramatically changed the country's parties and party system – rescinded the change and returned to parliamentarism in 2001.

Both countries' reforms introduced separate origin of the executive, breaking the single chain of delegation that characterizes parliamentarism. However, in terms of executive survival, Israel retained a critical feature of parliamentarism: the entire government – including the elected prime minister – remained dependent on parliamentary confidence to survive in office.[1] In France, the president enjoys separation of survival, even though the French National Assembly retains the right to oust the premier and the cabinet. Thus, while France adopted the premier-presidential variant of semi-presidentialism, Israel became a rare hybrid that combined separate origin with fused survival – an elected prime-ministerial regime.

In this chapter we leverage these two quasi-experimental cases to explore the impact of imposing separation of origin and/or survival on party organization and behavior. France and Israel are critical cases for

---

[1] To be specific, a vote of no confidence under the reformed system only removed the prime minister; if it passed, then the Knesset was also dissolved (Article 19A of the Basic Law, as amended in 1992).

Executive Origin

		Fused (From Assembly Majority)	Separate (Popularly Elected)
Executive Survival	Fused (Subject to Assembly Confidence)	Parliamentary	Elected Prime-Ministerial (Israel 1992–2001)
	Separate (Fixed Terms)	Assembly-Independent	Presidential

FIGURE 6.1. Executive Origin and Survival in Single-Executive Regimes: The Israeli Hybrid Compared to the Pure Types.

this book's argument because both shifted from pure parliamentarism to systems with direct executive election – and, in Israel's case, shifted back – under fully democratic auspices. If we see predictable changes in party organization and behavior following these reforms, our theoretical argument gains credence – even if we must temper our generalizations because we draw upon only two cases. Thus in what follows we first discuss the theoretical importance of these two cases. We then examine the reforms parties undertook, and consider their impact on party presidentialization.

CONSTITUTIONAL REFORMS AND EXPECTATIONS FOR PARTY ADAPTATION

How do parties adapt to change in the structure of executive-legislative relations? In this section we consider this question from the perspective of our neo-Madisonian framework. This approach emphasizes how the chain of delegation under different constitutional contexts confronts parties with different collective action and delegation problems. In particular, in Chapter 2 we noted that democratic regimes structure the origin and survival of executive authority in different ways. Figure 6.1 thus revisits Figure 2.1, which showed how the pure-type regimes enact similar relationships on both dimensions of executive origin and survival: parliamentary systems are fused on both, while presidential systems are separated on both. In contrast, hybrid constitutions with single executives combine origin and survival differently. Thus in the lower left cell we find assembly-independent regimes like Switzerland, while in the upper right cell we have elected prime-ministerial regimes, which Israel's brief experience exemplified. In this latter system, the executive enjoys separation of origin but depends on the confidence of the assembly majority to survive in office.

Of course, it is far more common to find hybrid regimes that have a dual executive. In semi-presidential systems the president enjoys separation of origin and survival, while the prime minister is dependent on the assembly majority for survival in office. The French and Israeli reforms thus created two distinct hybrids, which share the parliamentary feature of a prime minister accountable to the assembly majority and the presidential feature of an executive with separate origin. They differ on the question of the survival of the directly elected executive.

How much did these reforms presidentialize the parties, relative to their experience under parliamentarism? The constitutional changes in France and Israel should have predictable effects on those countries' parties. Moreover, those effects should differ across the two cases as a function of their differences in executive survival. In this section we first consider the impact on parties of shifting from fused to separate executive origin, which occurred in both cases, and we then discuss the impact on parties of different combinations of executive origin and survival.

The Impact of Shifting from Fused to Separate Origin of Executive Authority

A shift from fused to separate executive origin should have predictable effects on political party organization and strategy. As suggested in Chapter 2, the possibility of winning a popular executive election focuses parties' strategy on their viability in executive elections rather than on winning parliamentary seats. Parties that survive and thrive in such systems are those that discover how to address the challenge of fielding a competitive candidate in the national executive race. In contrast, parties that fail to field viable candidates in direct executive elections will remain "niche" parties in the legislature, relegated to a subordinate position in the political system relative to a viable coalition partner in a parliamentary system.

The opportunity to capture the executive branch directly provides parties with different organizational and behavioral imperatives than they encounter in parliamentary systems. Party presidentialization due to separation of origin is primarily a function of stronger "vote-seeking" incentives in direct-executive elections (Samuels 2002), relative to parties' "office-seeking" or "policy-seeking" incentives in parliamentary elections (Strøm 1990). Vote-seeking incentives are stronger when there is separation of origin because no parliamentary system has a threshold of exclusion for *legislative* elections as high as all separation of powers systems do for *executive* elections, in which the winner takes all the seats, so to speak.

Given the stronger vote-seeking incentives, parties will sacrifice policy commitments in executive campaigns, and executive candidates will develop autonomous campaign organizations unaccountable to party organs.[2] Candidates for prime minister in parliamentary systems often develop personal organizations, but ultimately the candidate and the content of the campaign both remain accountable to the party.

The opportunity to compete in a direct executive election is also fraught with potential challenges for parties' collective action problems because parties face the problem – also unknown in parliamentary systems – of having to coordinate electoral strategy across races for two institutions. Given the need to adopt a vote-seeking strategy in the executive race and the consequent incentive to nominate candidates with "outsider" appeal, the requirements for running successful campaigns in both races will not necessarily overlap. This challenge is complicated by the fact that the constituency of the median party legislator may differ substantially from the constituency that a viable presidential candidate might seek to target, as Chapter 5 suggested.

The impact of coattail effects and the electoral cycle (which by definition cannot exist in parliamentary systems) also exacerbate parties' organizational, financial, informational, and strategic challenges. For example, to the extent that an elected presidency is politically valuable, direct executive elections – whether held concurrently or not – can influence legislative elections. Parties' electoral dependence on their presidential candidate can become problematic because – as shown in Chapter 4 – after the election, a president often becomes the de facto party leader, with separation of survival.

In sum, separation of origin forces parties to strategize differently about whom to nominate to lead the party and how to campaign in both executive and legislative races. Given the political importance of the directly elected executive, parties with viable presidential candidates face strong incentives to concentrate their energies and resources on the executive election, at the potential cost of underinvesting in legislative races, and even considering the problems of adverse selection and moral hazard involved in the process. All parties in presidential or semi-presidential systems face these dilemmas, because all parties have

---

[2] In addition to the hybrid-system examples in this chapter, we also demonstrate these phenomena under pure presidentialism in Chapter 7.

strong incentives to present presidential candidates. The strength of such incentives varies as a function of parties' self-perceived viability in the presidential election: parties that believe they can compete for the presidency have relatively stronger incentives to adopt a broad, vote-seeking strategy, while parties that lack viable candidates for the direct executive election should concentrate on office- or policy-seeking through winning seats in the legislature.[3]

The Impact of Fused versus Separate Survival

Institutional reforms transformed both the French and Israeli systems of fused origin into systems of separate executive origin. Yet these countries' constitutional reforms differed crucially in terms of the mechanism of executive survival. France created a directly elected president with separation of survival for a fixed term, while Israel left the directly elected prime minister subject to assembly confidence. This difference in executive survival should also have predictable effects on parties' behavioral and organizational imperatives. Specifically, in a dual-executive hybrid like France's, we expect all parties to become presidentialized. In contrast, where origin is separate but survival fused we expect a bifurcation of the party system in which only the larger parties enter the direct executive election and become presidentialized, while the smaller parties forgo the presidential race and remain parliamentarized.

As noted earlier, in systems with separation of origin, even small parties have strong incentives to compete in both the executive and legislative races. Small parties often enter direct executive elections despite no chance of winning, hoping to benefit from media exposure for their policy positions as part of a long-term political strategy. Coattail effects can also help parties win legislative seats in hybrid systems even if the party does not expect to *win* the executive election (Tavits 2009), thereby providing additional incentives to run a candidate in the direct election. A small party that is unlikely to win a direct executive election could also decide to enter the executive race to leverage whatever popularity its

---

[3] The degree of vote seeking also depends on whether presidential elections involve one or two rounds. A one-round system distorts the votes-seats relationship somewhat less than a two-round system. In a one-round system, the candidate with the most votes wins. However, in a two-round system, the second-place finisher in the first round can eventually win. Thus, in a two-round system presidential candidates are relatively freer to conduct ideological campaigns in the first round. Both cases in this chapter employ or employed two-round majority rules.

candidate possesses *after* the election to bargain for concessions from one of the leading candidates or the eventual winner.

Given these incentives, parties that forgo running candidates in systems with separation of survival relegate themselves permanently to secondary positions in the political system. This is because under the separation of survival, to the extent that presidents can independently influence cabinet composition, switch policies (see Chapter 8), or dissolve the legislature, smaller parties have no guarantee that the president will hold up his end of any bargain to divide the spoils. A party that decides not to nominate a candidate for direct executive elections might continue to win votes from committed supporters, but it cannot guarantee its supporters anything in return for their support. After all, presidents stay in office for the duration of their term no matter what smaller parties demand.

Parties that operate as strictly "parliamentary" parties in systems with separation of survival thus possess relatively less leverage over directly elected executives who enjoy separation of survival, compared to parties' leverage over prime ministers in parliamentary systems. Given this, parties in systems with separation of origin rarely choose this parliamentary path – most executive elections in pure and semi-presidential systems feature candidates from smaller parties. However, parties in systems that combine separation of origin with fusion of survival should see a bifurcation of party strategies: larger parties will become presidentialized and concentrate on the direct executive elections, while smaller parties will remain parliamentarized and concentrate on the assembly elections. This is precisely what happened in Israel: in each of three direct prime-ministerial elections there were exactly two candidates on election day; Israel's myriad other parties all invested solely in the legislative contest.[4]

This bifurcation of party strategies is a function of the combination of separate origin and fused survival. As argued in previous chapters, systems that combine separate origin with separate survival tilt the balance of power toward the directly elected executive and away from *all* the parties in the system, including the executive's own party. In contrast, the combination of separate origin and fused survival creates a peculiar situation in which smaller parties can gain considerable leverage over the prime minister (as in a parliamentary system) while the prime minister's

---

[4] In 1999, the Centre Party's candidate (Yitzhak Mordechai) dropped out the day before the election after it became clear that his entry in the race had been a strategic mistake.

own party becomes a secondary actor (as in a presidential system). In an elected prime-ministerial regime, the winner of the popular election automatically becomes head of government, but a directly elected prime minister whose party does not win a legislative majority needs coalition partners to form a cabinet with assembly confidence, just as in a semi-presidential regime. However, in contrast to a president in a semi-presidential system, the elected prime minister also needs these parties' support simply to remain in office. Indeed, the Israeli reform required new prime-ministerial and assembly elections if the incumbent lost a confidence vote.[5] This rule gave smaller parties relatively greater bargaining power in an elected prime-ministerial regime than in a semi-presidential regime, because a prime minister's coalition partners could bring down the executive itself and force new elections.

This combination of separate origin with fused survival created intraparty agency problems for the prime minister's party unlike those seen in parliamentary systems. In parliamentary systems the prime minister depends not only on the confidence of the legislative majority but also on majority support within his or her own party. Given this, as shown in Chapter 4, parties in parliamentary systems can and frequently do swap out their premiers between elections – without even a vote on the floor of parliament. In this way, pure parliamentary systems maximize intraparty accountability. However, somewhat ironically, parties in a system with separate origin but fused survival cannot fire their prime-ministerial agents and substitute a co-partisan as parties in parliamentary systems can. Although prime ministers in hybrids like Israel's remain subject to parliamentary confidence – and thus in theory formally subject to intraparty dismissal – a party that seeks to discipline its agent in this way would have to immediately present a different candidate for another direct election – a highly risky prospect. This is because the system required new prime-ministerial elections – but not new assembly elections – if the prime minister resigned or was forced from office through a procedure other than a confidence motion.

Thus in elected prime-ministerial regimes, the prime minister's accountability to the assembly majority severely limits *intra*party accountability, while retaining *inter*party accountability. It is important to note that even

---

[5] This is true if the vote was a majority of at least 61 of the 120 Knesset members (Article 19A of the Basic Law as reformed in 1992). However, if more than 80 Knesset members voted in favor of a no-confidence motion, then the Knesset would remain and there would be elections only for the prime minister (Article 19B of the Basic Law).

if one party were to win a majority of seats, it would still have to call new prime-ministerial elections if it wanted to remove its own leader as prime minister. All in all, elected prime-ministerial regimes severely weaken prime ministers' parties relative to coalition parties. This suggests that the combination of separate origin and fused survival presidentializes larger parties but leaves smaller parties parliamentarized. We thus expect only the larger parties to adopt a vote-seeking strategy by nominating outsiders who will campaign on broad platforms, while smaller parties – those that conclude they have no chance to win the direct prime-ministerial election – should concentrate on the legislative race, consolidating their hold over an electoral "niche" and leveraging the hold they have over the prime minister to extract office and/or policy benefits.

We expect significant presidentialization of parties after the adoption of direct election of the president in France and the prime minister in Israel. In Israel we expect more extensive presidentialization for the parties that contest the separate executive election, while small parties should remain parliamentarized, emphasizing their legislative leverage rather than the remote possibility of winning the executive election. We now turn to each case to test the strength of these propositions.

PRESIDENTIALIZED PARTIES IN FRANCE

Constitutional reforms shifted the French political regime from pure parliamentarism to semi-presidentialism. In this section we explain how these reforms presidentialized French political parties. Undisciplined parties, a fragmented party system, and intractable governability problems characterized the French 4th Republic's (1946–58) pure parliamentary system. In the wake of the 1958 Algerian crisis – which almost resulted in a military coup in Paris – French leaders agreed to Charles de Gaulle's proposed constitutional reforms to anchor the political system with a strengthened executive (Cole and Campbell 1989, 176–77). The reforms initially retained the indirectly elected presidency, but in 1962 de Gaulle demanded and won a plebiscite that adopted direct presidential elections, first held in 1965. The 5th Republic thus became the model for many subsequent semi-presidential constitutions, as we noted in Chapter 2.

French presidents enjoy separation of origin and survival for a five-year term (originally seven). They also hold important formal constitutional powers, including authority to appoint the prime minister (Article 8), call referenda (Article 11), and dissolve parliament and call new elections (Article 12). Clift (2005, 223) suggests that de Gaulle's vision transformed the 4th Republic's largely ceremonial president from a "referee into a team captain." In reality, de Gaulle's reforms made the French president not just a team captain but an attention-grabbing star player his or her team anoints and depends upon entirely to lead them to victory.

This political transformation is important for our argument because experts on French politics concur that presidentialization of the parties and the party system occurred because of these *institutional* changes, which were adopted well before the social-structural changes Poguntke and Webb (2005b) suggest presidentialized parties in other European parliamentary systems. Writing in Poguntke and Webb's volume, Clift (2005, 241) confirms this point, adding only that "structural changes since the 1960s have induced further shifts, but the advanced starting point means subsequent presidentialization has seemed less dramatic than in many other cases."

France's reforms had immediate and obvious effects on the internal character of France's parties, reshaping the relationship between party leaders as presumed presidential candidates and their parliamentary groups and altering the dynamics of interparty competition (Machin 1989; Cole 1990a, 1993; Frears, 1991). The separation of executive origin has encouraged political personalization, a decline in the importance of ideology, and the marginalization of party organization from political campaigns. Let us examine these changes in some detail.

Presidentialization of Nomination and Campaigns

As the aggregate evidence in Chapter 3 suggests, presidentialization has forced France's parties to focus their energies and resources on finding credible presidential candidates and on winning the presidential election, as opposed to winning parliamentary elections. Even given France's two-round majoritarian presidential electoral system, in which parties may use partisan and ideological appeals to stand out in a crowded first-round field, credibility in the presidential race requires finding a candidate with a broad electoral base (Knapp 1990, 140).

Across the political spectrum, the desire to win the presidential election has pushed parties to find suprapartisan candidates, adjust their campaign strategies by reducing the importance of ideology, and limit the importance of the party organization. Cole (1990a, 13) notes that presidential candidates tend to "base [their] campaigns upon the notion of *rassemblement*, the ecumenical appeal beyond the political space represented by any one political tendency." This dynamic appeared first on the right side of the political spectrum. De Gaulle himself claimed to disdain parties, and the first "Gaullist" party to emerge (in 1958), the Union pour la Nouvelle Republique (UNR) – which was a direct descendant of a similar party organized to support de Gaulle under the 4th Republic – was regarded as completely "'at the service' of de Gaulle's 'plebiscitary monarchy'" (Duhamel and Grunberg 2001, 533).

De Gaulle's powerful personality united the UNR and obviated the need for a strong party organization (Knapp 1990, 154). Moreover, de Gaulle's popularity helped elect the party's legislative candidates, confirming the party's status as a mere tool of de Gaulle's ambitions. After de Gaulle departed the political scene for good in 1969 the UNR re-formed and renamed itself the Rassemblement pour la Republique (Rally for the Republic, RPR), but it remained highly presidentialized. As with the UNR, the RPR's main function was to elect its new leader Jacques Chirac president (Cole 1990a, 13).

Like the UNR/RPR, the Union for French Democracy (UDF), a non-Gaullist rightist party, was formed in 1978 as a "presidential-inspired confederation" (Cole 1990b, 126). In fact, the UDF was formed *exclusively* as a presidentialized party: when cobbling together the UDF, Valéry Giscard d'Estaing deliberately devoted few resources to building a grassroots support base and focused instead on creating a party that would merely "articulate the president's will" (Cole 1990b, 128). As a result, during campaigns, the UDF's presidential candidates tended to ignore the party organization.[6]

On the left side of the political spectrum, the vote-seeking incentives of the semi-presidential constitution hit the Socialist Party (PS) particularly hard. Gaffney (1990, 64) notes that in the 3rd and 4th Republics, the relationship between party organization, ideology, and electoral strategy in the PS was "relatively non-contentious." The party dealt with the trade-offs parties in pure parliamentary systems face fairly well in building its legislative delegation and augmenting its municipal bases of support. Yet facing the possibility of remaining permanently in the opposition, by the 1970s the PS was forced to confront the presidentialization of the

---

[6] Many leading UDF politicians joined with the RPR in 2002 to form the Union for a Presidential Majority (UMP), renamed later the Union for a Popular Movement (also UMP). As of 2007 the UMP was France's main conservative political party. Most of the rump UDF was subsequently incorporated in 2007 into a new party, the Mouvement Démocrate (Democratic Movement).

regime. Led by François Mitterrand, who only joined the PS officially *after* he had announced his presidential candidacy in 1974 (Clift 2005, 228), the PS began to direct resources and energy away from its parliamentary and municipal strategy and toward presenting a "nationally known, credible, and respected figure at its head" (Gaffney 1990, 64). This involved allowing Mitterrand to define himself as "larger" than the PS, in order to reach centrist voters.

The strategic reorientation of the PS diluted socialist ideology, personalized the presidential campaigns, and reduced the importance of the party organization and grassroots mobilization. Given the need to appear "above" his party, Mitterrand developed his own personal campaign organization that was free of the weighty democracy of the party's internal structure. The personnel who staffed this organization were responsible to Mitterrand alone, not to the party (Gaffney 1990, 65). Mitterrand distanced himself from the PS to such an extent that in 1981 his campaign headquarters had virtually no contact with the party organization (Cole 1990a, 13). In 1988, Mitterrand again ignored the party's platform and "stood on his own presidential platform" (Cole and Campbell 1989, 114), which was "pitched toward the center" (Northcutt 1989, 291) and swept the candidate's attachment to his party under the carpet. Overall, Mitterrand's rise to power "transformed his party into an organized representative of the presidential will" (Cole 1993, 57).

Presidentialization of Assembly Elections

The adoption of semi-presidentialism presented parties across the spectrum with new and different strategic challenges in terms of nominating and electing presidential candidates. The same can be said about parties' strategies in legislative elections, which after 1958 also increasingly responded to the ebb and flow of presidential politics. Clift (2005, 225) reports that the presidential electoral cycle rather than the rhythm of the parliamentary election calendar came to define the inner workings of all major French parties. This came about partly because presidential elections have greater "coattails" impact on legislative elections in France than they do in the United States (Pierce 1995, 189–99). An example of such influence comes from Mitterrand's early dissolution of parliament immediately following his 1981 inauguration. At the legislative elections held only six weeks later, the PS captured an absolute majority of the seats (Cole and Campbell 1989, 130). This is a classic example of what Shugart (1995) calls a "honeymoon election" – an election held early in a new president's tenure that generates even longer presidential coattails than a concurrent election.

However, the presidentialization of legislative elections can be a two-edged sword. Given unequal term lengths, a honeymoon assembly election early in the president's term (seven years long prior to 2002) would necessarily be followed by another later-than-midterm assembly election five years later (barring another parliamentary dissolution). If midterm losses are common in separate-powers systems, *late-term* election losses may even be greater (Shugart 1995). This was the case in the 1986 assembly elections, when the PS was unable to control its own fate. At that time, Mitterrand was unpopular, but given the separation of survival, the PS could not replace him. Thus Mitterrand's unpopularity – and not the unpopularity of the party or its prime minister – cost the PS its control of parliament (Gaffney 1990, 72). The result was the first case in France of cohabitation, with a conservative premier and cabinet serving alongside Mitterrand.

The presidential election cycle would continue to dominate assembly politics after Mitterrand won reelection in 1988. Mitterrand immediately dissolved parliament again, and the resulting assembly elections gave the PS the largest share of parliamentary seats. This allowed Mitterrand to appoint a cabinet with the "opening to the center" he had promised in his own campaign. This cycle of elections reveals that the incumbent president's popularity powerfully shapes the results of French legislative elections. When presidents are popular, parties depend on them for their survival in office. Yet when parties cannot remove an unpopular president from office, they will suffer at the next legislative election.

In addition to reorienting party ideology and the content of electoral campaigns, the creation of a separately elected president also reduced party organizations' influence in setting the government agenda. Cole (1990a, 10) goes so far as to state that Mitterrand's 1981 election transformed the Socialist Party's assembly caucus into "the prevalent model of the presidential party in the 5th Republic, the *parti de godillots* (party of bootlickers)," to illustrate parties' subservience to presidents and/or presidential candidates. After that election, the PS organization ceded influence over government policy and "rapidly gave up any pretence that it could lead government activity, rather than follow government's orders" (Cole 1990a, 10). This has become true of the other parties as well: presidents govern largely independently of parties and make their own decisions as to whether to stand for reelection (Gaffney 1990, 74; Cole 1993). In short, soon after the adoption of the 5th Republic's constitution, French parties became "presidential machines," vehicles for politicians' presidential ambitions and an organizational resource by which presidents could implement their programs.

Presidentialization of Interparty Politics

The adoption of direct presidential elections also changed the nature of *interparty* competition. In particular, direct presidential elections severely damaged the fortunes of the French Communist Party (PCF). By supporting the Socialist candidate Mitterrand in 1974, the PCF all but admitted that a communist could never be elected president. This move hurt the PCF because its supporters got used to splitting their tickets – voting for a socialist for president but a communist for assembly. The PCF's abstention from the presidential race also helped the PS in a different way, because it allowed the PS to reach out to centrist voters (Cole and Campbell 1989, 114). That is, the PCF early on smacked up against the vote-seeking requirements of direct presidential elections. Because it could not compete for the political center and lacked viable presidential candidates, its influence rapidly waned. As a result, fearing for its own survival, in 1978 the PCF withdrew from its alliance with the PS. In 1981 the PCF ran its own presidential candidate, but after Mitterrand won, the party's electoral fortunes continued to decline. In 2007, the party won only 15 of 577 assembly seats (2.6%). Under pure parliamentarism, interparty competition would not have revolved around presidential elections and the PCF might have not endured such a dramatic decline. In fact, while it is impossible to say for sure, it is likely that under parliamentarism either the Socialists would not have won in 1981 – because Mitterrand would not have had the autonomy to reshape his party toward the center – or they would have had to govern only with a coalition in which the PCF would have had much more leverage.

French Politicians React to Presidentialization

French scholars and politicians are perfectly aware that the hybrid constitution has presidentialized party politics (see e.g. Duhamel 1991). In order to reduce the likelihood of cohabitation, in 2000 French voters approved a referendum reducing the president's term from seven years to five. The National Assembly then passed a bill inverting the order of the 2002 elections so that the presidential election would precede the parliamentary election. Representatives of every party hotly debated this "calendar inversion bill," and their position depended largely on whether their party's health depended on its ability to field a credible presidential candidate and benefit from coattail effects (Bell and Criddle 2002; Jérôme, Jérôme-Speziari, and Lewis-Beck 2003). The PS and the UDF, which both had credible presidential candidates, both favored calendar inversion,[7] while the PCF and the Greens, which did not and which depended heavily on performing well in parliamentary elections, opposed it.[8] Yves Cochet of the Green Party stated that calendar inversion "would lead to the cannibalization of the parliamentary elections by the presidential elections."[9] President Chirac's RPR viewed the calendar inversion as a plot by Socialist Premier Jospin to promote his presidential candidacy,[10] but as we note below, the RPR ultimately benefited from the move.

In the wake of this reform, French parliamentary elections have become even *more* presidentialized than before.[11] In both 2002 and 2007, the party that won the presidential election regained (2002) or retained (2007) a majority in the National Assembly. The elections in both of those years illustrate several features of party presidentialization. In 2002, the left collectively suffered from its own fragmentation. The Socialists fielded Prime Minister Jospin in the presidential race, but four other leftist candidates each won at least 2% of the vote. Table 6.1

---

[7] Gerard Courtois and Cecille Chambraud, "L'avenir du quinquennat dépendra du calendrier électoral." *Le Monde* electronic edition, September 24, 2000. Jean Louis Saux, "Charles Pasqua souhaite à son tour que la présidentielle précède les legislatives." *Le Monde* electronic edition, September 27, 2000.

[8] Beatrice Gurrey and Jean Baptiste de Montvalon, "Le gouvernment ne paraît pas disposé à modifier le calendrier électoral de 2002." *Le Monde* electronic edition, October 6, 2000. Cecile Chambraud and Beatrice Gurrey, "Lionel Jospin déclenche la polémique sur le calendrier electoral de 2002." *Le Monde* electronic edition, November 28, 2000.

[9] Alain Beuve Mery, "Le PCF refuse un changement 'dangereux pour la démocratie.'" *Le Monde* electronic edition, November 30, 2000. Alain Beuve Mery, "Les Verts 'piégés' par leur base sur la question du mode de scrutin." *Le Monde* electronic edition, November 2, 2000.

[10] Raphaelle Bacque, "L'Elysée estime que le calendrier actuel sert Jacques Chirac." *Le Monde* electronic edition, November 30, 2000.

[11] A similar reform occurred in Romania in 2004. Since 1990, Romania had been one of the few semi-presidential systems to hold concurrent executive and legislative elections. Not surprisingly, legislators bemoaned presidential influence in "their" elections, and thus made a move in the opposite direction as France – to de-couple the two elections by lengthening the president's term by a year (Radu 2003). This change was designed to reduce presidential influence, but its most important effect was to increase the likelihood of cohabitation – which predictably followed in 2007, after the collapse of the president's coalition (Condon and Wagstyl 2007).

TABLE 6.1. *Results of the 2002 French Presidential Election*

Candidate	Party	First Round %	Second Round %
Jacques Chirac	Rally for the Republic	19.88	82.21
Jean-Marie Le Pen	National Front	16.86	17.79
Lionel Jospin	Socialist Party	16.18	
François Bayrou	Union for French Democracy	6.84	
Arlette Laguiller	Workers' Struggle	5.72	
Jean-Pierre Chevènement	Citizens' Movement	5.33	
Noël Mamère	The Greens	5.25	
Olivier Besancenot	Revolutionary Communist League	4.25	
Jean Saint-Josse	Hunt, Fish, Nature, Traditions	4.23	
Alain Madelin	Liberal Democracy	3.91	
Robert Hue	French Communist Party	3.37	
Bruno Mégret	National Republican Movement	2.34	
Christiane Taubira	Left Radical Party	2.32	
Corinne Lepage	Citizenship, Action, Participation	1.88	
Christine Boutin	Forum of Social Republicans	1.19	
Daniel Gluckstein	Party of the Workers	0.47	

Candidates of leftist parties in italics.

presents the results, with the leftist candidates' names placed in italics. Leftist fragmentation – combined with a stronger-than-expected showing by the far-right National Front candidate Jean-Marie Le Pen – meant that the left failed to place a candidate in the runoff round.

For our purposes, the 2002 presidential election and the subsequent parliamentary elections provide important lessons. First, it was clear that by 2002 nearly all parties had become presidentialized in one key respect: each saw advantage to presenting a presidential candidate. Presumably, leaders of parties such as Workers' Struggle or the Revolutionary Communist League did not believe they could actually win the presidency. Rather, they used the high profile of a presidential campaign to advertise their independence, which might serve them well in future parliamentary or regional contests, and perhaps also in the hope of extracting policy or office concessions from an expected Jospin runoff candidacy and potential presidency. However, this damaged the left's collective prospects.

Second, consider the performance of Le Pen. His party has established a national presence primarily due to its leader's perennial presidential candidacy. The National Front has never won more than one seat in a National Assembly election, except in 1986, the one election in which proportional representation was used. It has averaged just over 10% of National Assembly votes since 1986, but Le Pen himself frequently has won a higher vote share than his own party would in the next parliamentary election.[12] When Le Pen made the runoff in 2002, it was a national embarrassment, and voters – even those on the left – rallied to give the conservative Chirac more than 80% of the votes in the second round.

The parliamentary elections that followed one month after the second round of the 2002 presidential election only confirmed the right's strength. The parties that backed Chirac united after the presidential runoff into the Union for a Presidential Majority (UMP), which signaled by its very name its call to end cohabitation. A race to control the presidency and the legislature that had appeared close before the first round of the presidential election eventually turned into a romp for the right: the UMP won 357 of the 577 seats.

After 2002, presidentialization became entrenched even further. The shortening of the presidential term to five years – the same as the assembly – substantially reduces the possibility for future episodes of cohabitation, given that previous episodes had begun at least two years into a president's term.[13] With Chirac's retirement as his (shortened) second term drew to a close, his chosen successor, Nicolas Sarkozy, won the 2007 presidential election. The right subsequently again won a sizable majority of seats in the national assembly elections, held a month later. Commenting on the outcome of those elections, Prime Minister

---

[12] For instance, in 1988, Le Pen won 14.5%, while his parliamentary party would win only 9.7% later that year. In 2002, Le Pen won 16.9% but the party won 11.3% the same year. In 2007, the figures were 10.4% and 4.3%. Only from 1993 to 1997 were the percentages similar in both presidential and parliamentary elections.

[13] Thus far, cohabitation has occurred only after the late-term elections of 1986 and 1993, plus the early dissolution in 1997, two years into Chirac's seven-year first term.

François Fillon, whom Sarkozy had appointed even before the assembly election confirmed the majority, stated after the election that voters had made a "clear and coherent choice, which will allow the President of the Republic to implement his project" (CNN 2007).

France: Conclusion

Our theoretical predictions regarding the impact of the advent of separate executive and legislative origin and separate presidential survival hold up to scrutiny of the French case. Presidentialization of the French party system was fully evident by 1981 and, as we noted, has only deepened since then. In France, as Pierce (1995) and others have made clear, *national politics is presidential government*, not parliamentary "party government." Across the political spectrum, French parties no longer conform to a parliamentary model: presidentialism has transformed parties into "rallies" around their presidential leaders, in which the executive branch of each party dominates its legislative branch. Presidential candidates set the tone of party platforms; pursuit of the presidency, not of legislative seats, dominates electoral campaigns; presidential elections heavily influence outcomes in the legislative race; presidents frequently remove and replace prime ministers despite lacking the constitutional authority to do so; and presidents have come to dominate the policy-making process. The adoption of a dual-executive hybrid constitutional format has reduced the importance of ideology, decreased the importance of party organization in campaigns and in policy formulation, and increased the level of personalization in both interparty competition and intraparty politics. The effects are clearly a function of France's institutional reforms, and not of social-structural processes.

PRESIDENTIALIZED PARTIES IN ISRAEL

Presidentialization of the political parties also occurred in our second quasi-experimental case, Israel. Like France in 1962, in 1992 Israel adopted direct executive elections. Until that year, Israeli parties had competed in a parliamentary system in which all 120 Knesset members were elected in one at-large national constituency. The combination of this huge district magnitude together with a low threshold of exclusion generated considerable party-system fragmentation, which in turn generated nettlesome governability problems. By the 1980s, scholars and politicians had begun debating a proposal to directly elect the prime minister, separately from Knesset elections. Many believed this reform would energize voters, enhance the prime minister's legitimacy, and provide governments with stability and cohesion.

The resulting constitutional design was an elected prime-ministerial regime, which resembled presidentialism in adopting the separation of executive and legislative origin, but differed from presidentialism by retaining fused executive and legislative survival. That is, Israel kept the 120-seat national district for Knesset elections, but voters would cast two ballots – one for a prime-ministerial candidate, and one for a party-generated list of parliamentary candidates.[14] Yet the prime minister could lose office through a no-confidence vote, which would result in early elections. Under this system, direct prime-ministerial elections were held in 1996 and 1999 concurrently with Knesset elections. A third prime-ministerial election took place in 2001, without a new Knesset election, after the prime minister resigned due to interparty coalition problems (Diskin and Hazan 2002).[15]

Reform proponents had assumed that few voters would split their tickets (Rahat 2004, 469),[16] yet the aftermath of the reform proved its supporters dead wrong. Our neo-Madisonian framework helps explain why reformers' expectations were so off the mark. In each of three prime-ministerial elections, only the two largest parties ultimately ran candidates for prime minister. Other parties focused on entering a postelection parliamentary coalition with whoever won the direct prime-ministerial election, and thus concentrated all their resources on winning Knesset seats. The result was widespread ticket splitting, which pushed party-system fragmentation to new highs. As a result, government stability suffered – as one expects in a system in which postelection allies in parliament hold the keys to the prime minister's survival but bear minimal electoral consequences because they do not contest prime-ministerial elections themselves.

Given the disastrous consequences of the reform, after less than a decade Israeli politicians returned their country to pure parliamentarism. In what follows, we describe the ways in which the direct election

---

[14] Technically only 119 members of the Knesset (MKs) would be elected from the party-list ballot, because the directly elected prime minister was also a Knesset member. However, the proportionality was calculated based on the full 120 seats, and the prime-ministerial candidate was also the first-ranked candidate on the party list.

[15] As noted, new Knesset *and* prime ministerial elections were required following either a Knesset dissolution or a successful no-confidence vote, but not if a prime minister resigned.

[16] Israeli constitutional lawyers adopted this position while political scientists predicted considerable ticket-splitting.

of the prime minister radically and rapidly altered the nature of Israeli party politics. Both large and small parties strategically responded to the imposition of a new institutional context in ways our argument suggests. Even more radically and rapidly than in France, the major Israeli parties became "presidentialized" after the country moved away from parliamentarism and toward the separation of powers. Thus, as in France, the long-term structural factors that Poguntke and Webb (2005a) point to also cannot explain party presidentialization in Israel – and such factors certainly cannot explain parties' similarly rapid *de*-presidentialization following the reform's repeal (Hazan 2005).

Presidentialized Parties in the Electoral Arena

The combination of a national constituency for parliamentary elections with voters' ability to split their tickets generated the crucial "presidentializing" incentives in Israel and illustrate with a startling degree of clarity the imperatives that exist to greater or lesser degrees in all separate powers systems. This institutional combination divided Israel's parties into two camps: those that could credibly field a prime-ministerial candidate and those that could not (Stellman 1996). Only Labor and Likud, Israel's two largest parties at the time, opted to nominate prime-ministerial candidates in any of the three elections held under the hybrid system. Knowing that voters could split their tickets, smaller parties ignored the direct election completely and concentrated on winning Knesset seats, in the hope of entering the governing coalition as junior members.

These "two camps" result from combining separate origin with fused survival, as we suggested earlier. Labor and Likud had long been Israel's largest parties, yet neither had ever held a majority of seats in parliament, and the institutional environment had never forced them to seek a majority of votes. The adoption of direct prime-ministerial elections immediately transformed both parties' electoral and governing strategies – in similar ways. As in France, given the need to win a majority contest, Labor and Likud suddenly confronted a trade-off between sticking to their ideological roots and broadening their vote base. Both parties' leaders understood that in order to win the direct election, their prime-ministerial candidate would have to attract voters from other parties. Thus the first way in which we can observe presidentialization of the two main parties is in terms of candidate selection.

As our framework suggests would happen, the reform encouraged the two main parties to select radically different types of candidates.

Labor and Likud's strategies followed the logic we laid out in Chapter 3: to win a direct executive election, parties must recruit candidates who can appeal to a broad constituency, rather than choose a candidate based on long intraparty service. In 1996 Likud thus selected Benjamin Netanyahu as leader in only his second Knesset term, because of his personal leadership characteristics. In the same year Labor chose Ehud Barak as its parliamentary leader, less than a year after his first election to the Knesset. Hazan concludes that the two main parties had "entered a new era in which they were forced to 'accept' leaders who were thrust upon them – similar to parties in the United States – by the exigencies of the new electoral and political system" (2005, 299).

Following the nomination of candidates with far weaker partisan connections, as in France the large parties sought to appeal to the center of the political spectrum and reduce the salience of ideology in their appeals. Labor and Likud candidates sought to appear to be "above" parties (Hazan and Rahat 2000) and focused their campaigns on attracting undecided centrist voters (Hazan 1999, 163) – strategies they had never adopted under the pure parliamentary system. Labor explicitly moved to the center of the spectrum prior to the 1996 contest, enacting new articles in its charter that "downgraded its more dovish [partisan] tendencies in exchange for a more centrist path" (Hazan 2001, 356). Likud followed suit, as Netanyahu moderated his party's opposition to the peace process and distanced his party from far-right parties.

Believing that appealing to loyal voters was a waste of time and resources, both parties also held fewer public rallies, because only committed supporters tended to show up. Instead, in an attempt to attract undecided voters, they devoted more attention to television advertising. Hazan suggests that this shift to the center was even more pronounced in 1999, when "both sides decided to blur their differences in order to attract the undecided voters, with whom victory rested" (2001, 360). A move toward suprapartisan appeals is precisely what we expect given the introduction of separate executive origin, and this is similar to what we saw in France.

Like France's major parties, Labor and Likud also diverted resources away from the Knesset race to concentrate on the prime-ministerial race. Because the candidate elected prime minister would form the governing coalition and because one of the two main parties was bound to be in the opposition, for Labor and Likud winning the prime-ministerial race became much more important than winning Knesset seats. Both parties initially struggled internally over the question of favoring the prime-ministerial race over the Knesset campaign (Torgovnik, 2000), but in the end both devoted most of their resources to that race (Mendilow, 1999). Both large parties established separate election headquarters for the prime-ministerial election and for the Knesset election, and devoted most resources on prime-ministerial elections (Kenig, Rahat, and Hazan 2005).

One reason Labor and Likud downplayed the Knesset elections was that both parties' needed to attract *other* parties' supporters to win the prime-ministerial race. Under the pure parliamentary system parties competed intensely against each other for votes in Knesset elections. Under the reformed system, prime-ministerial candidates needed votes from their own party's supporters as well as from other parties' supporters to win the election. Given this, the large parties could not afford to compete intensely against their ideological rivals in the Knesset race because they feared that the smaller parties would urge their supporters to vote for the other party's prime-ministerial candidate.

Given this dynamic, to appease the smaller parties Labor explicitly toned down its campaign rhetoric in 1996 and adopted a policy of not responding to rhetorical attacks from any of its partisan rivals in the Knesset race. Bick (1998, 126) quotes Haim Ramon, head of Shimon Peres's campaign, as saying that "it is only important that Peres wins. There is no point ... if Labor ends up with fifty seats and Peres is not elected prime minister." This willingness to essentially dispense with the Knesset elections offers an important contrast with France. In France, as long as the opposition does not control the National Assembly (in which case cohabitation results), separation of survival affords the French president relatively greater leverage over the cabinet compared to the influence of Israel's prime minister under the reformed system. This is because Israel's fusion of survival implied not only that the elected prime minister had to negotiate with other parties over the composition of a cabinet, but also that parties *other than the prime minister's* would hold the entire executive's survival in their hands. Of course, such power only accrued to parties *within* the governing coalition. It genuinely would be of little use to a party to have lost the prime minister's election yet have won a substantial number of Knesset seats – because that party would be in the opposition, unable to bring down the government and force new elections. For any large party, winning the prime-ministerial election was absolutely imperative.

The large parties appeared willing to sacrifice their legislative contingent to support their prime-ministerial candidates' ambitions. In 1996 for example, Likud gave one-third of the spots on its own parliamentary list to two smaller parties in exchange for those parties' support in the prime-ministerial race. Both major parties engaged in a similar practice in 1999 (Hazan and Rahat 2000). These sorts of intra- and interparty dynamics are unknown in parliamentary systems, because under parliamentarism the personal success of the prime-ministerial candidate, no matter how "presidentialized," remains connected to the collective electoral fate of his or her co-partisans.

In the theoretical section of this chapter we noted that the combination of separate origin and fused survival should produce a bifurcation of the party system, with the high presidentialization of the major parties accompanied by continued parliamentarization of the smaller parties. The willingness of Labor and Likud to sacrifice the legislative branch of their party to enhance the viability of the executive branch of their party is one element of this dynamic. As for the small parties, they quickly perceived the strategic implications of voters' ability to split their tickets and their own ability to influence the survival of the directly elected prime minister. They knew that the two larger parties would adopt a broad vote-seeking strategy in order to concentrate on the prime-ministerial race, so they concentrated exclusively on the Knesset race and encouraged their supporters to split their tickets (Goldberg 1998, 71; Mahler 1997; Stellman 1996, 659). In 1996, nearly half of all voters split their votes between a smaller party for the Knesset race and a larger party for the prime-ministerial race (Bick 1998, 126–28). The results of the reform grew crystal clear: as Table 6.2 reveals, after the reform Labor and Likud lost seats in the Knesset while smaller parties gained.

Several smaller parties had always sought out a niche in the Knesset's 120-seat single constituency, but the constitutional reform enhanced these parties' incentives to get voters to split their tickets. When voters can split their tickets, they can employ two distinct decision processes in each election – something they cannot do under parliamentarism. The separation of origin thus opens up new possibilities for party electoral strategies, particularly when (as in Israel but not in France) the system is bifurcated into parties that run executive candidates and those that do not. Thus in Israel, Kenig, Rahat, and Hazan (2005) note that candidates for prime minister competed primarily on foreign policy and domestic security, while "Knesset" parties competed on completely different issues. The smaller parties correctly concluded that they could do so while remaining neutral on the question of Israeli foreign policy, divorcing the executive and legislative campaigns from each other. Parties that benefited from voters' ability to split their tickets emphasized

TABLE 6.2. *Number of Seats Won in Israeli Knesset: Last Election before Direct Election of Prime Minister (1992) and Two Elections Concurrent with Prime-Ministerial Election (1996 and 1999)*

Group	Party	1992	1996	1999
Large Parties	Likud	32	32*	19
	Labor	44	34	26
	Large parties total	76	66	45
Sectarian Parties	Shas	6	10	17
	National Religious Party	6	9	5
	Yahadut Hatorah	4	4	5
	Shinui	–	–	6
	Yisrael B'aliyah	–	7	6
	Yisrael Beitenu	–	–	4
	Ra'am	2	4	5
	Sectarian parties total	18	34	48
Nonsectarian Parties	Meretz	12	9	10
	Tsomet	8	–*	–
	National Union	–	–	4
	Moledet	3	2	–
	Center	–	–	6
	Third Way	–	4	–
	Hadash	3	5	3
	Balad	–	–	2
	Nonsectarian Parties Total	26	20	25
Others	One People	–	–	2
	Total seats	120	120	120
	Number of parties in parliament	10	11	15
	Effective # of parties in parliament	4.4	5.6	8.7

* In 1996, Likud, Gesher, and Tsomet presented a joint list. The two smaller parties were each allocated the third seat on the list, alternating. So 10 of the 32 seats went to these two parties – 5 each for Gesher and Tsomet.
Source: Rahat (2004).

a narrowly defined identity politics, such as the social cleavages between religious and secular Israelis, Ashkenazi and Sephardic Jews, or new immigrants versus native Israelis. The adoption of the direct prime-ministerial election thus transformed Israel's two largest parties into vote-seeking parties and away from their ideologically rooted policy-seeking origins, but gave smaller parties even more powerful incentives to seek out and hold onto a narrow niche in the hope of joining the winning candidate's cabinet coalition.

Presidentialized Parties in the Governing Arena

The adoption of direct prime-ministerial elections clearly impacted parties' electoral strategies and affected election results. Moreover, contrary to proponents' predictions, the constitutional reform also proved disastrous for governability by complicating the relationships between prime ministers and their own party, and between prime ministers and other parties.

Not surprisingly given small parties' growth, the separation of prime-ministerial and parliamentary elections had a clear "before and after" effect of weakening executive control of the legislature. Because of small parties' hold over the premier's fate, they could demand a higher price for their support (Rahat and Hazan 2005, 347). Thus after the reform, prime ministers spent far greater time and effort on coalition management – on "maintaining, rather than on heading" the government (Hazan 2005, 304). The Knesset increasingly rejected or overturned government decisions, even as the distribution of budget resources tended to increasingly favor smaller coalition partners (Nachmias and Sened 1999). Hazan (1997) also shows a dramatic increase in "private members'" bills as a proportion of the total legislation passed immediately after the reform, evidence that the government had lost control of the agenda.

Direct elections also changed a system that had relied on the mutual dependence of leaders and followers into a system in which prime ministers felt they should govern independently of their own party. This is a key indicator of presidentialization, because no matter how personalized campaigns become in parliamentary systems, parties and prime ministers can never go their separate ways. While on the campaign trail, the candidates for prime minister ran "above" their parties, ignoring or even disparaging their parties in the process. Their personal constituencies also differed substantially from their parties – a phenomenon that is common under separate origin (as we saw in Chapter 5) but unheard of under parliamentarism. Prime ministers who won direct election could legitimately believe that they did not owe their *personal* political success to their *party's* political success, and they assumed that direct election had given them legitimacy and authority to run the government regardless of their party's desires.

Direct elections thus weakened the influence of the prime minister's party, virtually eliminating the notion of collective responsibility essential to parliamentarism. For example, after winning election, Benjamin Netanyahu (1996–99) "virtually ceased to function as a party leader" in terms of fostering unity of purpose and organizing collective decision making by Likud ministers and members of Knesset (Medding 2000, 195). Netanyahu's leadership style consequently "failed to establish the necessary *esprit de corps* ... upon which the principle of collective cabinet responsibility rests" (Medding 2000, 196). Similarly, Ehud Barak (1999–2001) ignored his party and personally chose his own ministers, acting as if the new system "specifically precluded" his party from having any say in cabinet appointments (Medding 2000, 203). Not surprisingly, members of prime ministers' parties grew disgruntled and expressed increasing reluctance to support their leaders. Medding concludes that the new system "retained the formal principle of collective responsibility, but deprived it of its party core" (Medding 2000, 205). No scholar has argued that such dynamics characterized *pre*-reform Israel.

Israel's reformed system severely presidentialized the prime minister's own party in another key way. Although prime ministers remained accountable to the assembly majority, *they became unaccountable to their own party.* Unlike in a pure parliamentary system, the prime minister's party in Israel could not "fire" its agent and swap in a new premier without taking the issue to the floor of the legislature. In a pure parliamentary system the prime minister's office "belongs" to a particular party until the next election or until that party can no longer sustain a government. In the Israeli hybrid *only a direct election could constitute the executive.* A party that sought to oust its prime minister from the party and force a resignation had no guarantee that it would retain the premiership in a new election. As a result, prime ministers enjoyed de facto separation of survival from their own (severely weakened) parties, but not from allied parties. As our framework predicts, prime ministers' parties grew increasingly presidentialized while the smaller parties remained parliamentarized. Given this, as one might expect in a pure presidential system but not in a parliamentary system, members of the prime minister's party abstained and withheld support with greater frequency following the reform (Hazan 2005; Rahat and Hazan 2005).

In sum, the Israeli hybrid left executive-legislative relations in an unstable political no-man's land – the prime minister expected legislative deference from his own party based on separation of origin, but allied parties expected prime-ministerial deference based on the fusion of survival. The reform thus made coalition maintenance a "full-time, practically impossible, task," and even running day-to-day routine government affairs became a "chronic crisis of confidence" (Medding 2000, 196). In the end, Hazan concludes, "the directly-elected PM was unable to rein in the anarchy within both his coalition and his party" (2005, 304). As far as we know, scholars of parties in parliamentary systems have never claimed that "presidentialization" has generated decreased cohesion *within* a prime minister's party.

The Return to Parliamentarism and Parties' "De-Presidentialization"

The dramatic consequences of the Israeli constitutional reform seriously embarrassed the reform's original proponents. Rahat (N.d., 18) writes that those who had advocated reform "found it more and more difficult to market their original claims, as their promises collapsed one after the other: they promised stability, but governments collapsed prematurely; they promised an end to coalition politics, but the increase in the number of effective parties and in the power of the small sectarian parties made coalition maintenance at least as difficult as it was before; they thought that the popular mandate of the directly elected PM would supply him with political legitimacy that would improve governability, but legitimacy vanished quickly." As the negative repercussions continued to mount, reform proponents switched tacks and defensively argued that "society," rather than the reform itself, had caused the problems.

Initial efforts to overturn the reform stalled because of opposition from Labor and Likud party leaders – that is, from the only politicians who had gained under the new system (Rahat N.d., 5). However, mounting evidence that presidentialization exacted too high a cost added fuel to a movement to repeal the reform. Ironically, Rahat writes that "almost all the MKs who supported reform became its victims," while the only sizable party that had initially opposed the reform, the ultra-orthodox Shas party, emerged as the only winner (Rahat 2004, 469).

The impact of Israel's 1998 local elections proved critical to the repeal effort. Local elections followed the same formula as the national elections, meaning that mayors were elected directly, independently of city council members. As in the prime-ministerial race, many mayoral candidates thus sought out the middle ground and downplayed party attachments. The 1998 election results revealed substantial losses for both Labor and Likud, strengthening the argument that ticket splitting was a grave threat to those parties' survival (Rahat N.d., 7). The local election results finally convinced most Labor and Likud members of the Knesset that the reform had hurt their interests. The only parties that continued to support the reformed system were the smaller sectarian parties.

The 1999 national elections reconfirmed the larger parties' decline, clarifying even to the most skeptical Knesset members that the new system was killing the larger parties and helping only the smaller parties. Thus the day in 2001 that Ariel Sharon's government was sworn in, the Knesset repealed the direct prime-ministerial election and returned the country to pure parliamentarism starting with the 2003 elections. Knesset members from parties that had shrunk over the previous three elections supported the repeal, but 36 of the 41 votes opposing the repeal came from smaller parties (Rahat N.d., 19).

As most Israelis expected and as our argument implies would happen, the return to the old system substantially and rapidly changed party and voter behavior yet again, reversing much of what had occurred during the hybrid experiment. In particular, prime ministers are "once again elected because of and together with their party, rather than individually and at times despite their party" (Hazan 2005, 307). Repeal of direct prime-ministerial elections increased the parliamentarization of *all* parties, especially the larger ones, by linking the party leader – no matter how personally authoritative – to the collective fate of his or her party and giving the party, rather than the assembly majority, the possibility of holding the leader to account. Thus following the return to parliamentarism, government coalitions became more stable, and "the parties, which were practically absent in the two previous elections, returned to the forefront" of election campaigns (Hazan 2005, 307). Repeal also altered the major parties' electoral strategies, weakening religious and ethnic sectarian parties (Kenig, Rahat, and Hazan 2005). For example, several small immigrant parties, realizing they were facing extinction, quickly merged with Likud or other right-wing parties. Abolishing the direct elections thus reversed the decline of the large parties and the gains of the sectarian parties.[17]

Israel's 1992 electoral reform rapidly and fundamentally altered the relationship between candidates and parties, changed the incentives of each party "branch," and made coordinating across party branches more difficult both on the campaign trail and in government. Like the French case, the Israeli experiment with moving away from pure parliamentarism by adopting separate executive and legislative origin supports our hypothesis that parties organize and behave differently when confronted with the greater vote-seeking incentives of a direct election. Indeed, the effects in Israel were so obvious, rapid, and ultimately disastrous – and exacerbated by the combination of intrapartisan separation of survival with prime ministers' dependence on allied parties for survival in office – that after less than a decade politicians moved to repeal the reform and return to pure parliamentarism.

CONCLUSION

Scholars and politicians both know that even relatively small institutional changes can have large effects on the balance of power both within political parties and within entire political systems. It stands to reason that larger institutional changes would have larger effects. In this chapter we examined two quasi-experimental case studies of important changes in executive-legislative relations. Evidence from France and Israel confirms this book's main point that constitutional structure shapes parties' organizational and behavioral imperatives. A shift away from pure parliamentarism and toward the separation of powers in both countries altered parties' collective action and delegation problems, changed their electoral strategies, and damaged party organizational cohesion and strength – all evidence of presidentialization as we defined it in Chapter 1. Only these institutional reforms, and not other factors, can plausibly explain the rapidity and depth of party transformation in both countries.

In France, the adoption of separate presidential origin *and* survival presidentialized the parties dramatically. We saw evidence of this dynamic as parties nominated different types of candidates, shifted

---

[17] The adoption of a constructive vote of no confidence after the repeal of direct prime-ministerial elections also contributed to coalition stability.

resources away from their legislative contingents and toward their presidential candidates, and reduced the extent of ideological and policy-based competition for assembly seats. Consistent with the broader patterns of intraparty accountability described in Chapter 4, the 5th Republic constitution shifted the balance of intrapartisan power to such an extent that presidents have effectively reversed the party-president principal-agent relationship. In the 4th Republic all changes in prime minister resulted from interparty conflict, yet in the 5th Republic nearly all cases of prime-ministerial turnover have resulted from intraparty conflict – not from within parties' assembly delegations, but from presidents' influence over their parties. Breaking the single chain of parliamentary delegation has dramatically altered party politics in France.

In Israel, which adopted separate origin while retaining fused survival through executive dependence on parliamentary confidence, constitutional reform immediately transformed party and voter behavior. Moreover, consistent with our expectations for elected prime-ministerial regimes, we saw an immediate bifurcation of the party system. The two largest parties completely presidentialized their organizations and electoral behavior by nominating relative outsiders, downplaying ideology and organization in the executive election, and focusing on maximizing votes in the executive election at the expense of Knesset seats. In contrast, the smaller parties remained parliamentarized and did not even present prime-ministerial candidates. Instead, they concentrated all their energies on the Knesset race and conducted "office-" or "policy-seeking" campaigns.

Critically, the Israeli reform also created a situation in which prime ministers enjoyed de facto separation of survival from their parties, but remained highly dependent on their coalition partners. This weakened prime ministers' connections to their parties while making coalition management even more difficult than it had been under the pure parliamentary system. Ultimately, presidentialization of Israel's two largest parties was so rapid and profound that it threatened their organizational survival. As a result, it was repealed less than a decade after it had been enacted. And as our theory of the impact of executive structure on parties would lead us to expect, we saw an equally rapid "re-parliamentarization" of Israel's large parties.

Several other countries have undertaken reforms from one variant of pure or semi-presidentialism to another (See Table 2.1), but few countries have undertaken reforms to their constitutional structure as extensive as those in France and Israel. The few other cases of change from parliamentarism toward any form of separated powers have been in new and/or unstable democracies, and thus the impact of these changes may have escaped scholarly notice. Moves in the opposite direction from the separation of powers toward parliamentarism are even less common: Israel excepted, if a country has ever had separate executive elections, it will not change to pure parliamentarism – a fact that helps explain the worldwide trend toward more presidential and semi-presidential systems. Indeed, we suspect that the rarity of within-country changes in the core elements of executive-legislative relations helps explain why scholars have paid relatively little attention to this book's core claim, that constitutional structure has a critical impact on party organization and behavior.

7

Parties' "Presidential Dilemmas" in Brazil and Mexico

As we suggested in Chapter 2, the extent to which the executive and legislative branches of a party part ways is a function of party organizations' ability to rein in their agents – both on the campaign trail and in government. Managing the principal-agent relationship between party and leader is an ongoing challenge, one that all parties in separation of powers systems inevitably confront. To illustrate these challenges empirically, in Chapter 5 we explored the extent to which the electorates of presidents and their legislative parties diverge, and in Chapter 6 we explored the impact on parties of constitutional reform away from pure parliamentarism and toward a hybrid constitutional format.

To further illustrate the empirical implications of our theoretical framework, in this chapter we explore the tension between the executive and legislative branches of parties in two very different pure presidential systems – in Brazil and Mexico. We focus on Brazil's center-left Partido dos Trabalhadores (PT, Workers' Party) and Mexico's conservative Partido de Acción Nacional (PAN, National Action Party), although we also briefly consider Brazil's centrist Partido da Social Democracia Brasileira (PSDB, Party of Brazilian Social Democracy) and Mexico's centrist Partido de la Revolución Institutional (PRI, Revolutionary Institutional Party) and leftist Partido de la Revolución Democrática (PRD, Party of the Democratic Revolution).

Brazil has a highly fragmented party system, while Mexico has emerged with stable three-party competition. In comparative perspective, Brazil's president is institutionally powerful and its parties organizationally weak, although the PT is an exception to this characterization. In contrast, Mexico's president is institutionally weak but its parties are comparatively strong. Thus the PT and the PAN are ideological opposites, they compete in different political contexts, and their social and political support bases vary widely. If the executive and legislative branches of such different parties in such different party systems can "go their own ways," then we have good reason to believe that such divergence could happen in any separation of powers system.

In fact, evidence we present here suggests that quantitative analysis of electoral separation of purpose presented in Chapter 5 tends to *understate* the true extent of intraparty conflict. Recall that in Chapter 5 we showed that all Mexican parties exhibit relatively low electoral separation of purpose. However, evidence in this chapter reveals that these numbers do not tell the whole story. The PAN is thus a particularly important case for our argument about the impact of the separation of powers on party politics, because if parties confront uniquely "presidential" strategic dilemmas in Mexico, where the combination of low electoral separation of purpose and weak presidential powers means that parties might resemble parliamentary parties about as much as in any pure presidential system,[1] then the separation of powers is presumably a factor that parties must reckon with in all presidential systems.

PRESIDENTIAL DILEMMAS IN BRAZILIAN PARTIES

Our exploration of the presidential dilemmas that parties confront begins with Brazil. In this section we explore the impact of separation of origin and survival on two parties that have recently alternated executive power in Brazil, focusing mainly on the PT or Workers' Party, and then turning our attention to the PSDB.

Separation of Origin and the PT

The PT has roots in union, social-movement, and Catholic Base Community mobilization during Brazil's redemocratization (1979–85). In a system dominated by "inchoate" parties and party competition, the PT has emerged as Brazil's most cohesive and organizationally strong political party (see e.g. Keck 1992; Mainwaring 1999). Since the late 1980s, the PT has had the highest proportion of partisan identifiers among all of Brazil's parties, by a considerable margin (Samuels 2006).

---

[1] Leaving aside those with fused ballots.

Although the party has moderated its political radicalism considerably since its early days (Samuels 2004; Hunter 2007), the party's policy-oriented roots, relative organizational strength, and deep roots in the electorate might imply that the PT is a relatively "parliamentarized" political party. However, this is not the case. In fact, the PT exhibits many of the features that typify presidentialized parties. By implication, to the extent that we observe presidentialization in a party like the PT, we have good reason to expect similar dynamics in organizationally "weaker" political parties.

In what follows we detail the growing separation between the PT and its longtime leader, Luis Inácio Lula da Silva. Lula, as he is generally known, helped found the PT in the late 1970s, led the party for many years as its president, and served in Brazil's Congress from 1987 to 1990. He ran for president in 1989, in Brazil's first direct election following the end of a long military dictatorship. He ran again in 1994 and 1998, finally won on his fourth try in 2002, and then won reelection in 2006. Despite being the leader of a union-based party and its only presidential candidate through five consecutive elections, Lula is by no means a stereotypical Latin American populist leader in the vein of Argentina's Juan Perón or Venezuela's Hugo Chávez. Lula has always taken a reformist path, working through existing institutions rather than attempting a radical transformation of Brazil's political system. Thus it would be wrong to characterize Lula as the sort of political leader who from the start has sought to use his party merely as a tool to advance his personal vision of politics.

Nevertheless, since at least his second presidential election defeat in 1994, Lula sought to pull the PT toward the political center in order to enhance his own electoral viability. Up through the mid-1990s, the PT held steadfastly to its original leftist ideological principles (Azevedo 1995; Árabe 2001). That is, up through that year the PT remained a good example of what Strøm (1990) called a "policy-seeking" party. For example, in 1993, as leftist parties the world over were rethinking and reforming their principles, the PT's 1993 National Meeting reaffirmed the party's "revolutionary and socialist character" (Azevedo 1995, 209), condemned a "conspiracy of elites" to subvert democracy (Partido dos Trabalhadores 1998, 545), affirmed the party's advocacy of "radical agrarian reform and suspension of the external debt" (Partido dos Trabalhadores 1998, 556), and concluded that "capitalism and private property cannot provide a future for humanity" (Partido dos Trabalhadores 1998, 561). In 1994, party resolutions echoed this radical rhetoric yet again, condemning the "control by the dominant classes over the modes of production" (Azevedo 1995, 212) and reaffirming the PT's commitment to socialism (Partido dos Trabalhadores 1998, 581). Thus as of 1995 – after Lula had been defeated twice – the PT had not altered its official ideology (Azevedo 1995, 243).

Although the PT resisted moderating its policy-seeking stance, Lula and his supporters fought to broaden the party's appeal and tone down the party's rigid platform positions. After his 1994 loss, Lula demanded greater autonomy from the PT and sought to make his electoral viability dependent on his own charisma and political positions rather than the party's positions and its organization. He also urged the PT to adopt a more "pragmatic" alliance strategy, primarily to boost his presidential candidacy rather than help the party elect more legislators (Samuels 2004). The party thus confronted a classic partisan dilemma under the separation of powers: delegate more autonomy to Lula, which would essentially make him a free agent, or seek to maintain control over the content of Lula's platforms and over PT alliance strategy, which might limit his electoral viability. Up through the year 2000, the PT statutes even contained a provision designed to hold its presidential nominees formally accountable to the party: specifically, PT candidates for executive offices were subject to party executive committee "guidance."[2] This meant that candidates technically lacked autonomy from the group that controlled the PT's national executive committee. This dependence was problematic for Lula in 1989 and 1994, when he had to submit his decisions to a council on which his allies did not hold a majority (Alves 1998b).

Parties in presidential systems *ought* to impose such rules, if they want to minimize moral hazard and thus keep their presidential candidates true to the party line. However, this form of contract design inevitably led to repeated conflicts between Lula and his party (Alves 1998c); Lula complained that a key factor in his two electoral losses was his lack of political autonomy (Alves 1998a). Consequently, prior to the 1998 campaign Lula demanded carte blanche from his party (Alves 1998c) and made a take-it-or-leave-it demand: he would have total autonomy to run his campaign or he would refuse the party's nomination (Alves 1997). These events mark an early phase in the PT's presidentialization.

---

[2] See article 76 of the party's 1980 statutes and article 103 of the 1995 version of the statutes. Article 103 was simply deleted from the statutes in 2000.

Given that Lula was the PT's only viable candidate, the party had little choice but to let him adopt a vote-seeking strategy. This agreement did not involve *coordination* over a joint presidential and legislative electoral strategy; it merely let Lula and the PT part ways. Lula's third presidential campaign platform thus cut out many proposals he considered too radical, and completely eliminated any mention of socialism (Árabe 2001). For its part, the PT did not repudiate Lula's platform, but its leaders gave a nod to the emerging distance between the party and its candidate by lamely noting that Lula's personal campaign platform "should not be confused with the socialist program of the PT" (Partido dos Trabalhadores 1998, 675). This sort of statement is unthinkable in a parliamentary system.

Lula also cemented his autonomy by demanding that the PT create an independent institutional vehicle for his presidential campaign. This became the Instituto Cidadania (Citizenship Institute [IC]), created in 1996. Lula presided over the IC from its creation until he assumed Brazil's presidency in January 2003, at which time it became moribund. The IC enhanced Lula's autonomy by putting him in control of an organization independent of the PT bureaucracy, staffed by his handpicked associates rather than party bureaucrats. This let him prepare his platform and develop his public image free of party influence. In 2002, when the IC released Lula's preliminary campaign proposals, the media discussed the document for two months *as if* it were a party document, even though it was not. Only after Lula and his advisors gauged public reaction did they present the document for internal party debate. Not surprisingly, many PT members accused the IC of "usurping party functions" (Alves 1997.).

Lula's strategy paid off in 2002, when he won the presidential election handily. Again, although the PT has a reputation as Brazil's most cohesive political party, Lula and the PT have never gained votes from the same sets of voters. Recall from Chapter 5 that the median Electoral Separation of Purpose index (ESP) in all concurrent presidential elections was 8.38.[3] As Table 7.1 reveals, the PT has never come close to this level, with its lowest ESP being 16.44 in 1994. From that point, the PT's ESP scores have increased. By 2006, when Lula won his second term, the score reached almost 40, the second-highest value in our data for any party in a concurrent election.[4] The fact that the PT's ESP increased over

---

[3] Ignoring cases with fused ballots.
[4] The highest value, 46.64, also belongs to a Brazilian party, the PSDB, when it won its first presidential contest in 1994.

TABLE 7.1. *Electoral Separation of Purpose (Average % Difference), PT*

1994	16.44
1998	18.18
2002	30.33
2006	39.98

time suggests that Lula's strategy of deliberately distinguishing himself from his own party paid off – for him. This strategy did not, however, translate into close correspondence between the party's and the president's electoral bases. Electorally, Lula and the PT have parted ways.

We can provide more precise information about Lula and the PT's distinct bases of support by exploring Brazil's 2002 National Election Survey. Samuels (2006) considered the factors associated with partisan identification with the PT. We repeated Samuels' analysis, seeking to discover the extent to which the factors that predicted PT partisanship *also* predicted a vote for Lula in the first round of the 2002 presidential election.[5] Doing so permits us to identify the nature of divergence between Lula's and the PT's vote bases. This approach reveals that the issue in presidential systems is not simply that presidential candidates typically adopt *broader* vote-seeking appeals than their party, but that presidential candidates make *different* sorts of appeals – their campaigns can diverge in substantive content from their party's campaign platform, and thus appeal to quite distinctive electorates.

Table 7.2 thus compares the results of two similar regressions, one seeking to identify the correlates of *Lulismo* (a vote for Lula in the presidential election) and one seeking to identify the correlates of *petismo* (self-declared partisan identification with the PT). This sort of analysis could be conducted in any presidential system and could be used to identify the sources of tension or divergence between a president and his or her party. The Brazilian case is illustrative. To keep the discussion simple, we report only whether coefficients were significant or not, and their direction.

---

[5] While these are not precisely comparable dependent variables, we do not consider this an egregious case of comparing "apples with oranges." Both dependent variables involve multiple-choice options and thus involve the use of multinomial logit regression analysis. Results are available upon request from Samuels. The 2002 Brazilian National Election Study is available through the Comparative Study of Electoral Systems website.

TABLE 7.2. *Factors Associated With ...*

	Petismo	Lulismo
Active in politics?	+	+
Leftist?	+	+
Active in social movements?	+	−
Knowledgeable about politics?	+	
Believe in efficacy of the vote?	+	
Dislike clientelism?	+	
Dislike corruption?		
Educated?	+	
Live in developed municipality?	+	
Catholic?		+
Income		

Consider first the variables associated with *petismo*. First, *petistas* self-identify as "leftists" on the typical scale employed by electoral surveys. Several variables also confirm the conventional view of the PT: it does best among better educated Brazilians who actively participate in politics and/or social movements. Such Brazilians are also more likely to live in one of Brazil's more developed municipalities (using the UNDP's "Human Development Index" as the proxy for development). In addition, PT identifiers tend to believe voting can make a difference, and they dislike clientelism. Note, however, that *petistas* appear no more or less likely to dislike corruption than other Brazilians.

Now consider the factors associated with a vote for Lula. The contrast is stark. Only two of the eleven variables in the regression returned similar results – political activism and leftism. *Petismo* and *Lulismo* had no other factors in common. Lula supporters are actually less likely than average Brazilians to be involved in "non-political" forms of social action such as a social movement, church group, neighborhood association, or nongovernmental organization (NGO), and they are more likely to declare themselves religious Catholics than *petistas*, who tend not to be religious. In short, the profiles of the average PT supporter and the average Lula supporter are distinct. This is not simply a function of the fact that Lula is a presidential candidate in a multiparty system but of Lula's strategic efforts to portray himself in a particular way, and of the PT's strategic choice to retain greater emphasis on policy seeking rather than moderate its platform.

The Impact of Separation of Survival on the PT

Not surprisingly, given Lula's efforts to distance himself from his party, once he had finally won a presidential election he and his party repeatedly came into conflict. The results of the 2002 legislative elections shaped Lula's options: the PT became the largest party in Brazil's Chamber of Deputies, but it still only had 17.7% of the seats (and even fewer in the Senate). (The parties in Lula's electoral coalition won only 25.3% of the seats.) To get anything done, much less to reach the 60% threshold required to pass constitutional amendments for important reforms, Lula had to bring other parties into his cabinet – including parties that had supported the prior administration and his opponent in the presidential election.

Although Lula had sought to win on his own terms, the PT regarded Lula's administration as *its* chance to rule and expected not only to dominate Lula's cabinet but also to have extensive influence in the policy process. Yet in addition to interparty squabbling over the distribution of cabinet portfolios, *intra*party *inter*branch clashes soon emerged over policy proposals, plum political appointments, and the distribution of pork-barrel budgetary funds. For example, Lula maintained the conservative fiscal and monetary policies of previous president Fernando Henrique Cardoso of the PSDB, leading many critics from within the PT to complain that the president was ignoring the PT's long-standing goals of increasing spending on social policy (see e.g. Sallum and Kugelmas 2004; Hunter and Power 2005; Hochstetler 2006a).

Specific proposals also further alienated Lula from the PT. For example, soon after taking office Lula proposed cutting public sector pensions in order to reduce a massive social security system deficit. Cardoso had tried a similar reform, but the PT had opposed it because public sector unions comprise an important element of the PT's vote base. Nevertheless, once in office Lula fought to pass this reform, distancing himself from his party's policies and from its powerful organized labor supporters. Lula won passage of a social security reform only because he reached out to conservative opposition parties that had supported the previous administration.

Lula's focus on macroeconomic policy continuity and his attack on several PT sacred cows came at a high political cost, at least temporarily. Perceiving a growing disjuncture between the administration's policies and its political and social support bases, many *petistas* publicly criticized Lula's pragmatism and reacted viciously at his perceived betrayal.

Lula's choices alienated many of his closest political allies and weakened the government's support in the legislature. For example, when the PT was in opposition its cohesion on roll call votes was extremely high. However, the party's legislative unity declined rapidly immediately after Lula's inauguration, spoiling the new president's "honeymoon" (Carey 2009, 155–57). Such lack of consensus when a party has just entered government is very rare in parliamentary systems, but the PT's experience is emblematic of the tensions inherent to party presidentialization. After passing the social security reform, the PT even expelled several members who had refused to support the government proposal.

Coalition government in any political system strains both intra- and interparty relations. However, in a parliamentary system a prime minister who heads a coalition does not enjoy the legitimacy of winning a direct national election. And of course, a prime minister's party can lose control of the national executive if a coalition collapses. A president, by contrast, commands the executive from a position of relative autonomy and personal legitimacy, and he or she faces no such threat of removal if a coalition collapses. The separation of survival means that the president can choose to pay relatively less attention to the demands of both his allies and his own party. Because of this intraparty tension, in presidential systems both party cohesion (Carey 2009) and legislative productivity (Cheibub, Przeworski, and Saiegh 2004) are lower than in parliamentary systems. Lula's first term clearly illustrates that in multiparty situations the separation of origin and survival strains intraparty relations in different ways than under parliamentarism. (We discuss other implications of this tension for governing in Chapter 8.)

The Impact of Lula's Reelection on the PT

Presidents can survive in office without consistent support from their own party and can even successfully seek and win reelection while pushing the party further aside. Parties are loath to deny renomination to an incumbent president because incumbency offers such a powerful electoral advantage – for example, retrospective voting studies typically include a dummy variable for "incumbent running for reelection" because incumbency of an individual has such a powerful effect on presidential election outcomes (e.g. Samuels 2004).[6] This fact says a great deal about parties'

---

[6] Indeed, we know of no cases of a party explicitly denying renomination to an incumbent president. Two of the rare cases that we know of when incumbents withdrew their

TABLE 7.3. *Brazil: Correlations with*
State-Level Human Development

Year	PT vote	Lula vote
1994	0.68	0.16
1998	0.38	0.15
2002	0.51	0.32
2006	0.30	−0.57

(as principals) inability to use the threat of "not renewing the contract" when making a deal with a prospective presidential candidate (as agent).

Thus, although Lula helped found the PT and spent years leading it and building up its organization, as his first term drew to a close he sought to distance himself even further from his party, relying on his administration's successes and his personal appeal. As Table 7.1 showed, Brazilian voters responded to Lula's efforts: the gap between Lula's and the PT's electorate was larger in 2006 than ever. The PT's base remained rooted in Brazil's middle class, found mainly in Brazil's better developed municipalities (Samuels 2008b), while Lula's support increasingly came from voters in the lower classes, who live in Brazil's poorer municipalities (Hunter and Power 2007).

Evidence of this "divorce" between Lula's and the PT's electorate can be found by simply correlating the percentage of the vote Lula and the PT received with the level of human development in Brazil's 27 constituencies (UNDP 2003).[7] Table 7.3 provides the results: the correlation between the PT vote in legislative elections and a state's level of human development is always higher than for the correlation between Lula's vote and state-level human development, even though both vary over time.[8] Lula has always done better among Brazil's poorer citizens than the PT. The correlations for 2006 reconfirm what Table 7.1 showed – that electoral divergence between Lula and the PT had reached its greatest level that year.

After Lula's reelection, leaders of the PT meekly requested a meeting with the president in order to "fashion a re-approximation."[9] Lula

candidacies due to intraparty challenges are US President Lyndon Johnson in 1968 and Finland's Martti Ahtisaari in 2000. However, both of these presidents withdrew well before the party's final decision was due and were thus not explicitly "denied" renomination.

[7] The inspiration for this paragraph comes from Power (2006).

[8] Variations over time are due to the different nature of interparty and intercandidate competition in each election.

[9] Vera Rosa, Clarissa Oliveira, and Vanice Cioccari, "PT articula reaproximação com o presidente." *O Estado de São Paulo*, October 31, 2006.

responded by encouraging the party to rotate out all of its leaders. The party's former president acknowledged that different forces drove the destiny of Lula and the PT – that "the success of Lula's government does not guarantee the permanence of the PT as an alternative for this country." Given that the party and the president had chosen different paths, the PT still had to learn how *not* to damage its own president's political project. Lula's presidency muted the PT's role in the Brazilian party system and short-circuited its efforts to construct its own image (Samuels 2008a). Indeed, by 2007 Lula's centrism had placed the PT in the uncomfortable position of lamely claiming "autonomy" from the president and reaffirming its right to adopt a critical stance regarding Lula's administration, a position hardly imaginable in a parliamentary system.[10]

Intrapartisan Dilemmas in the PSDB

To illustrate that the intrapartisan dilemmas derived from the separation of origin and survival in Brazil are not limited to the PT, we briefly turn to the PT's main rival, the PSDB, and focus on the legislative arena. Given the separation of origin and survival – and the potential that presidents and their parties sometimes will have different vote bases and thus divergent incentives – parties and their presidents will sometimes work at cross-purposes when the time comes to put proposals to a vote. A way to measure the degree of divergence between a president and his or her party is by analyzing roll calls. Using Poole and Rosenthal's w-Nominate method, scholars can impute actors' positions in policy space. Thus, for example, analysis shows US Presidents Kennedy, Johnson, and Carter further to the left than the median House Democratic legislator, while Nixon and Reagan were more conservative than the median House Republican.[11] A similar pattern emerges for Brazil. Leoni (2002) revealed that Brazilian presidents are typically some distance in policy space from the median member of their party. Figure 7.1 illustrates this for the PSDB in Brazil's 1995–98 legislature.

In a "parliamentarized" party, the prime minister should be located close to the center of his or her party's position in policy space. However, the separation of origin and survival (and varying rules regarding presidential vetoes) opens up the possibility that a president's position will

---

[10] Ricardo Amaral and Natuza Nery, "PT tem de ceder espaços ou vai se isolar, diz Tarso." *O Estado de São Paulo*, January 8, 2007.

[11] Compare the figures "Presidents, and House and Senate Means, 1st Dimension of Joint Space" and "Figure 3A: House, First Dimension" from Keith Poole's website, www.voteview.org, accessed November 15, 2006.

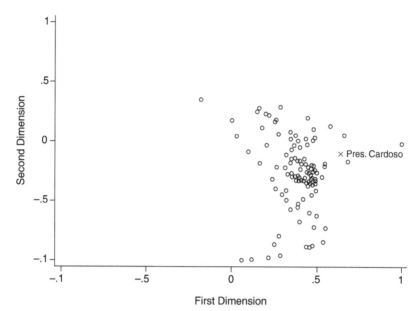

FIGURE 7.1. Placement of PSDB Legislators and President Cardoso in Two-Dimensional Policy Space (derived from w-Nominate scores).
Source: Leoni (2002), data provided by Eduardo Leoni.

not align closely with his or her party's median member. As Figure 7.1 shows, Brazilian President Fernando Henrique Cardoso sat far to the right of the median member of his party. (Cardoso sat to the right of his entire legislative coalition as well.)

Figure 7.1 actually reveals only the tip of the iceberg: roll calls represent the final stage in a long and complex cross-branch negotiating process. By the time a vote is called, much intra- and interparty conflict has been bargained away. Thus if we observe a clear difference between a president and his party at the *last* stage of the policy-making process, we have good a priori reason to expect that such divergence characterizes the entire policy-making process. In short, although tension may exist between prime ministers and their parties, in separation of powers systems intraparty tension has different roots: electoral separation of purpose due to voters' ability to split their tickets, and the separation of survival.

PRESIDENTIAL DILEMMAS IN MEXICAN PARTIES

We now turn our attention to the presidential dilemmas that parties in Mexico have faced. We focus primarily on the National Action Party

(PAN) and its two very different victorious presidential candidates, in 2000 and 2006. The PAN is an especially good case to contrast against the PT. The PT's experience showed that presidentialization can occur in a leftist party that deliberately organized itself to counteract the incentives of Brazil's institutional environment, which promotes the personal vote (Samuels 1999). This suggests that presidentialization is not simply a characteristic of personalistic or organizationally weak political parties. When we turn to Mexico, we see that presidentialization can also occur in a conservative party in a system with considerable overlap between a party's legislative and executive constituencies (as in Chapter 5). By exploring the center-right PAN in its very different institutional context, we increase the variance in our comparative analysis. After discussing the PAN, we turn briefly to an examination of the two other main Mexican parties.

Separation of Origin in the PAN

The PAN formed in 1939 as a voice for Mexican conservatives and religious Catholics alienated from the leftist rhetoric and populist policies of the ruling party, the forerunner of the PRI, which dominated Mexican politics for most of the 20th century. Although the PAN participated in Mexico's controlled elections under PRI hegemony, it eschewed a vote-seeking strategy and instead signaled that its primary motivation was pursuit of principle and not power (Ard 2003, 10). Electoral participation let the PAN play the role of the "conscience of the regime," and its quixotic policy-seeking strategy attracted support only from those convinced of the righteousness of the party's doctrine. This choice meant that the party approached nominations and campaigns with an acute sense of ambivalence: although many *panistas* (PAN supporters) wanted to compete against the PRI, others believed that elections in an obviously authoritarian regime were not for winning but rather for political and social theater.[12] These principled *panistas* feared that broadening the party's appeal would compromise its ideals (Mizrahi 2003, 8).

In the early 1970s, the PAN's leader sought to make the party more competitive. This effort to reshape the party's profile caused severe internal dissension (Shirk 2005, 80). Parties everywhere face trade-offs between policy seeking and vote seeking, between adhering to the party's ideology and wanting to actually win the election.

---

[12] Mexico's Polity IV score began exceeding 5 only in 1997.

Factional battles or leadership struggles typically resolve these debates one way or another. The PAN's experience illustrates the particular way in which parties in presidential systems confront this fundamental strategic dilemma: not through the selection of a party leader, but through the selection of a presidential candidate, who may or may not be the party's de jure leader. This process does not occur in parliamentary systems – and its political consequences are unique to separation of powers systems.

As we have suggested, *presidential* nomination processes tend to exacerbate intraparty tensions over *legislative* electoral strategy. For example, in 1975, the PAN's national convention failed to agree upon a candidate for the 1976 presidential election. The "pragmatic" candidate, who urged the party to broaden its appeal, obtained a majority of the votes at the nominating convention. However, the party's internal threshold for winning nomination was set at 80% of all delegates.[13] The losing candidate, a PAN "traditionalist," refused to step aside, alleging that doing so would violate the party's "moral integrity" (Shirk 2005, 83). As a result, the PAN failed to nominate anyone for president. Not surprisingly, this decision proved disastrous for the party in congressional elections because of the lack of coattail effects from the presidential race (Ard 2003, 102). (It is worth noting that parties in parliamentary systems never choose *not* to have a "nominee" for prime minister.)

The PAN has long imposed unusually restrictive rules for rank-and-file membership and even tighter ideological qualifications for selection to the National Executive Committee (Shirk 2005, 117). Such rules seek to prevent dilution of the party's ideology. However, this self-imposed purity has repeatedly forced PAN presidential nominees to distance themselves from the party organization. Once nominated, candidates faced the inevitable trade-off between adhering faithfully to the party line (and thereby alienating the majority of Mexican voters) and appealing to voters across the spectrum (and thereby alienating faithful *panistas*). The party's 1988 campaign exposed this rift: the party's candidate, Manuel Clouthier, adopted a broad campaign platform that ignored PAN doctrine (Shirk 2005, 104). Clouthier expressed "discomfort" with his connection to the party on several occasions (Mizrahi 2003, 86; see also Loaeza 1999, 447), and his campaign alienated PAN activists, who wanted him to toe the party line.

---

[13] This rule was changed in the 1990s to a simple majority (Ard 2003, 13).

Vicente Fox and the PAN's 2000 Campaign: Winning While Divided

The gulf between the PAN and its presidential candidate widened considerably in the run-up to the 2000 election, which resulted in Mexico's first democratic transfer of power from one party to another. In 1997, the PAN's leader Felipe Calderón (later president of Mexico) implemented even more stringent party membership rules. Not surprisingly, these changes worked to reduce the party's membership rolls (Shirk 2005, 117).[14] The PAN also chose to refuse its allotment of public campaign funds for that year's midterm legislative elections and decided to centralize campaign operations for all its congressional candidates. Both actions were designed to keep candidates "on message" (Shirk 2005, 119), and suggest that the PAN's leaders had opted for a policy-seeking strategy at that time; David Shirk concludes that "The PAN made strategic decisions that favored activists who were loyal to party leaders and principles and isolated the party's more pragmatic elements (Shirk 2005, 118). Yet what seemed desirable to hard-core party activists proved counterproductive in the electoral arena, as the party sank from second to third place in the Chamber of Deputies after the elections (Shirk 2005, 119).

At precisely the moment the PAN's leaders were tightening the party's membership criteria, turning down campaign funds and generally seeking to implement a policy-seeking strategy, Vicente Fox was plotting behind the scenes. After winning the gubernatorial election in the state of Guanajuato in 1995, Fox immediately began preparing the ground for a presidential bid, independent of the PAN's central organization (Shirk 2005, 123). Fox's ambitions encountered resistance from party officials, and he soon realized that if he were to let the process run its traditional course he would have no chance of winning the nomination (Mizrahi 2003, 100). He therefore sought to cut the party organization and its leadership out of the process by publicly declaring his candidacy immediately after the 1997 congressional elections. This gave him a head start and intimidated other potential candidates (Ard 2003, 180). Fox focused on fortifying his support outside the PAN's "narrow conservative base"

---

[14] Given the membership decline following the tightening of the rules, in 1998 the party encouraged recruitment of "adherents," a new category one step below full-fledged "member." A 2001 party reform allowed adherents to become full members after six months, but candidates for party membership still had to endorse the party's principles, take a "doctrinal course," and agree to comply with a series of prerequisites, such as "having an honest way of life" (Mizrahi 2003, 98).

(Shirk 2005, 125), for example by organizing a US-style political action committee called Amigos de Fox (Friends of Fox), which amassed huge campaign contributions independent of party constraints.

Eventually Amigos de Fox became "larger" (Mizrahi 2003, 101) and "more formidable" (Ard 2003, 181) than the PAN itself. Fox's organizational success discouraged all other PAN aspirants from placing their hats in the ring, and Fox arrived at the nominating convention as the sole candidate. Members of the PAN's executive committee discussed ways to block Fox's candidacy, knowing that Fox's candidacy created a difficult trade-off: the party could win the election with him and thus gain dramatically in the short term, but doing so might risk indelibly compromising the party's ideological profile over the long term. Yet they also knew that if they impeded Fox's candidacy they might not have a candidate at all, which could be politically suicidal in both the short and the long term. After all, predictions pointed uniformly toward 2000 as a good year to finally defeat the PRI (Shirk 2005, 125). Such trade-offs are never so intense in pure parliamentary systems because the danger of moral hazard is far lower: party leaders know that they can always rid themselves of a wayward prime minister and are far less likely to select an outsider like Fox to begin with.

Fox's success at gaining the nomination by circumventing his party meant that he and the PAN would inevitably have an ambivalent relationship after the election. Party insiders saw Fox as an interloper, and they knew Fox's strength did not lie with his links to party faithful or in his commitment to PAN's principles, but rather with his carefully crafted media image, broad popular appeal, and ability to build an independent campaign organization (Mizrahi 2003, 88). Given his "outsider" status, during his campaign Fox drew little support from PAN leaders, its organizational structure, or even its membership base (Shirk 2005, 176); he even confronted the "open hostility of some of the most prominent leaders of the party" (Mizrahi 2003, 88). Such feelings were mutual: Fox largely ignored the PAN organization during his campaign (Romero 2005, 10) and appealed to voters "over and above" the party (Mizrahi 2003, 145).

Of course, many candidates for president or for prime minister hire outsider campaign consultants. What is distinctive and paradoxical about this story is that Fox announced his candidacy and organized his campaign autonomously from the PAN *at precisely the same moment that the PAN's national executive committee moved to restrict membership, centralize control over candidate nomination, and narrow the party's message.* That is, Fox adopted a vote-seeking strategy while his party adopted a policy-seeking strategy. In the end, the PAN's leadership disagreed with the thrust of Fox's campaign, but – much as we saw in the case of the PT and Lula – the party could do very little about it (Romero 2005, 10). This case reveals that even highly structured party organizations that tightly control their nominations for legislative office confront entirely different strategic dilemmas when nominating and electing a presidential candidate.

The Impact of Separation of Survival: Divergence in the Governing Arena under Fox

We argued in Chapter 3 that adverse selection problems are worse in separation of powers systems because the profiles of successful presidential candidates differ from the profiles of successful prime-ministerial candidates in pure parliamentary systems. Adverse selection suggests that parties face a trade-off in selecting their agents: a candidate who is more likely to win is also more likely to later act adversely to the principal's interest. The PAN illustrates this trade-off well. Fox won the election, but he also epitomized a party outsider – someone distant from the party's organizational leaders as well as from his co-partisans in the legislature (Mizrahi 2003, 102). After the election, Fox fulfilled this agency theory prediction by doing little to minimize tension with his party.

Indeed, in many ways Fox acted to exacerbate the tension between the executive and legislative branches of the PAN. For example, three days after winning and already facing pressure to nominate PAN members to his cabinet, Fox reaffirmed his independence and simultaneously lowered his party's expectations by explaining, "The PAN must respect the president's authority to choose his own cabinet. At the end of the day, the one who governs is Fox, not the PAN" (Romero 2005, note 2). The distribution of cabinet posts is a clear indication of the relative weight of each party in a government administration. It is also an important indicator of the degree to which a party can monitor and control its agent, whether a prime minister or a president. Although Fox had incentives to reach out to other parties because the PAN did not hold a legislative majority, he nominated far fewer PAN members to the cabinet than its legislative weight would have predicted. In parliamentary systems, parties almost always hold cabinet portfolios in direct proportion to their weight in the legislative coalition. However, Fox named only three *panistas* to his first cabinet, which had 23 posts. This pattern of discrimination continued throughout his administration. Fox's indifference toward his party angered PAN leaders and legislators (Shirk 2005, 189) and fed the tension between Fox's government and the PAN organization (Romero 2005, 17).

In response to Fox's perceived slights, PAN legislators significantly modified Fox's 2001 fiscal reform proposal as well as an important presidential proposal on indigenous rights that was designed to end the long-standing conflict in the state of Chiapas with Zapatista rebels. Tension between Fox and his party pervaded the administration's first year to such an extent that PAN president Luis Felipe Bravo felt compelled to remind attendees at the party's annual convention that "the PAN is President Fox's political base." At the same event, Fox had to beg for the PAN's help in governing (Romero 2005, 2).

Following a comprehensive exploration of president-party conflict in recent Mexican history, Romero (2005) concluded that although such tension has always been present, a qualitative difference distinguished conflicts between Fox and the PAN from earlier episodes. Conflicts during PRI administrations were *factional* or *individual*, yet when push came to shove the party always officially supported its president. In contrast, during Fox's administration open conflict emerged between the president and the PAN's highest institutional organ, the National Executive Committee, and also emerged between Fox and the party's legislative leaders, including between Fox and Felipe Calderón, the PAN's – but not Fox's – choice for party leader in the chamber of deputies. President-party conflict was far more problematic under Fox because *the party as a whole* – as opposed to a subgroup or an individual – was coordinating to oppose its own elected president.

Nevertheless, Romero concludes that the PAN ultimately gave more to Fox than it received in return (2005, 20). The party agreed to such an imbalanced exchange because like all governing parties in presidential systems, it had little choice. Under the separation of powers, a party is better off supporting its president and getting little in return than not supporting its president and getting nothing – which might be possible, given the separation of survival. Parties in parliamentary systems never find themselves in such situations. For his part, Fox incurred relatively little cost by keeping his party at arm's length. The PAN suffered at the midterm elections, but Fox remained in office. A party in a parliamentary system could replace such a demanding and unresponsive leader, but the PAN could not.

Separation of Origin in the PAN's 2006 Campaign:
Winning through Unity

Perhaps the PAN's dissatisfaction with Fox served as a learning experience, because in 2005 the PAN nominated a very different type of candidate for the 2006 presidential election. The contrasts between these two nominating processes and their results illustrate our point that under the separation of powers delegation problems can vary considerably over time within a single political party, depending on how party leaders weigh the trade-offs between different goals, and depending on whether they resolve contracting problems with their agents.

In 1999 Vicente Fox successfully skirted the party bureaucracy and won the nomination in an uncontested primary. In 2005, the PAN's internal primary was highly competitive. Three candidates sought the nomination: Fox's interior secretary Santiago Creel; former governor Alberto Cárdenas; and Felipe Calderón, who ultimately emerged victorious. How did Calderón win the nomination? Many factors were at work, but we should first note that the internal nomination process did not differ much from 2000 to 2006. In both years the PAN employed a closed primary in which only fully accredited party members could vote. A closed primary in a party with comparatively strict membership criteria should produce "policy-seeking" candidates who pledge to protect the party's image and ideals. It should also favor insider candidates over outsiders. Given the result in 2000, when Fox preempted the process and undermined the incentives of the party's institutions, it should be clear that nomination rules cannot always predict the type of candidate a party will nominate (cf. Siavelis and Morgenstern 2008a).

Calderón was the consummate party insider, and partly for this reason he was not a well-known public figure, particularly relative to Creel. Calderón had served a term in the legislative assembly of the Mexico City Federal District, and two nonconsecutive terms in the chamber of deputies (1991–93 and 2001–03). As noted, in his second legislative term he also served as the PAN's leader in the chamber of deputies. He lost a gubernatorial election in his home state in 1995, but he also served as the PAN's secretary-general (1993–95) and party president (1996–99). After his second term in the chamber of deputies he served briefly in Fox's administration as director of a public credit agency and as secretary of energy.

In contrast to Fox, Calderón had no independent electoral base. Observers even suggested he had the *least* electoral appeal of the PAN's three presidential aspirants. Also working against him was the fact that both Fox *and* the PAN's president preferred other candidates (Shirk 2006, 7). Nevertheless, a decades-long history of involvement with the PAN's organization at the highest levels had given Calderón time and opportunity to cultivate extensive personal connections to *panista* activists. This credibility as a committed partisan worked in Calderón's favor as he built support for the internal primary. Ultimately, the fact that he was not Fox's favored candidate worked in his favor (and against Creel) – because many *panistas* held a grudge against Fox (Shirk 2006, 10). Many *panistas* were eager for a candidate who would represent and uphold the party's ideals.

Still, parties that nominate candidates who embody the preferences of the median party activist undertake a significant risk, since that candidate's attractiveness to party members may not translate into widespread popular support. Indeed, voters may perceive such a candidate as too ideologically extreme. Still, in 2006, many *panistas* opposed nominating a candidate with external appeal but who had a weak attachment to the party. Instead they chose a candidate who offered the chance of "winning the election without losing the party" (Romero 2005, 16).

Calderón therefore knew that unlike Fox, he could not depend on his personal popularity and financial independence to win the election. His career history helped him win the party's nomination but placed him in a strategic situation vastly different from Fox's in 1999: in 2000 Fox knew that he could win *without* the PAN's organizational support, whereas in 2006 Calderón knew that he could win only *with* his party's support. Thus in a significant departure from Fox, Calderón actively sought to portray himself as a party insider and signaled that he "intended to serve as a devout standard bearer" for his party if he won (Shirk 2006, 11). In contrast to Fox in 2000, he was heavily involved in preparing the PAN's 2006 electoral platform.[15] To demonstrate his loyalty, shortly after winning the nomination he enjoyed a Christmas feast at a Mexico City hotel, at which he signed a "unity agreement" with PAN cabinet members, legislators, and high officials.[16]

Parties in separate powers systems face a dilemma: by nominating an insider and aligning the executive and legislative races, as parliamentary parties do, a party may nominate a sure-fire loser. Yet in nominating

---

[15] Lilia Saúl, "AN se reúne para aprobar plataforma electoral." *El Universal*, November 12, 2005.
[16] Daniel Pensamiento, "Cierran filas los panistas y candidato." *Mural*, December 7, 2005.

an outsider, a party risks selling its soul if its candidate wins. Parties in separation of powers systems confront this dilemma repeatedly – at each presidential election. In contrast, leadership selection bias toward insiders (Chapter 3) and intraparty accountability mechanisms (Chapter 4) attenuate this problem in parliamentary systems. In Mexico, the PAN had luck on its side in both 2000 and 2006, winning both times after pursuing a vote-seeking strategy in 2000 and a policy-seeking strategy in 2006. The latter strategy, however, clearly entailed greater risk: whereas Fox had won by a margin of 6.4 points (42.5%–36.1%), Calderón won a tight three-way race by less than one point (36.7%–36.1%).

The contrasting experiences of the PAN's 2000 and 2006 campaigns illustrate that tension between the executive and legislative branches of a party emerges partly as a function of how well that party balances its vote-seeking and policy-seeking goals in the presidential nomination process. A presidential candidate who stakes a claim as being larger than or above the party (à la Fox) may be more likely to win, but such cases are likely to generate considerable intraparty tensions in the electoral and governing arenas. Outsiders of this sort rarely rise to the top of parties in parliamentary systems, and in any case a prime minister who strays from the party line risks being ousted from power via an internal leadership challenge. In contrast, when presidential candidates admit they are "smaller" than their party (à la Calderón), separation of purpose is likely to be low – even though the party runs a greater risk of losing the election. The PAN managed to eke out a victory in 2006, but it took the riskier path to Los Pinos, the Mexican White House.

Separation of Origin in Mexico's 2006 Campaign: The PRD and the PRI

The PAN illustrates that tension between executive and legislative branches of a party can vary within parties over time. A brief comparison of the PAN against Mexico's other two main parties – the PRI and the PRD – reveals that the degree of tension can also vary from party to party at the same election. In 2006, while the PAN was nominating an insider who pledged to stick to the party line, a different dynamic emerged in the PRD and PRI. Following the procedure developed for the Comparative Manifestos Project for European parties, Kathleen Bruhn (2006) compared the party platforms of the PRI, PRD, and PAN against the campaign platforms of those three parties' presidential candidates.

FIGURE 7.2. Left-Right Placement, Mexico 2006.
Source for placement data: Bruhn (2006).

In 2006, the tension between the PRI and its candidate Roberto Madrazo and between the PRD and its candidate Andrés Manuel López Obrador (known by his initials as "AMLO") echoed the PAN's experience in 2000. For example, López Obrador expressed no interest in helping to formulate the PRD's platform and actively distanced himself from his party's organization during the campaign. According to one interviewee, "López Obrador did not participate actively in the assemblies held by the party to debate the content of its platform, responding 'that is your business, not mine' when asked to do so" (Bruhn 2006, 16).

During the campaign the PAN desperately (and successfully) sought to portray AMLO as a radical firebrand. However, as Figure 7.2 reveals, AMLO's own campaign document was actually far more *conservative* than his party's, as was Madrazo's. In truth, AMLO wanted to position himself as a centrist – which meant that his stated platform resembled the PAN's more than the PRD's! For example, AMLO's platform mentions economic orthodoxy 18 times more often than his party's platform. Given facts like these, Bruhn concludes, "López Obrador intended to campaign as a moderate, against his party's expressed preferences" (Bruhn 2006, 17).

Clearly, intraparty conflict in Mexico is not simply a function of the degree to which voters split their tickets. As noted in Chapter 5, electoral separation of purpose in all three main Mexican parties is comparatively low, but intraparty conflict emerges nonetheless. Moreover, intraparty tension is not unique to the PAN's experience in 2000, when a party outsider gained the party's presidential nomination. In 2006, the PAN managed to contract with an insider candidate (Calderón released no independent platform, signaling the degree to which his positions aligned with his party's), but internal strife plagued the other main parties. The candidates of the PRD and PRI both sought to distance themselves from their parties. This strategy almost worked for AMLO, who polled consistently ahead of his own party. Attempting a suprapartisan appeal was probably the only way that a PRD candidate could win – and AMLO lost to Calderón by the narrowest of margins.

As in Brazil, separation of purpose can characterize Mexico's main parties both at elections and in government. The fact that the PAN and the PT are so unlike each other further supports our point that separation of purpose can characterize parties with any sort of sociological profile in separation of powers systems. The PAN also illustrates that tension between the executive and legislative branches can vary over time within the same party, without any change in the institutional context that might alter the incentives that shape the relationship between the party and its agent.

CONCLUSION

When leaders are autonomous from or even gain ascendance over their parties – to the point that some presidential candidates prepare their own platforms! – then parties lose their place as standard-bearers of representative democracy, and not only when those candidates' platforms are at odds with or even contradict their parties' platforms. It is certainly true that intraparty tension divides all political parties, regardless of constitutional format. However, parties in parliamentary systems simply do not experience the same sorts of problems as described in this chapter. Parliamentary systems permit little preference divergence between executive and legislative branches of the same party,[17] and intraparty tension in pure parliamentary systems can never follow from different vote bases. Prime ministers cannot offer separate and/or different platforms from their party's legislators, and their preferences in the legislative arena cannot diverge so starkly from their party's. In contrast, considerable divergence can emerge between branches of a single party when executives enjoy separation of origin and survival.

What does the research in these two chapters tell us about the *sources* of intraparty contracting problems? First, this chapter's case studies

---

[17] Even cases that evince tension between a party and a prime minister are telling. For instance, Japanese prime minister Junichiro Koizumi – sometimes said to embody a case of presidentialization – famously vowed to "destroy" his own Liberal Democratic Party in his pursuit of economic and other structural reforms. Yet he rose to his position precisely by having been voted in by the rank and file, and when he called a snap election in an effort to garner support for a pet project in 2005, he still had to appeal for voters to support LDP candidates – after all, there was no way to reelect Koizumi's authority without giving the LDP itself an expanded mandate. And of course, after Koizumi resigned, the LDP remained in power under a new leader, with no new election called. This experience is nothing like what we have seen in this chapter and elsewhere in this book for truly presidentialized parties.

revealed that divergence between the executive and legislative branches of a party can emerge in any kind of party, irrespective of ideological profile or social base. Second, institutional variables do not exert a consistent effect on the degree of intraparty tension. For example, although nonconcurrence tends to increase presidents' distance from their party, such distance can also arise in concurrent elections, as the Mexican examples illustrate. Third, intraparty institutions also do not exert a consistent effect on the type of candidate selected and thus have an uncertain effect on intraparty contracting problems. Presidential candidates in both the PT and the PAN are nominated via closed primaries, but the depth of each party's internal problems has varied over time.

Finally, the "type" of candidate does not necessarily predict the extent of contracting problems. Fox was a relative outsider while Calderón was an obvious insider, and the degree of intraparty tension paralleled these characterizations. Yet while Lula counts as an insider, he gradually grew convinced of his need to *become* an outsider because he had lost three consecutive presidential elections. We might also note the experience of US presidential candidates in this regard: generally speaking, US presidential candidates are outsiders, but tension between presidents and parties has varied over time. In fact, the idea that insiders should have good relations with their parties does not seem to hold in the United States: for example, Lyndon Johnson was a relative insider, but he and his party deeply clashed on the campaign trail and during his presidency. In contrast, George W. Bush was an outsider yet he fit the Republican Party's increasingly conservative profile very well in 2000.

Our research has merely scratched the surface of the ways that the separation of origin and survival impacts intraparty politics. Several additional avenues cry out for investigation. First, comparativists could measure presidents' positions in policy space relative to their parties, using any of several potential sources of information, including the content of legislative proposals, content analysis of speeches, or positions on final roll-call votes. We predict the following: to the extent that presidents and their parties clash over the content of campaign platforms or electoral alliance strategy, or receive votes from different groups or for different reasons, they are likely to clash in the legislative arena and over the allocation of resources such as cabinet portfolios. These sorts of intraparty squabbles may exist in parliamentary systems, but not as much as under the separation of powers, and not for the same reasons.

Kathleen Bruhn's analysis of presidential and party campaign platforms in the 2006 Mexican elections also carries broad comparative implications for the study of party politics. No research similar to that of the Comparative Manifestos Project exists for presidential systems (but see Bruhn 2004 for a small sample of leftist parties in Latin America). Should some group of scholars undertake such a project, the evidence in this book serves as fair warning not to assume that parties and presidential candidates (or elected presidents) occupy the same "location" in political space. Any comparative study of the evolution of parties' ideological and/or policy positions will need to assess the positions of not only parties but also presidents.[18] Similar efforts could employ expert surveys (e.g. Wiesehomeier and Benoit 2007) or voter surveys such as the Comparative Study of Electoral Systems.

---

[18] Another way to explore this facet of separation of purpose would be to use CSES survey results to explore how voters place presidents, prime ministers, and parties in political space, for example, on a left-right continuum. If we are correct, all else equal, we ought to see greater variance (not necessarily a greater absolute difference) in the placement of *party leaders* versus *parties* on the continuum in presidential versus parliamentary systems, with semi-presidential systems representing a middle ground. In parliamentary systems, voters should recognize that party leaders represent the median member of the party – but are less likely to perceive or believe this in a pure presidential system.

8

Presidents, Prime Ministers, and Mandate Representation

Thus far in this book we have focused on the impact of constitutional structure on such aspects of party presidentialization as agent selection and dismissal, campaign dynamics, the degree to which the electoral constituencies of different branches of a single party overlap, and on intraparty governance problems. In this chapter we turn our attention to the key policy decisions executives make – and the extent to which those decisions reflect what parties say they will do once in office, which is ostensibly the reason citizens voted that party and its candidate for the executive into office in the first place. In other words, in this chapter we ask, What is the impact of fusion or separation of powers on policymaking and representation?

We follow Pitkin (1967) generally in defining representation as a relationship between citizens' interests and political outcomes in which rulers act to meet the interests of the public. Since elections signal citizens' interests in modern democracy, we also follow Manin, Przeworski, and Stokes (1999) in focusing on electoral responsiveness – what they call "mandate representation." Critically, conventional political science wisdom asserts that this sort of representation requires political parties. According to this view, representation requires prospective voting, in which governments "represent" citizens' interests when voters signal what they would like government to do, parties compete by proposing alternative policies, citizens use their vote to choose the best policies, and the party or parties that form the next government implement the proposed policies.

This view of the connection between parties, elections, and representation permeates theoretical and empirical political science research.[1] It also reflects the way we have understood the process of democratic politics in this book, in which parties occupy a prominent position in a chain of delegated authority:

VOTERS → PARTY → EXECUTIVE → POLICY

If there were no slack in this idealized delegation chain, executives would be perfect agents of their party, and parties in turn would be perfect agents of the electorate. Under such conditions we would get "perfect" mandate representation – that is, we would never see deviations from parties' electoral mandates because parties would anticipate voter sanction for deviating. Thus in election campaigns the platform of the party and its executive candidate would be indistinguishable, and in governing, the executive's policy choices would embody the party's platform. In turn, voter preferences would determine the party's platform. If any of these conditions for perfect mandate representation were violated, the principal would punish the agent, which could take the form of the party dumping its leader or, ultimately, the voters switching their votes to another party at the next election.

As Manin, Przeworski, and Stokes (1999) note, no democracy literally enforces mandate representation – and with good reason: when circumstances change, voters might want parties to violate their mandates in order to respond adequately to the new conditions. Moreover, no chain of delegation – even one in which agents are reliable and honest and the contracts are perfectly designed – is ever so free of friction as our stylized account suggests. While consensus exists that parties do seek to promote mandate consistency, scholars also agree that perfect representation is a fantasy.

Nevertheless, for our purposes, understanding *why* representation tends to deviate from this theoretical ideal requires asking whether certain constitutional formats systematically shape this chain of delegation so that some parties can put the ideal into practice more easily than others. The study of political representation has a long history, yet although a majority of the world's democracies now have popularly elected presidencies, neither normative nor positive political theory has adequately

---

[1] See e.g. Klingeman, Hofferbert, and Budge (1994); Manin, Przeworski, and Stokes (1999); Powell (2000); Stokes (2001); Cox and McCubbins (2005); Benoit and Laver (2006).

explored the implications of the separation of powers for democratic political representation.[2] An influential example illustrates this problem. G. Bingham Powell's (2000) wide-ranging study of the relationship between elections and representation focuses on differences between "majoritarian" and "proportional" democracies but ignores potential differences in representational outcomes between presidential and parliamentary systems.

From our perspective this approach is problematic, because neither pure nor semi-presidential systems can be shoehorned easily into either of Powell's ideal-types. For example, a two-party pure presidential system is not as majoritarian as a two-party parliamentary system, and a multiparty pure presidential system is not as proportional as a multiparty parliamentary system. Likewise, semi-presidential systems can be strongly majoritarian if the president's party has a majority in the assembly and thus controls the cabinet, but they can also be quite proportional if a coalition cabinet is in place or if the dual executive is divided between opposing parties, as under cohabitation. The wide range of possible configurations under pure and semi-presidentialism suggests that these systems do not fit neatly into the famous typologies of "majoritarian" versus "proportional" (or "consensus") governance that comparativists have long employed (e.g. Lijphart 1984; 1999; Powell 2000).

In earlier work (Samuels and Shugart 2003) we addressed this conceptual gap and considered the impact of the separation of powers on representation, using Manin, Przeworski, and Stokes's (1999) distinction between electoral responsiveness and electoral accountability. We argued that pure presidentialism tends simultaneously to maximize accountability – in which voters retrospectively assess politicians for their performance – and minimize responsiveness. Samuels (2004) and Hellwig and Samuels (2008) have empirically confirmed that the separation of powers does enhance retrospective accountability, at least on one measure of economic performance. Here, we turn our attention to electoral responsiveness.

---

[2] One can also note the absence of attention to the presidency as a source of representational influence in the United States in Miller and Stokes (1966), an absence repeated in Converse and Pierce's study of France (1986). Generally, in the US politics literature, "mandates" are typically explored from the president's point of view (e.g. Kelley 1983; Dahl 1990), or legislators' point of view (e.g. Weinbaum and Judd 1970), or parties' point of view (e.g. Edwards 1989; Jones 1999) – but the interplay of the party and the president in terms of representation has been largely ignored. Our approach most resembles that of Jones.

Our argument in this chapter builds on existing research on the conditions that foster or impede mandate representation. We suggest that all else equal, the separation of origin and survival creates relatively greater disincentives for consistent mandate representation. Following the theoretical arguments we have advanced in this book, we examine how different political institutions influence the chain of democratic delegation and thus impact the probability that parties are likely to fulfill their stated mandate. Parliamentary systems tend to more closely resemble the idealized chain of democratic delegation and accountability. Presidential and semi-presidential systems, in contrast, are far less likely to embody that ideal. This implies, quite simply, that *mandate representation should be less common as we move away from the ideal-typical parliamentary chain of delegation.*

Preceding chapters laid the theoretical foundation for this claim. We have demonstrated how the separate origin and survival of the executive breaks the chain of delegation by (1) encouraging parties to recruit candidates who may be less-than-faithful agents; (2) encouraging executive candidates to campaign independently of their parties; and (3) limiting parties' ability to sanction executives who enjoy separate survival. This chapter explores the empirical implications of these findings for democratic representation.

To test the impact of democratic regime-type on mandate consistency systematically, we explore the incidence of *violations* of mandate consistency. In doing so, we build on Susan Stokes's (2001) research on Latin America in the 1980s and 1990s. Like Stokes, we call violations of mandates "policy-switches." Politicians may betray their stated campaign commitments in any policy area; we focus here only on economic policy, as did Stokes. As we explain in more detail below, campaigns can be oriented toward either "security" or "efficiency" in economic policy. A policy-switch occurs when a candidate campaigns with one orientation but then pursues policies with the opposite orientation after assuming power.

We test our hypotheses on a much broader sample than Stokes, and our results support our claim: policy-switches are about four times as common under pure presidentialism as under parliamentarism. Moreover, we find that the separation of powers overwhelms the causal impact of the factors Stokes identified. We find that two conditions enhance the likelihood of policy-switches in pure and semi-presidential systems: (1) close presidential races, which increase the incentive of presidential candidates to tailor their campaign messages for their own electoral benefit; and (2) presidents who lack a legislative majority after an election, a situation that gives them greater discretion in forging governing and policymaking strategy.

As we explain later in the chapter, close presidential elections and minority legislative support are the real-world political conditions under which we are most likely to see problems of adverse selection and moral hazard. In this way our findings in this chapter are consistent with the implications of our principal-agent theoretical framework. We have suggested that parliamentary systems minimize adverse selection and moral hazard – and in this chapter we find that close elections and minority legislative support matter *only* in pure and semi-presidential systems, but not in parliamentary systems. In parliamentary systems neither the competitiveness of *legislative* elections nor whether a prime minister has a majority of seats make a switch more likely.

In sum, patterns of mandate consistency and inconsistency across democracies derive from differences in the chain of democratic delegation. This finding has huge implications for the study of parties' ability to fulfill one of their primary purposes in modern democracy – to represent citizens' interests. As long suspected but never shown in comparative politics, "responsible party government" is in fact less likely under systems with directly elected presidents. Before turning to our data and findings, we first offer a more thorough theoretical consideration of how the separation of powers affects mandate representation.

PARTIES, PRESIDENTS, AND POLITICAL REPRESENTATION

Scholars have long criticized the separation of powers as an institutional structure that impedes "responsible party government." This essentially Anglophile view has a long pedigree in American political discourse. Woodrow Wilson (1908) decried the lack of "responsible" parties from his perch at Princeton's Department of Politics before he had to deal with those parties as president of the United States. Critics such as E. E. Schattschneider (1942), who headed the American Political Science Association's "Committee for a Responsible Party System" (1950), blamed party irresponsibility on the separation of powers, and his argument still resonates (see e.g. Sundquist 1992).

It is true that scholars currently see US parties as having grown more cohesive (e.g. McCarty, Poole, and Rosenthal 2006), a situation that some believe would "delight" critics such as Schattschneider (Bartels 2008, 290). Yet the fact that US parties are currently more ideologically cohesive does not suggest they have finally bridged the separation of powers; it only suggests to the historically minded that US parties (or parties anywhere) can cycle in and out of relatively more or less "responsible" phases, not that Wilson's or Schattschneider's dream of "parliamentarizing" US parties has been realized. Are "responsible" parties unlikely – in the United States or in any other separate-powers system – or in any democracy, for that matter? Are "irresponsible" parties a function of the separation of powers itself, or are they simply the fruit of American exceptionalism?

The responsible parties thesis finds a loud echo in the mandate-representation notion of how democracy *should* work: parties articulate distinctive platforms, voters make decisions based on those distinctions, and parties govern according to their platforms. Several scholars have applied the conception of mandate representation in empirical research. For example, Klingeman and his colleagues (1994) noted a substantial degree of mandate *consistency* across eight established democracies, including the United States. In contrast, Stokes (2001) found substantial mandate *inconsistency* across pure presidential systems in Latin America.[3]

As noted, no research has considered the variable impact of the fusion or separation of powers on either responsible parties or mandate consistency. In this section we discuss the obstacles that the separation of powers places in the way of mandate representation. We consider politicians' incentives to switch under any system, and then explore the particular incentives to stick with or abandon a mandate under each of our three main democratic constitutional designs. We argue that executives' incentives to break the chain of democratic delegation and diverge from their party are stronger under systems with popular presidential elections. By implication, this means that the conditions Stokes (2001) identified as most likely associated with policy-switching – in particular, minority government – may actually be important only under the separation of powers.

First Principles: Executives' Motivations to Stick or Switch

Why might a politician promise one thing during a campaign and then repudiate that promise once in office? To understand why party agents in the executive confront different incentives in different institutional contexts, we must start with first principles about politicians' motivations. Politicians desire power and its trappings. If they reach the pinnacle of

---

[3] Her cases include Peru, which, as we have noted, is technically a president-parliamentary regime.

their party organization and win the office of president or prime minister, they presumably want to retain that position as long as is feasible
and ultimately to exit office with their reputation intact.

To accomplish this under democratic auspices, politicians must propose
and enact policies that please voters. Yet in terms of mandate consistency,
there is a more important question: to what extent must candidates for
executive office propose and enact policies that also please the party members who put those politicians in position to win executive power to begin
with? Stokes (2001) assumes that there is no fundamental incompatibility
between what presidents want, what their parties want, and what voters
want. Thus she assumes that some presidents switch policies because they
believe doing so will simultaneously advance both their personal goals and
advance their parties' interests. She states that presidents measure their
success as "victory of one's own party at the next election" (Stokes 2001,
66) even when term limits prevent a president from running for reelection.
This means that presidents switch policies believing they are acting as
good party agents – *even if party members vehemently disagree.*

Stokes also argues that some presidents switch because they believe
they are acting as a good agent of citizens' interests – again, regardless
of whether citizens might vehemently disagree. To justify this assumption
Stokes argues that neither international financial agencies (Stokes 2001,
74, 92) nor the prospect of personal financial gain (85) motivates switches.
Instead, she suggests that policy-switchers believe that voters underesti-
mate the effectiveness of efficiency-oriented policies and know that they
must hide this belief and advocate populist "security-oriented" policies on
the campaign trail in order to win office. Presidents who switch are thus
dissembling on the campaign trail when they later switch policies and
enact what they believe to be citizens' *true* interests, even though they are
not responding to citizens' *expressed* interests, and even though they are
violating their *party's* stated policies (Stokes 2001; see pp. 19, 56, 65).

Although Stokes hinted that presidentialism might be driving her findings (189), her hypotheses about why presidents sometimes violate their
mandates are not derived from theoretical claims about how the separation of powers per se shapes presidents' incentives. For instance, she
argues that term limits – which are virtually unknown in parliamentary
systems[4] – do not influence the likelihood of a policy-switch.[5] What then

---

[4] Botswana and South Africa are exceptions. The Liberal Democratic Party in Japan has
a term limit for its leaders who serve as prime minister.
[5] We accept Stokes's assumption that presidents desire the victory of their own party at
the next election. However, as we showed in Chapter 5, presidents and their parties

are the sources of executives' incentives to stick with or violate their party's mandate? We have no *a priori* reason to believe that Stokes's motivational assumption – politicians switch because they believe doing so is in their personal interest, their party's interest, and in voters' interest – should differ across constitutional formats. Yet even if we assume that politicians everywhere have similar motivations, the pertinent question that remains is whether different democratic institutions *channel* politicians' motivations in different ways, constraining their options or providing new opportunities. If so, we should observe policy-switching at different frequencies under different constitutional formats. Thus in the remainder of this section we explore both intra- and interparty incentives to switch under parliamentarism, presidentialism, and semi-presidentialism.

Incentives under Parliamentarism

There is some baseline nonzero probability that a political leader will wake up one day and decide to switch policies. Such incentives are minimized under parliamentarism, both within and across parties. First, as discussed in Chapter 3, parties spend a great deal of time vetting their potential prime ministers. This leadership selection process implies a low probability that a prime-ministerial candidate would harbor policy preferences at variance with his or her party – a necessary condition for a policy-switch. Once in office, certain intraparty conditions might marginally increase the propensity to switch: perhaps a crafty prime minister could feel so secure in office – either because of personal popularity or a lack of viable replacements – that party colleagues could not retaliate following a mandate violation.[6] Nevertheless, the

---

sometimes have only partially overlapping electoral constituencies. Thus presidents eligible for reelection may judge their own success by whether they win reelection or not, even at the expense of their parties. Moreover, presidents limited to only one term may not always believe that election of another candidate from their party – one with a different electoral constituency – fulfills their legacy. Still, even given the potential that term limits affect the degree of incentive overlap between presidents and parties, term limits are not essential to explaining policy-switching across democratic regimes. As we saw in Chapter 4, prime ministers may have shorter time horizons than presidents because they are more likely to be deposed *by their own parties* before the end of the term. This suggests that the separation of origin and survival, and not the potential for reelection, fundamentally determine the incentives for executives to act as faithful party agents while in office.

6 The likelihood could also be shaped by the institutional context – for example if the parliament requires a "constructive" vote of no confidence, which requires that an alternative government be ready to fill the expelled prime minister's shoes immediately. However, these sorts of factors are likely to have relatively minor importance.

core institutional fact of parliamentarism remains: even prime ministers who feel "secure" in office remain subject to both parliamentary and/ or partisan no-confidence votes in the event that the party rejects the prime minister's policies or if things go badly. This generates powerful intraparty constraints on our hypothetical prime minister who wakes up one day intending to switch policies. The risks of getting fired are simply too high.

In cases of coalition government, *inter*party constraints also lower the likelihood of a switch in pure parliamentary systems. This is because the nature of parliamentary coalitions limits unilateral switching and makes such decisions a matter of *inter*party transactions. Many coalitions (up to a third, depending on how they are counted) are formal, public agreements sealed before the election campaign begins (Strøm and Müller 1999; Golder 2006; Carroll and Cox 2007). And even in the absence of a formal pre-election "contract," coalitions commit parties to sets of policies and to processes of interparty coordination and consultation. Indeed, many parliamentary coalitions employ interparty mechanisms that let parties "keep tabs" on their partners, such as the allocation of junior minister posts or legislative oversight committee chairs (Thies 2001; Clark and Jurgelevičiūtė 2008; Martin and Vanberg 2004).

Any premier heading a coalition cabinet in a parliamentary system is an agent of multiple parties and is thus accountable to multiple principals. Consequently, all parties to a coalition must consent to implement a proposed switch – and in the absence of such consensus, a switch will not happen. Thus, just as prime ministers cannot unilaterally impose a switch on their own parties, prime ministers *or their parties* cannot impose a switch *on other parties* that could bring down the government were the switch successfully implemented. Coalitions in parliamentary systems place both intra- *and* interparty obstacles in front of prime ministers who want to switch policies. And prime ministers heading minority governments – whether of a coalition or not – should confront even stronger constraints, given the fragility of minority governments. In short, switches should be highly unlikely in parliamentary systems, and still less likely under coalition or minority governments.

Incentives under Pure Presidentialism

In contrast to prime ministers, executives in pure presidential systems face far weaker intraparty constraints on their own actions. For one, presidents win their job through a popular election, which gives them a source of legitimacy distinct from their party. Moreover, the separation of origin tends to generate incentive incompatibility between a party's executive and legislative branches, based on a party's need to recruit a presidential candidate who can win a direct executive election (Chapter 3) and on the fact that the party's executive and legislative constituencies may not completely overlap (Chapters 5–7). Such incentive incompatibility only emerges when executives compete in popular elections. Moreover, when an election is expected to be close, incentive incompatibility may lead presidential candidates to be less-than-forthcoming about future policy choices, if they believe that being "too honest" might put their own election at risk.

In addition to incentive incompatibility derived from separate origin, parties' ability to control their agents once they have assumed office is more difficult under the separation of powers. As we showed in Chapter 4, the separation of survival means that parties have extremely limited ability to hold their leaders accountable between elections. As such, presidents should have relatively greater liberty to switch policies than prime ministers under parliamentarism. Presidents can switch *despite* the preferences of their co-partisans in the legislature, because their co-partisans cannot credibly threaten them with removal.

What about interparty constraints when a president's party does not control a legislative majority? We suggested above that coalition and minority situations make prime ministers in parliamentary systems *less* likely to switch. Yet for presidents, minority situations should have the opposite effect. This is because presidents can forge coalitions without the consent of their own party, a possibility that is unthinkable in parliamentary systems. Although coalition cabinets are common in presidential systems (Amorim Neto 2002, 2006a; Cheibub, Przeworski, and Saiegh 2004), formal *interparty* agreements are uncommon (Carroll 2007).[7] This is partly because the president is the *formateur* of the coalition, but also because the president cannot be fired. In pure presidential systems, presidents – not parties – lead and agree to coalition deals. Thus whereas prime ministers are at their *most* constrained when their parties are lacking a majority, presidents are at their *least* constrained under comparable conditions. Depending on their own personal preferences,

---

[7] To our knowledge, Bolivia is the only case of pure presidentialism where there have been formal interparty agreements about the allocation of executive and legislative portfolios, due to congress's selection of the president when no candidate obtains a popular-vote majority.

they can force their own party to "agree" to a coalition – or reach across the aisle to pass a particular policy proposal – without fear of intra-partisan repercussion. As a result, policy-switches should be most likely under presidentialism when there is no majority party.

Theoretically, we are agnostic as to whether presidents switch policies and then say, in effect, "My coalition partners made me do it,"[8] or abandon their party's mandate on their own accord and then find partners in the legislature to support their choice. Given the nature of agency relationships under presidentialism, either scenario is plausible. However, both scenarios are less plausible for prime ministers in parliamentary systems. If presidents switch policies because they need support in the legislature from parties favoring a switch, their own parties are in a weak position to stop them, for all the reasons we have given. If, on the other hand, they initiate the switch and then cobble together a supportive coalition afterward, they still face minimal constraints from their own party compared to prime ministers in parliamentary systems. They are relatively unconstrained both to govern and to initiate consultations with other parties, and face even fewer constraints to do so when they face a legislature without their party in the majority – which is precisely the case in which presidents may feel they have a personal mandate above that of the party and hence the freedom to shuffle alliances and switch policies.

Incentives under Semi-Presidentialism

Now let us consider the case of semi-presidentialism. Three theoretical possibilities exist. First, it could be the case that semi-presidential systems generate both intra- and interparty constraints on *both* elements of the dual executive – similar to the constraints on prime ministers in parliamentary systems – due to the need of the cabinet to have parliamentary confidence. Second, these systems could generate incentives similar to pure presidential systems, due to the separate origin and survival of one half of the dual executive, the presidency. Or third, semi-presidential systems could fall somewhere in the middle in their propensity to switch policies – a hypothesis that seems as safe as it is theoretically uninteresting.

We argue that semi-presidential systems are more like pure presidential systems in their tendency to give the executive – *whether a president or a*

---

[8] This may be the case in Bolivia in 1989. See Stokes (1999), pp. 122–23.

prime minister – considerable leeway to switch policies. This hypothesis might seem intuitive for presidents in president-parliamentary systems because in that subtype the president is clearly the strongest actor in the political system both within and across parties, due to unrestricted dismissal power.

However, there are good reasons to believe this hypothesis will hold even for prime ministers in such systems, as well as for both presidents and prime ministers in premier-presidential cases. Although the formal rules of premier-presidentialism imply a strong parliamentary logic and intraparty obstacles to policy-switching, we have already seen evidence of partisan presidentialization in these systems: a tendency for outsiders as both premiers and presidents (Chapter 3), a propensity for presidents to terminate the premier's tenure (Chapter 4), and often considerable electoral separation of purpose (Chapter 5). Other scholars have also found presidential influence over cabinet composition across all semi-presidential systems (e.g. Amorim Neto and Strøm 2006). All of this suggests a strong presidentializing logic for party politics, even in relatively "parliamentarized" premier-presidential cases. Even though semi-presidential systems retain the link between the parliamentary majority and the cabinet, we expect these presidentializing intraparty dynamics to increase the likelihood of policy-switching relative to parliamentary systems.

The path to executive power in semi-presidential systems adds additional "breaks" in our idealized chain of delegation, enhancing incentives for policy-switching. Recall from Chapter 3 that a large percentage of presidents in semi-presidential systems served as premier immediately before being elected president: 24% in premier-presidential systems and 19% of presidents in president-parliamentary systems. And of course, many more premiers *pursue* the presidency than manage to win it. This suggests that the goal of winning presidential elections shapes the incentives of both prime ministers *and* parties, across all semi-presidential systems. In the end, the existence of a popularly elected president may overwhelm the "parliamentary" features of semi-presidentialism. Thus to the extent that separate origin and survival of the president make switches more likely, we should observe more switches in semi-presidential systems than under parliamentarism.

Finally, pursuit of the presidency in semi-presidential systems implies that both new presidents as well as new premiers after a legislative election may be likely to switch. Most semi-presidential systems have non-concurrent legislative elections. And as we saw in Chapter 2, cabinets are typically constitutionally required to resign after a new parliament is elected.[9] While a newly installed prime minister after a nonconcurrent election might seem to be the most shielded from presidential influence, a nonconcurrent assembly election typically means that the next *presidential* election will come sooner than the next *parliamentary* election, which in turns implies that the next test of parties' popularity will come in a presidential contest, *in which the newly installed premier may be a candidate.* Thus if premiers perceive that a switch may help them win the next presidential election, they may be able to initiate a switch notwithstanding their dependence on parliamentary confidence. Presidentialization of the entire political system means that parties must give freer rein to their leaders because of the need to build supraparty support in the electorate. As we have argued in other chapters, this electoral dynamic is present in semi-presidential systems nearly as much as under pure presidentialism. In sum, although the logic differs from pure presidentialism, the distinct presidentializing incentives of semi-presidential systems makes mandate consistency less likely than under pure parliamentarism.

Theoretical Argument: Summary

This chapter's argument flows from the theoretical framework we have used throughout this book: the separation of origin and survival generates distinct imperatives that parties simply do not encounter in parliamentary systems. Both intra- and interparty constraints on executive freedom of action are greater under pure parliamentarism than under either pure or semi-presidentialism. Likewise, the incentives to abandon a party's expressed mandate are stronger under systems with separate executive origin and survival. We are not saying that executives in pure or semi-presidential systems will *never* act as faithful agents of their parties. It is certainly possible for presidents to act as faithful partisan agents, just less likely than for prime ministers under pure parliamentarism.

Presidents' and parties' greater incentive incompatibility is partly due to the fact that presidents must seek suprapartisan coalitions in the electorate. Moreover, the separation of survival makes policy-switching a much less risky option for presidents, compared to prime ministers. The separation of origin and survival thus encourages voters to see presidential

---

[9] Typically, especially in the premier-presidential subtype, the prime minister is not required to resign after a new president is inaugurated. However, as we saw in Chapter 4, they often do so anyway. This is a clear indication of presidentialization and an informal practice that opens up the potential for a policy-switch led or instigated by a new president, who would then attempt to build a sympathetic cabinet.

candidates as distinct from their parties, even if they are longtime "party politicians." We expect the logic of this argument to hold even for prime ministers in semi-presidential systems. Parties in semi-presidential systems must tolerate greater agency slack in the relationship with their prime minister because they know that they must field a viable presidential candidate – and their best choice may turn out to be the incumbent premier. Consequently, presidents or premiers in semi-presidential systems may propose policies that are not aligned with those of their party, and the party may either tolerate the switch (in the case of a premier) or be powerless to impede it (in the case of a president). In short, executives are less accountable to their party in pure and semi-presidential systems, and thus more likely to violate campaign promises.

POLICY-SWITCHING OR MANDATE REPRESENTATION: A GLOBAL EXPLORATION

To test our hypothesis about the impact of the separation of powers on mandate representation, we analyze campaigns and postelectoral policy choices around the world between 1978 and 2002. As in previous chapters, a country is included if it scored a 5 or better on the Polity IV index of democracy for five consecutive years.[10] In presidential systems we analyzed the presidential candidates' campaign and governing strategy. In parliamentary systems we looked at the prime minister's party. In semi-presidential systems we looked at both presidential and parliamentary election campaigns, except in the few cases where elections were concurrent.[11] Our database contains entries for 401 election-observations, almost 10 times as many as Stokes considered.

We employ Stokes's definition of a policy-switch: during a campaign, "politicians will pronounce themselves in favor of job creation, growth, improvement in real wages, industrial policy, a gradualist approach to inflation stabilization, and limited repayment of the foreign debt, only to impose austerity and liberal reforms when elected" (Stokes 2001, 43).

---

[10] The shorter time period than in other chapters allows us to focus on the "third wave" of democratization after the mid-1970s, after which there is a more diverse set of democracies of all types.

[11] There is no reason to consider both presidential and legislative campaigns when they are concurrent because it would not be feasible to separate the two (unless the election resulted in cohabitation, which has never been the outcome under concurrent elections). In pure presidential systems we ignore legislative campaigns, even when non-concurrent, because in such systems legislative campaigns are by definition not about control of the government.

This is a switch from a "security-oriented" platform to an "efficiency-oriented" set of policies; the reverse sort of switch can also occur. Given these definitions, we coded winning candidates'[12] campaigns according to their stated future policy orientation: either (1) "security-oriented," (2) "efficiency-oriented," or (3) too vague to classify. We then gathered information on the policies that the winning candidate subsequently pursued: again, either (1) "security-oriented," (2) "efficiency-oriented," or (3) too vague to classify.[13] Comparing the two codings lets us determine which governments had followed through on campaign promises and which had switched policies.

Examples of Policy-Switches

Some policy-switches are well known, especially given Stokes's systematic exploration of the Latin American cases. For example, Argentine president Carlos Menem (1989–99) campaigned on his Peronist party's historic platform, advocating a "nationalist and expansionist" economic policy (Stokes 2001, 45) that would avoid imposing hardships on the working and middle classes. Yet once in office, "Menem's economic team fashioned policies like the ones his opponents had advocated" (Stokes 2001, 47), including currency devaluation, spending cuts, privatization, and trade liberalization. Similarly, Venezuelan president Carlos Andrés Pérez (1989–93) violated his party's long-standing left-of-center reputation by implementing austerity programs following his inauguration. Other cases of policy-switching in Latin America follow a similar pattern: leaders campaign on what Stokes calls "security-oriented" policies but govern with "efficiency-oriented" policies.

Our research yielded several examples of similar policy-switches from outside of Latin America. One such case comes from South Korea in 1997. Presidential candidate Kim Dae-Jung had gained wide respect as an advocate for democracy. His core constituency consisted of farmers, small business owners, and union members. Big business distrusted him, particularly because he had called for slashing the power of Korea's economic conglomerates, the *chaebols*. Kim had also opposed Korea's

---

[12] In the case of semi-presidential systems, this means the prime minister after a legislative election as well as the president after a presidential election (except that we consider only the president when elections are concurrent).

[13] Our research, as well as Stokes's, relied heavily on news media accounts of campaigns and subsequent policies. We employed the Lexis-Nexis Academic online search engine, which consults hundreds of global news sources.

entry into the OECD, saying that the country was "not ready" to open its markets (*Financial Times* 1997). Given his trajectory, one business executive said, "You know what his economic policy will be" (*Financial Times* 1997). Moreover, during his campaign Kim allied with the United Liberal Democrat party, with which he shared "the same economic policy based on nationalism and a strong state role in guiding business."

Given this campaign, observers expected policies to favor "entrenched vested interests that would slow down controversial economic reforms" (*Financial Times* 1997). A week before election day, Kim even took out front-page newspaper ads promising to renegotiate an International Monetary Fund (IMF) austerity package if elected, which was "seen as a ploy to please an electorate worried that the IMF package would cause massive job layoffs" (Chandler 1997a). Academic experts did not expect Kim to tone down his anti-IMF rhetoric after the election. Overall, the campaign did little to dispel Kim's image as a populist (Baker 1997; Mi-young 1997).

Nonetheless, almost immediately after the election – and even months before his inauguration – Kim "partly reversed himself" (*New York Times* 1997) and signaled a change of course (Agence France Presse 1997b). He used meetings with outgoing administration advisors "as a pretext to commit his new government fully to the IMF's harsh recovery program and to ditch an unrealistic election promise that he could stimulate the economy into full recovery within 18 months" (Chandler 1997b). Kim's one-week conversion suggests considerable dissimulation on the campaign trail, given that immediately after the election he proposed a "sweeping package of monetary policy and financial market reforms" (Chandler 1997b), including labor-market flexibility in exchange for an IMF bailout. Not surprisingly, Kim's supporters regarded this turn-around as traitorous (Agence France Presse 1997a; Alford 1997).

Prominent Examples That Are *Not* Switches

Two well-known cases might be thought of as switches but actually are not, at least by our definition: France after the 1981 election and New Zealand in 1984. In May 1981 French Socialist leader François Mitterrand won election as president. Less than six weeks later the Socialist party smashed its rivals in the parliamentary elections, winning 269 of 491 seats. Finally given the chance to put their ideas into practice, Mitterrand and his party initially made a hard left turn, nationalizing important industries and aggressively using fiscal policy to pump up France's economy.

Unfortunately for the Socialists, this strategy backfired badly and by 1983 Mitterrand had abandoned it (Schmidt 1996). This "Great U-turn" is clearly a policy-reversal, but it is not an example of a policy-switch, because Mitterrand campaigned as a socialist, *and earnestly tried to govern as a socialist.* In our view as well as Stokes's, a policy-switch suggests that a president or prime minister makes no real attempt to follow through on his or her campaign promises. Mitterrand reversed course only in the face of evidence that his policies were not working; policy-switching requires no such evidence. Moreover, Mitterrand only switched after almost two years in office; our definition (which follows Stokes's) requires switching after six months or less.

A second "nonexample" comes from New Zealand. In 1984, the Labour Party defeated the incumbent National government and imme-diately embarked upon a radical program of economic liberalization that contradicted the party's long-standing programmatic reputation. In a very short time, New Zealand moved from having one of the most protected economies among the rich countries to having one of the world's most open economies. Much of the literature on New Zealand (e.g. Bollard 1994; Nagel 1998) refers to this move as a violation of Labour's manifesto commitments and points to public-opinion evidence that suggests voters believed that Labour had broken its promises.

However, our review of the campaign – as well as our ability to place this campaign in perspective of hundreds of other cases – suggests that Labour was *vague* about its commitments on the campaign trail and on several occasions even suggested to voters that a difficult period of eco-nomic adjustment would lie ahead. For example, the then-shadow (and future) finance minister, Roger Douglas, had even authored a book enti-tled *There's Got to Be a Better Way* (Douglas 1980) that sharply criti-cized the National Party's welfare-oriented policies and openly advocated "efficiency-oriented" economic reforms. Thus, while the government that came to power indeed implemented policies at variance with the long-standing reputation of the Labour Party, it is not a case of a policy-switch because the party's 1984 campaign gave voters no clear indication that it was committed to maintaining economic "security" policies.

Policy-Switches around the World

Let us now turn to the analysis of policy-switching. We were unable to classify 62 of the 401 campaigns (15.5% of the total) in our data-base as either "efficiency-oriented" or "security-oriented" because the campaign was vague (as in the New Zealand case sketched above) or because we lacked sufficient information.[14] This leaves us with 339 cases in which we could determine whether candidates had switched or not after winning office.[15] As noted, we consider a case to be a policy-switch only if the government reneged relatively quickly on its campaign position, consistent with Stokes's definition (2001, 43). We took this to mean "within six months of inauguration." If a government changes policy after six months, one could reasonably argue that conditions had shifted sufficiently that the government was reacting to events (as in the case of Mitterrand) and perhaps acting in response to public opinion. Of our 339 cases, we found 27 policy-switches (8% of the total),[16] listed in Table 8.1. We do not break semi-presidential systems into the two subtypes because of small sample sizes.[17] The total number of security-oriented campaigns is 66, or 19.5% of the total; all of the switches except for one came following security-oriented campaigns (see below).[18]

Our findings reveal that policy-switching is rare but by no means unique to Latin America or to pure presidential systems.[19] Six policy-switches

---

[14] Stokes could not classify 6 of the 44 elections held between 1982 and 1995 in Latin America (13.6%), for similar reasons.

[15] Thus, both our analysis and that of Stokes preclude analysis of "strategic ambiguity" on the part of prospective presidents *or* prime ministers. This merits additional exploration.

[16] For the Latin American cases, our classifications agree with Stokes's in every case except one: Colombia 1982, which Stokes classified as a switch and we do not. President Betancur campaigned on a security-oriented platform and was elected in May 1982. We found no evidence that he switched policies within six months of taking office; media coverage indicates that Betancur continued the "security-oriented" policies after he took office. For example, in November 1982 the *Washington Post* called Betancur a "populist" (Diehl 1982). A December 2 *New York Times* article indicated no change in the president's policies (*New York Times* 1982). Echoing his "populist" appeal, in November Betancur warned that he might resort to nationalizations in an attempt to stabilize the economy (*Latin America Weekly Report*, November 19, 1982). It is true that a year later, Betancur was forced by changing circumstances to adopt heterodox policies to combat an economic downturn. Nevertheless, he continued to resist orthodox shock therapy. Betancur does not qualify in Stokes's sense as a policy-switcher because he did not switch from "security" to "efficiency" policies within the first six months of his administration and only partially switched due to changing circumstances. Of course, including Betancur in our analysis would only bolster support for our hypothesis.

[17] In semi-presidential subtypes we found only one switch in a president-parliamentary system: Peru 1990. Our data include only 26 elections under president-parliamentary systems, compared with 95 for premier-presidential systems. The percentages by regime-type that we report below would hardly change if we reported on only premier-presidential systems.

[18] The exception is Germany 1998.

[19] Another recognized difficulty with this kind of analysis is that we do not measure policy-switches that were attempted but that failed or switches that were desired but were not attempted – but the same could be said of Stokes.

TABLE 8.1. *Policy-Switches Worldwide, 1978–2002*

Country	Year	System
Argentina	1989	PRES
Australia	1983	PARL
Bolivia	1989	PRES
Costa Rica	1990	PRES
Costa Rica	1994	PRES
Dominican Republic	1982	PRES
Dominican Republic	1990	PRES
Ecuador	1988	PRES
Ecuador	1992	PRES
Ecuador	1996	PRES
Ecuador	2002	PRES
France	1995	SEMI-PRES[a]
France	1997	SEMI-PRES[b]
Germany	1998	PARL
Greece	1981	PARL
Greece	1985	PARL
India	1991	PARL
Ireland	1987	SEMI-PRES[b]
Korea	1997	PRES
Panama	1994	PRES
Moldova	1996	SEMI-PRES[a]
Moldova	2001	PARL
Peru	1990	SEMI-PRES[c]
Poland	1993	SEMI-PRES[b]
Romania	1992	SEMI-PRES[c]
Venezuela	1988	PRES
Venezuela	1993	PRES

Notes regarding election type in semi-presidential systems:
a. Nonconcurrent presidential election.
b. Nonconcurrent legislative election.
c. Concurrent presidential and legislative elections.

occurred in parliamentary systems, and 7 in semi-presidential systems, in addition to the 14 in presidential systems. For semi-presidential systems, because both presidential and parliamentary elections may be a path to government change, notes at the bottom of Table 8.1 indicate which type of election preceded a switch: four followed presidential elections

TABLE 8.2. *Frequency of Policy-Switching, 1978–2002, All Cases*

	Switches	Total Cases	%
Parliamentary	6	157	3.8
Semi-Presidential	7	99	7.1
Presidential	14	83	16.9

(including two cases of concurrent elections) and three followed non-concurrent parliamentary elections. Of the latter subset, two followed elections that resulted in cohabitation (Poland 1993 and France 1997).

Switches by Regime-Type

Table 8.1 makes clear that even in the narrow yet important area of macroeconomic policy, parties do switch policies from time to time under each of the three main democratic institutional formats. Table 8.1 certainly suggests that *more* switches have occurred in presidential systems than in other democratic constitutional frameworks, but it says nothing about the *relative frequency* of policy-switches under different democratic regimes. Table 8.2 provides these relative frequencies by regime-type.

The frequencies tend to conform to our predictions regarding the impact of regime-type. Policy-switching is about four times as likely in presidential systems as in parliamentary systems. Semi-presidential systems occupy a middle ground, seeing switches about twice as often as parliamentary systems, though less than half as often as in presidential systems.

Switches by Campaign Type

Table 8.2 considered all campaigns. However, as noted earlier, all switches except one occurred after a "security-oriented" campaign. Thus in Table 8.3 we repeat the analysis in Table 8.2, but control for the type of campaign by including only security-oriented campaigns. In contrast to the pattern in Table 8.2, the patterns for both semi-presidential and presidential systems converge, with the propensity for switching now almost twice as great in pure and semi-presidentialism as under parliamentarism. Thus, the semi-presidential systems occupy an "intermediate" position in Table 8.2 only because security-oriented campaigns occur somewhat less frequently under semi-presidentialism than under pure presidentialism. Once we control for the type of campaign,

TABLE 8.3. *Frequency of Policy-Switching, Security-Oriented Campaigns Only*

	Switches	Cases (% of total)	% of Subtotal
Parliamentary	5	21 (13.4)	23.8
Semi-Presidential	7	16 (16.2)	43.8
Presidential	14	29 (34.9)	48.3

the propensity to switch turns out to be similar under semi- and pure presidentialism: over 40% of security campaigns under both variants of separated powers result in postelection switches.

Switches by Country Wealth

It is possible that policy-switching is less likely in wealthier countries, perhaps because rich countries see less demand for security-oriented policy promises (because voters better understand that efficiency-oriented adjustments are sometimes necessary) or less need for adjustments (because of more diverse and better managed economies). Thus Tables 8.4 and 8.5 consider the incidence of switches in only middle-income and poorer countries. This exercise also partly controls for the rich-country bias against pure presidentialism: aside from the United States, all the world's richest democracies are parliamentary or semi-presidential. By the same token, removing the richest countries also results in a much more balanced sample across democratic regime-types. However, as the two tables show, the patterns we saw in Tables 8.2 and 8.3 hold up when we remove wealthier countries from the sample. This suggests that country wealth does not help predict whether a country will undergo a switch.

Switches by Region?

If we looked only at Table 8.1, we might conclude that switching was largely a Latin American phenomenon, given that all but one of our presidential policy-switches occurred in Latin America. Yet although security-oriented campaigns *and* switches were common in Latin America,[20] the similar frequency in Table 8.5 of switches from security-oriented campaigns in semi-presidential and pure presidential systems means the economic, cultural, or political factors found only in Latin

---

[20] Among Latin American presidential elections in our sample, 42.4% (28 of 66) featured security campaigns.

TABLE 8.4. *Frequency of Policy-Switching, Excluding the Richest Countries (those with GDP per capita over US$15,000), All Campaigns*

	Switches	Total Cases	%
Parliamentary	4	75	5.3
Semi-Presidential	5	72	6.9
Presidential	14	76	18.4

TABLE 8.5. *Frequency of Policy-Switching, Excluding the Richest Countries (those with GDP per capita over US$15,000), Security-Oriented Campaigns Only*

	Switches	Cases (% of total)	% of Subtotal
Parliamentary	4	14 (18.7)	28.6
Semi-Presidential	5	11 (15.3)	45.5
Presidential	14	29 (38.2)	48.3

America cannot explain the incidence of policy-switching in general. After all, we find semi-presidential systems on every continent on the planet except Australia. Given this, the propensity to switch – regardless of campaign type – cannot be a "Latin" phenomenon.

Predicting Switches from Security-Oriented Campaigns

Our theoretical discussion earlier in this chapter on the intra- and inter-party constraints that parties impose on executives focused on switches without regard for the content of the campaign that preceded the switch. Table 8.2 confirms our primary hypothesis, that switches are most likely in pure presidential systems and least likely in parliamentary systems, with semi-presidential systems occupying an intermediate position. However, Table 8.3 revealed the importance of concentrating on security-oriented campaigns: although such campaigns are most frequent under pure presidentialism, the propensity to switch from security to efficiency policies remains greater under both pure and semi-presidential systems compared to parliamentarism.

For whatever reason, switches from security-oriented campaigns to efficiency-oriented policies were more likely around the world during the time period we explored. We can surely attribute some of this pattern to worldwide trends such as increased globalization and the decline of leftist parties. Under these conditions, advocating populist "security-oriented" policies could still reap votes for some candidates and their parties, but actually implementing such policies grew more difficult. Given a broad set of economic and political conditions, "security to efficiency" switches thus grew common. However, the fact remains that such switches were far more common under certain institutional contexts than others, controlling for country wealth. Let us therefore consider in greater detail why governments in pure and semi-presidential systems are almost twice as likely to switch from a security-oriented campaign as governments in parliamentary systems.

To be clear, we are not seeking to explain why candidates adopt a particular campaign strategy. In fact, regression analyses (not shown) failed to predict security-oriented campaigns. At present we lack a way to predict what causes security campaigns, even in our global sample. We thus agree with Stokes, who argued the likelihood that some candidates who end up switching are dissimulating while others truly believe they will implement security policies but then find that conditions make such policies unwise. Instead, what we want to do is predict, once a candidate has campaigned on security-oriented policies, whether that candidate will switch. Our large dataset – almost 340 campaigns, about 20% of which were security-oriented – makes this investigation feasible in a way that has not been possible before, including for Stokes. As suggested earlier, two variables are particularly important: the competiveness of the election for chief executive, and the postelection legislative status of the chief executive's party.

The Impact of Electoral Competitiveness

Stokes suggested that electoral competitiveness might predict switches. She argued that tighter races encourage dissimulation while big leads encourage politicians to truthfully reveal their future proposals (Stokes 2001, 58). Her results on this variable were ambiguous, but our larger and more diverse sample makes it possible to test our own version of this hypothesis, which is that tighter races would be associated with a greater propensity to switch policies *only in presidential contests*. Because presidential candidates are delegated considerable discretion to shape their own campaigns – a key aspect of our definition of presidentialized parties – they may be less revealing of their future plans when they fear that doing so might jeopardize their chances of winning the election.

TABLE 8.6. *Margin of Victory (%) and 95% Confidence Interval in Switch and Non-Switch Elections, by Election and Regime-Type, All Campaigns*

Switch or No Switch	Presidential Elections, Pure Presidential Systems	Presidential Elections, including Semi-Presidential	Parliamentary Systems
No Switch	11.9 (9.5–14.3)	15.1 (12.4–17.7)	8.7 (6.6–10.7)
Switch	6.8 (3.5–10.0)	8.6 (4.9–12.4)	13.7 (0.9–26.5)
Significance of Difference	.03	.03	.17

TABLE 8.7. *Margin of Victory (%) and 95% Confidence Interval in Switch and Non-Switch Elections, by Election and Regime-Type, Security-Oriented Campaigns*

	Presidential Elections in Pure Presidential Systems	Presidential Elections, including Semi-Presidential	Elections in Parliamentary Systems
No Switch	15.4 (9.0–21.7)	14.8 (9.3–20.3)	9.4 (2.1–17.8)
Switch	6.8 (3.5–10.0)	8.6 (4.9–12.4)	15.3 (−0.8–31.4)
Significance of Difference	.01	.03	.17

Table 8.6 offers support for this hypothesis: policy-switches indeed are more likely to follow close presidential elections in both pure and semi-presidential systems.[21] In contrast, switches are less likely in parliamentary systems following a close election, though the effect is not statistically significant. In Table 8.7 we repeat the analysis on the subsample of security campaigns. The results again support our hypothesis: closer presidential elections are more likely to result in switches, but no such relationship exists in parliamentary systems.

Why does margin have no impact in parliamentary systems?[22] Part of the answer lies in the much greater range of margins in parliamentary systems, which derives directly from institutional variables. In presidential systems, negative margins are rare: they can happen only where

---

[21] In the case of two-round systems we take the votes from the decisive round.

[22] Margin also does not matter in legislative elections in semi-presidential systems, a result we do not show here.

electoral institutions permit a candidate to win who does not obtain even a plurality of the vote, as with the US electoral college in 2000 or in Bolivia, where the legislature may select as president a candidate other than the plurality winner of the popular vote. In parliamentary elections, on the other hand, it is common for parties other than the largest to obtain the premiership as a result of a coalition or via an informal support agreement under a minority cabinet.[23] This means that "competitiveness," measured as margin of victory, simply does not mean the same thing in parliamentarism as it does in systems with popular presidential elections, regardless of the nature of the legislative party system.[24] Because parties in parliamentary systems can and frequently do win the premiership even by "losing" the election, the incentives either to dissimulate or tell the truth on the campaign trail will differ. And in any case, the prima facie incentives to tell the truth are much stronger in parliamentary systems to begin with, due to the weaker adverse selection problems we highlighted in earlier chapters.[25]

[23] The greater tendency of negative margins for the incoming executive is clear from summaries of the data distribution. The mean *margin* of victory in all our data is 11.2 (standard deviation 12.9, range −25.1 to 64.4). In presidential systems the mean is 11.0 (standard deviation 9.3, range −3.4 to 37.0), while in parliamentary systems the mean is 8.8 (standard deviation 12.9, range −25.1 to 56.8).

[24] Negative margins occur in some parliamentary elections under first-past-the-post or alternative-vote electoral systems when the party with the second most votes wins the most seats. Nonetheless, most negative margins in our data are cases of coalition governments led by parties other than the largest.

[25] It is theoretically plausible that under certain conditions in parliamentary systems, competitive races for an anticipated majority would have a similar effect as competitive races for a presidency – in particular, if the system were a two-party system. Indeed, at least three of the five switches in parliamentary systems following security campaigns took place under essentially two-party competition for the premiership: Greece in 1981 and 1985 (elections won with a majority by PASOK – the Panhellenic Socialist Movement – against a single main competitor, New Democracy) and Australia 1983 (when a Labor majority replaced a previous majority by the Liberal–National Coalition). Another similar case is the Congress Party's return to power in India (albeit with less than a majority) in 1991. The fifth case is Moldova in 2001, where the Communist Party was hegemonic, having won by a margin of 36.8 percentage points over its closest competitor. All of these cases support our hypothesis except Moldova, but small sample sizes prevent testing this argument statistically for parliamentary systems. Note that this suggestion does not indicate that switches should be a function of party-system "size" in all democratic regimes – only in parliamentary systems. In elections with direct presidential elections, it is not the number of significant legislative parties but the competitiveness of the *presidential* election that influences switches. This means that dissimulation is not necessarily more likely under separate powers systems – only when *presidential* races are competitive. Since this happens frequently, dissimulation should happen more frequently.

Our findings suggest that the competitive context of popular presidential elections makes policy-switches more likely. Although we were unable to predict when executive candidates or their parties would choose one type of campaign or the other, we would certainly expect that competition to win a national plurality or majority would force parties to search for electorally appealing platforms even if they had no real intention of implementing them, simply to gain the necessary number of votes. And we would certainly expect such a result to be even *more* likely when the candidates campaigning to implement such policies were far less accountable to their principal, the party. This is, as noted in Chapter 2, part of our definition of "presidentialization." The logic of presidentialization suggests that close competition – as captured by electoral margins – makes it more likely that a candidate will campaign on policies he or she (once elected as executive) is unable or willing to implement.[26]

The Impact of Legislative Status

Earlier we suggested that presidents who lack legislative majorities would be least constrained, whereas the incentives would be reversed for prime ministers, who would be most constrained when in a coalition or a minority-government situation. We thus predict that policy-switches would be more likely for minority presidents and less likely for minority prime ministers. In Table 8.8 we provide a breakdown of the frequency of policy-switches by regime-type, by majority or minority situation, and by type of campaign.

When all campaigns are considered, the expectations follow our predictions. However, the only statistically significant difference in the frequency of switches appears between majority and minority situations in semi-presidential systems, where all of the switches occurred when the executive lacked an assembly majority. When we consider only security-oriented campaigns, the frequency of switches also follows our hypothesis, and the differences are statistically significant in each of the three

[26] The data in Tables 8.6 and 8.7 also hint at a potential reason that security campaigns are less common in semi-presidential systems: the average margin of presidential elections is significantly higher in semi-presidential systems (20.0%) than in pure presidentialism (11.0%). This difference seems unlikely to be a product of the regime-type, per se. Nonetheless, if we are on the right track to suggest that switches are more likely when a close presidential race has encouraged dissimulation, then observed differences in margins across these two regime-types may explain at least part of the lower frequency of security campaigns (as shown in Table 8.3) in semi-presidential systems, compared to pure presidential. This notion could be tested only with data from future campaigns.

TABLE 8.8. *Switches by Regime-Type, Legislative Status of Executive, and Campaign Type*

Executive Status in Assembly	Presidential		Semi-Presidential		Parliamentary	
	All Campaigns	Security Campaigns	All Campaigns	Security Campaigns	All Campaigns	Security Campaigns
Majority Party	.11 (2 of 19)	.20 (2 of 10)	.00 (0 of 22)	.00 (0 of 3)	.06 (4 of 68)	.36 (4 of 11)
Minority Party	.19 (12 of 62)	.63 (12 of 19)	.10 (7 of 74)	.54 (7 of 13)	.02 (2 of 89)	.10 (1 of 10)
Significant Difference?	No	Yes (at 98% confidence)	Yes (at 93% confidence)	Yes (at 95% confidence)	No	Yes (at 91% confidence)

regime-types. In pure presidential systems, switches occurred in 63% of the cases of security-oriented campaigns that preceded a presidential minority government, while they occurred only 20% of the time when the president's party had a majority after a security-oriented campaign. For semi-presidential systems, switches occurred in 7 of the 13 cases of security-oriented campaigns that preceded a government in which the president's party lacked a majority.

Turning to parliamentary systems, we expect the relationship between legislative status of the executive and policy-switching to be reversed: more switches should follow security campaigns when the prime minister's party controls a majority. This is what we find: just over one-third of majorities result in switches, against only 1 of 10 cases of no majority after a security-oriented campaign.[27] Indeed, while the sample is small, the difference is significant at 91% confidence. With so few cases of either security campaigns or switches under parliamentarism, we must be cautious with these results, but they are at least consistent with our theoretical expectations.

Part of the problem with teasing out the sources of policy-switches in semi-presidential systems is because single-party majorities in such regimes are so rare. In any case, the more important "legislative status" consideration for semi-presidential systems may be whether there is cohabitation. As noted, two of our seven switches in semi-presidential systems occurred under cohabitation: Poland in 1993 and France in 1997. Our sample in this chapter includes 15 cases of cohabitation, 11 of which, like these 2 switches, followed a legislative election. In both switches under cohabitation, the next election in the cycle was a presidential election – a looming event that might make switching more likely, even when initiated by a newly elected premier who is in opposition to the incumbent president. With only 15 cases of cohabitation – and none of single-party majority – we are unable to test whether cohabitation or minority status of the president's party is relatively more important. Regardless, the results suggest that our theoretical reasoning about the differential impact of legislative status under fused or separated powers

---

[27] In fact, the only case of a switch made by a coalition government in a parliamentary system is also the one case of a switch following an *efficiency* campaign. After Germany's 1998 election, the Social Democratic Party formed a coalition with the Green Party. Our reading of contemporary accounts suggests that the coalition may have been a key factor in producing the switch to security policies. All other switches in parliamentary systems were made by single-party governments, only one of which (India 1991) had less than a majority of seats.

is on the right track: when the president's party lacks a majority in the assembly, a policy-switch is more likely.

The Impact of Economic Factors

It may seem commonsensical that economic factors should influence the frequency of policy-switches, but our analysis suggests that the institutional and partisan factors we have considered swamp economic factors. Stokes hypothesized that we ought to see policy-switching in economic crises (Stokes 2001, 97). We thus estimated multivariate regression equations including both economic and political variables. We use the percentage real growth of GDP in the year of the election if the election was held in the third or fourth quarters of the year, and GDP growth in the year prior to the election if the election was held in the first or second quarters, and we also considered the impact of inflation in the current quarter as well as the four quarters prior to the election. In addition, building on the hypothesis we considered earlier, we also explored whether poorer countries (*per capita GDP*) and those more exposed to international markets (*trade as a % of GDP* and *foreign direct investment as a % of GDP*) are more likely to see policy-switches.[28] If these factors were associated with policy-switching, they would predict a switch anywhere in the world.

However, we found that *none* of these variables predicted a switch in a global sample, strongly suggesting that institutional differences between parliamentary and pure and semi-presidential systems are far more important.[29] We do not show the results because they come with a large caveat: we could not generate *any* significant statistical results for semi-presidential systems, on any variable. Unfortunately, it is impossible to estimate the impact of political and economic variables in semi-presidential systems because all switches in those regimes occurred under minority government. Given this "perfect prediction," the statistical program drops all semi-presidential cases from analysis. Additional statistical analysis must await accumulation of more campaigns – and more policy-switches – in semi-presidential systems, or explore a different manifestation of mandate representation across democratic regimes.

---

[28] Data for all of these variables came from World Bank (2007).

[29] Following Stokes, we also tested for the impact of *Age* of the prime minister's or president's party, and *Years* since a country's transition to democracy, to explore the hypothesis that switches are associated with less-institutionalized parties or party systems. Neither of these variables had any impact.

Yet even given this caveat, our results clearly point to the impact of variation in democratic regime-type on the likelihood of policy-switching.

CONCLUSION

Traditional notions of "responsible party government" and of parties' ability to serve as citizens' agents in government include both the enactment of new policies and the preservation of established policies. Parties' promises to do both – through efforts to establish and maintain a collective reputation – are viewed as the key to their survival and as the main normative criterion by which we should judge whether party government is operating successfully.

To what extent can parties fulfill their promises under different constitutional regimes? For parliamentary systems, the conventional conceptualization of democratic representation assumes that the executive and legislative branches of political parties always act in unison – on the campaign trail as well as in government. Yet following Shugart and Carey (1992); Manin, Przeworski, and Stokes (1999); Stokes (2001); and Samuels and Shugart (2003), we argued that political parties in pure and semi-presidential systems are unlikely, under most conditions, to act as voters' representational agents as they do in parliamentary systems. Indeed, voters can expect members of a party who occupy the executive and legislative branches of a presidential system to represent their interests in different ways. Among other things, this implies weaker mandate consistency in systems in which executives enjoy separate origin and survival.

Stokes (2001) considered whether parties' organizational "strength" – their cohesiveness and ability to maintain their brand name – is associated with mandate representation. Her findings confounded conventional scholarly wisdom because she found no connection at all between party strength and mandate representation: leaders of both weak *and* strong parties engaged in policy-switches. We agree that parties would not grow more "responsible" if politicians were to suddenly heed scholarly exhortations to strengthen parties' organizations and roots in society. Mandate violations occur under both strong and weak parties, across all democratic systems. However, they occur far more frequently under certain conditions in pure and semi-presidential systems – the situations that maximize divergence between the members of the executive and legislative branches of a single party. The implications of this finding are important: *the roots of "responsible parties" do not lie with parties per se, but with the way the separation of powers impacts political parties under particular party-system configurations.*

Policy-switches are thus not a function of a simple dichotomy between "parliamentary" and "not parliamentary" systems, but of the interaction between the regime-type, the party system, and the way in which intra-party politics differs under different regimes. Political representation differs across democratic regimes because institutional context makes the parties different. Where incentives between branches of a single party overlap, policy consistency is likely – even under pure presidentialism. Yet incentive incompatibility is more likely under the separation of origin and survival, because parties cannot control their agents either on the campaign trail or in office. When parties cannot control their agents, they cannot hold them to the party's stated platform – and that's when you'll see switches.

Specifically, parties – or at least their leaders – do switch, under common situations in separate-powers systems: close presidential elections and minority government. In close presidential elections, parties delegate the most discretion to their candidate to shape the campaign, to maximize the chances of winning. And under minority government, presidents are most free to choose coalition partners and push policy independently. These two conditions maximize the core feature of presidentialization that we have emphasized throughout this book: a political party in which the executive is an unreliable agent. Under parliamentarism, analogous situations are inconceivable. Indeed, we found no effect of competitiveness on policy-switching under parliamentarism – and as for legislative party size, we found that switches are more likely when prime ministers have a *majority* in parliament.

In this chapter we attempted to reconceptualize how we think of representation across different democratic regimes. Representation – the links between citizens and elected officials – involves different processes given different constitutional structures, so perhaps it should come as no surprise that the quality of representation also differs under presidential, semi-presidential, or parliamentary government. What might be surprising is the relative lack of scholarly research confronting this issue. We hope this chapter provides useful direction for future research, since our analysis of policy-switches in macroeconomic policy has merely scratched the surface of the ways in which political representation differs across democratic regimes.

9

Conclusion

Constitutional systems with directly elected executives now comprise a majority of all democracies around the globe. However, the comparative study of political parties remains conceptually wedded to the European experience with parliamentary democracy. The notion that parties might be "presidentialized" is not, of course, new. In fact, the trend toward presidentialization identified in some of the literature (e.g. Poguntke and Webb eds. 2005a, 2005b) reflects a long-standing scholarly concern with parties' deafness to popular demands. This particular concern has deep roots, even in the West European parliamentary context – it goes back at least to Michels (1911 [1962]) if not before, and in some ways is also an extension of Kirchheimer's (1966) lament about the emergence of catch-all parties.

We do not deny that Parliamentary parties can become "presidentialized" in one sense, by becoming increasingly reliant on an individual leader. This too is not a new concern; Max Weber famously made this specific point in the early 20th century, pointing out that the problem had characterized 19th-century British parties (Weber 1958 [1919], 103–07). Clearly, political parties have failed to live up to the high standards scholars set for them ever since they have existed. Yet this reliance on an individual leader is more accurately identified as *personalization* than as presidentialization, and our notion of presidentialization differs fundamentally from the concept of personalization. In our view, parties in parliamentary systems can never become truly presidentialized because the fusion of electoral origin and survival gives parties tools to minimize both adverse selection and moral hazard problems. Parliamentary parties can pick different kinds of candidates – candidates with different skills, interests, and goals – than parties in presidential systems, and they can fire leaders who do not live up to expectations.

It is worth noting that the notion of personalization is well known in the literature on legislative parties: it describes candidates who enjoy some personal reputation distinct from their party's collective reputation (Cain et al. 1987; Cox and McCubbins 1993; Carey and Shugart 1995). By extension, as we noted in Chapter 5, the idea of personalization can be applied fruitfully to executives and their parties. However, presidentialization means something more than personalization. A president is not simply a strong personality with a reputation distinct from that of his or her party. He or she is an official who heads a branch of political authority constitutionally separate from the legislature. It is in this sense that we have employed the concept of presidentialization – to illuminate the transformations that parties undergo when they compete not only for legislative seats, but also for a separately elected and separately surviving executive.

At the core of this book is the question of how political parties organize and behave when they must bridge the gap between the legislature and the executive. When constitutional design pushes parties down a path to control of (or a share in) the executive branch that does not pass exclusively through the legislature, it also requires parties to place their faith in an individual candidate for a separate and powerful office. This institutional context means that collective, organizational control over that candidate, once elected, cannot be guaranteed. And it further implies that the party must downplay the importance of the collective representation that is the hallmark of parties' legislative organization and behavior. The key question is, What difference does this sort of party presidentialization make?

We have argued that the internal collective action and delegation problems that political parties face vary as a function of differences in the executive-legislative structure of government. This argument has wide-ranging implications. Most broadly, this book suggests that many of the alleged differences in governance between democratic regimes – between presidentialism and parliamentarism, for example – are not a function of regime-type per se but are a function of the ways in which political parties function under different democratic regimes. The interactions to which we have called attention are not with the *number* of parties, as much previous research has claimed, but with their *nature* – the ways they organize and behave. This in turn suggests that the literature on presidents and assemblies in comparative politics has jumped the conceptual gun, because one cannot meaningfully consider the potential clash of incentives across separate branches of government without first considering the potential clash of incentives across branches of political parties.

These incentives come into conflict because of the ways democratic constitutions shape executive and legislative authority. Parliamentary constitutions offer parties comparatively simple and easy mechanisms of intraparty accountability, minimizing moral hazard. Because the executive emerges from the parliamentary majority, intraparty politics directly determines *who* runs the government as well as *how* those people run the government. Thus when parties select their agents from within their own top ranks and maintain effective control over those agents after they ascend to the top executive position, we can speak of parliamentarized parties. In contrast, to the extent that parties delegate discretion to agents who may have been selected for characteristics unrelated to their faithfulness to the party itself and who cannot be recalled, we can speak of presidentialized parties. To the extent that a separately elected presidency matters for any of the things that parties seek – votes, office, or policy – then the separation of powers does not merely split one branch from the other; it splits parties *internally*, posing particular dilemmas for members of the same party who occupy or seek to occupy different branches of government.

Our findings suggest that parties rarely reunite what constitutions divide. The separation of origin and survival shapes party strategy about whom to nominate for both executive and legislative office, whether or not to form electoral and/or governing coalitions, the content of electoral campaigns, and the content of and degree of support for executive policy proposals. Incentive incompatibility between branches of a political party can emerge in all types of parties, irrespective of ideological profile or social base, and regardless of the "type" of leader (insider or outsider). The breadth of the gap between party branches can also vary over time within a particular party, suggesting that parties' efforts to bridge the separation of powers are only inconsistently effective.

Indeed, presidents' insulation from intraparty deselection relative to prime ministers suggests that presidents may often engineer a de facto reversal of the party-executive principal-agent relationship. That is, presidents may come to control parties for their own purposes. We saw this most clearly in Chapter 8. As party scholars from Woodrow Wilson (1908) to Susan Stokes (2001) have suggested and our research confirms (at least for one measure), the roots of "responsible parties" do not lie with the parties per se. It is not, for example, a matter of the strength or weakness of the party as an organization, but rather the way the separation of powers impacts parties, under particular party-system configurations. By implication, the nature and quality of interest representation differ across democratic regimes. Where there is little incentive incompatibility between branches of a political party, policy responsibility and mandate consistency is likely. Yet where the separation of origin and survival generates incentive incompatibility and moral hazard problems, irresponsible parties are the likely result.

Responsible parties as conceived in the literature cannot exist under the separation of powers. This is an important point in light of recent developments in US party politics. The dramatic decrease in what we termed "electoral separation of purpose" in the United States in the early years of the 21st century does not suggest that parliamentarized "responsible" parties have suddenly emerged. It is true that overlapping executive and legislative constituencies are a necessary feature of responsible parties, but low electoral separation of purpose is just one of the ways parties might bridge separately elected institutions. Quite apart from the fact that the relatively low levels of electoral separation of purpose in recent US elections (e.g. ESP for the Republicans = 10.98 in 2004) remain short of the total fusion (ESP = 0.00) of parliamentarism, these other indicators remind us that the increased discipline and polarization of US parties do not imply responsible or parliamentarized parties.

For example, both scholarly and popular critiques of George W. Bush's presidency decried the increased use of unilateral executive powers (and not only in security and foreign affairs – see Cooper 2005) alongside the increased use of congressional "earmarks" in allocation of spending items.[1] *Neither* of these is a typical concern of parliamentary parties that resemble the responsible-parties ideal: prime ministers' powers are necessarily shared with their cabinet colleagues (Lijphart 1994) and members of parliament typically enjoy few opportunities to claim credit for special favors outside of the party's more general policies. However, if US presidents can use their "primary proposer power" to target spending to favored districts (Berry, Burden, and Howell 2009), they may be

---

[1] The NGO Citizens against Government Waste, for example, records a greater than 50% increase in what it defines as "pork-barrel spending" from 2001 to 2006, and then a sharp drop after the 2006 congressional elections resulted in divided government. See http://www.cagw.org/site/PageServer?pagename=reports_porkbarrelreport#trends (accessed March 29, 2009).

able to make their parties *responsible to the president* rather than the other way around, as parliamentarization would imply.

Consider also that had George W. Bush been a prime minister in a parliamentary system, he never would have survived in office as long as he did. The separation of survival cost the Republicans' presidential candidate and congressional candidates dearly in the 2008 elections.

Finally, consider the fact that it did not take long into Barack Obama's administration for journalists to note that the new president's priorities were overshadowing the preferences of his own party's legislative leaders (e.g. Nicholas 2009). Despite all the changes that US party politics has undergone toward more cohesive and ideological profiles and more consistent cross-branch electoral constituencies, both parties remain clearly dependent upon an unaccountable presidency to advance their goals. This remains the case even though US presidents possess notably weaker formal powers than their counterparts in other pure (and many semi-) presidential systems (Shugart and Carey 1992; Alemán and Schwartz 2006; Tsebelis and Rizova 2007).

Of course, many parties in separation of powers systems exhibit high electoral separation of purpose. They explicitly seek to work within the incentives the system offers and take a path that is by definition unavailable in pure parliamentary systems by gaining votes in legislative and executive races from distinct pools of voters. We saw a striking example of high separation of purpose in Brazil's Workers' Party in 2006: where the party's president gained votes in his successful reelection bid, the party's congressional candidates performed poorly. A party with such limited electoral reach for its legislative candidates would be unlikely to win control over the executive branch in a parliamentary system, a point that only underscores another way that parties can be presidentialized: rather than have a presidential candidate whose popularity and "coattails" generate low electoral separation of purpose, a party can instead have a presidential candidate who builds an almost entirely separate electoral constituency that far transcends the electoral appeal of the party itself!

The point is that party "responsibility" is not a function of cohesiveness or low electoral separation of purpose. To the extent that a political party depends on its presidential leader's electoral and governing success, it cannot be a "responsible" party as Woodrow Wilson or V. O. Key would have understood the term. It is instead a presidentialized party, because it must subordinate its collective pursuits to a single leader who remains unaccountable. The lack of intraparty leadership accountability is a critical implication of our theoretical framework: to the extent that presidents are unaccountable to their own co-partisans, Madison had it wrong in *Federalist #51*: constitutional checks and balances do not result in "ambition countering ambition" but rather in an agent's ambition running wild. The success of a system of checks and balances in preventing tyranny – whether of a majority or of a single powerful leader – thus depends crucially on factors Madison failed to consider: leaders' personalities and intraparty norms and rules, rather than the interparty balance of power, or what Madison termed the "factional" balance of power.[2]

We can forgive Madison this omission because political parties did not exist in his time. However, contemporary scholars who offer twists on Madisonian theories of representation, accountability, and policymaking have failed to appreciate the implications of differences in intraparty politics across democratic regimes. In saying that scholars of political institutions may have jumped the conceptual gun we do not mean to engage in finger-pointing, simply because we might not like what we see in the mirror – see Shugart and Carey (1992), Samuels (2007), or Samuels and Shugart (2003), for example. This book is an effort to bridge the literature on parties and on constitutional design. Neither literature has fully come to grips with the impact of the separation of powers on parties.

By saying that the prevention of tyranny depends on factors Madison failed to consider we are also saying that in modern democracy, constitutional structure shapes the way and extent to which parties can fulfill the key tasks that theorists of democracy assign to them – channeling citizens' interests into government and giving citizens the possibility of holding government to account. Presidentialized parties suffer from an intraparty accountability deficit. Theorists of democracy in the pluralist tradition such as Schumpeter (1942), Dahl (1971), Bobbio (1989), and Sartori (1987) tend to downplay or simply ignore intraparty politics (Van Biezen 2004, 10). Instead, they conclude that the key to democracy lies with maintaining an *inter*party balance of power. No matter how they organized themselves, as long as more than two "teams" of politicians

---

[2] In any case, as Kernell (2003) notes and we discussed in Chapter 2, Madison originally formulated the theory of factional balance before he and his colleagues in the Constitutional Convention had invented separate origin and survival of the executive. The notion of factional balance thus applied to a proposed constitutional design that more resembled what today is understood as parliamentary government than presidentialism.

compete regularly for power – and would relinquish power if voted out – the system was democratic. Everything else was superfluous detail (Schmitter and Karl 1991).

Yet even within the theory of democracy embodied by the line of argument traced from Schumpeter through Schmitter and Karl, our findings suggest that not all parties fulfill the "minimalist" criteria of democracy similarly. For one, it is not at all obvious that we should assume that parties act as unitary actors in presidential systems. And even if we can, to the extent that presidents *reverse* the principal-agent relationship, the dynamics of intraparty politics clearly differ across systems. A "responsible" party, after all, requires that the executive be responsible to the party and not the other way around – and certainly cannot allow executives and their parties to go their separate ways. In addition, voters have different opportunities to hold government to account in different systems. In parliamentary regimes, citizens very often do not have a chance to express their views about executive performance, precisely because the executive depends both on partisan and assembly confidence (Chapter 4). Parties can and do punish poorly performing executives in the hope that voters will *not* punish them at the next elections. In contrast, under the separation of powers, parties cannot hold their own leader to account; only voters can reward or punish the party's candidates for national executive. Some evidence suggests that the possibility of intraparty accountability under parliamentarism weakens electoral accountability (Hellwig and Samuels 2008). However, it remains unclear whether voters in presidential elections are retrospectively punishing an individual, a party, or both.

In short, the separation of powers creates presidentialized parties, not merely personalized parties. Variation in institutional context generates distinct intraparty dilemmas and dynamics across democratic regimes that have important political consequences for all the activities parties undertake: candidate selection, campaigning to represent citizens' interests, governing. Parliamentary parties can be personalized, but they can never become presidentialized.

SEMI-PRESIDENTIALISM IS MORE PRESIDENTIAL THAN PARLIAMENTARY

Another key implication of this book is that everything we have said above tends to hold true in both pure *and* semi-presidential systems. In this way, our theoretical framework helps explain why the distinction between prime-ministerial "insiders" and presidential "outsiders," as Linz (1994, 26–29) would have it, is untenable. Linz's distinction between insiders and outsiders does appear to hold between the two pure regime-types. However, the distinction is less helpful when applied to semi-presidential regimes, which suggests that the position of president and/or prime minister is not the critical factor that determines the "type" of candidate selected for each office. Instead, the constitutional balance of authority between the two positions is important. Thus in nearly all semi-presidential systems, the existence of a directly elected president tends to "contaminate" the parties, interfering in the principal-agent relationship between parties and their prime-ministerial agents in the legislature.

Given this, prime ministers in semi-presidential democracies have distinctive career paths relative to their counterparts in pure parliamentary systems (Chapter 3). This suggests either that parties care relatively less about adverse selection problems under semi-presidentialism – which seems unlikely – or that presidents play a powerful role in prime-ministerial selection. And as we showed in Chapter 4, semi-presidential regimes also give presidents influence over prime-ministerial deselection. Critically, these findings tend to apply even in premier-presidential systems, in which the premier is formally accountable only to the assembly majority, and not to the president.

Despite the absence of formal accountability of the premier to the president in premier-presidential regimes, our findings also illustrate that a premier in such systems typically becomes the de facto agent of the president, as long as the president's opposition does not control the assembly majority. Indeed, under unified government, premiers frequently become personal representatives of the president within the assembly, rather than co-equals in a dual executive structure. In cases of cohabitation, control over the cabinet clearly shifts to the assembly majority. In the more common situation in which the president's party has a strong legislative contingent – not necessarily a majority – presidents' place in the chain of delegation between parties and prime ministers complicates parties' ability to hold *either* their prime ministers *or* their presidents to account. In a crucial way, presidents' "contamination" of the party–prime minister relationship thus attenuates parties' control over the composition and direction of government.

Our findings suggest that treating semi-presidential systems as largely parliamentary, and the parties within those systems as parliamentarized, is misguided. Politics in most semi-presidential systems is highly presidentialized, most of the time. Weber's and de Gaulle's desire for a president "above" and more powerful than the parties – a temporary elected monarch – has become the norm in hybrid systems. The Irish and Austrian cases of essentially parliamentarized politics are exceptional, and pretending that they are anything but exceptional is wishful thinking. Presidents' *formal* influence in president-parliamentary systems makes this conclusion rather obvious; their *informal* and *partisan* influence in premier-presidential regimes offers additional evidence that one cannot simply equate this subtype with parliamentarism. When presidents' parties and/or allies control the assembly majority, intraparty politics becomes highly presidentialized and we see a reversal of the party-leader principal-agent relationship: the prime minister becomes the *president's* agent, rather than the party's.

PURE TYPES AND HYBRIDS: IMPLICATIONS OF TRENDS IN CONSTITUTIONAL DESIGN

Our theoretical framework and the results it generates also help explain underappreciated aspects of trends in constitutional reforms around the world. Around the year 2000, semi-presidential hybrids came to represent a narrow plurality of all democracies. The spread of this regime-type suggests that politicians frequently seek a "best of both worlds." Hybrid constitutional designs and the ongoing tinkering (or debating about tinkering) within hybrid formats appear to offer politicians the opportunity to balance the advantages of a direct executive agent of the electorate with the parliamentary accountability of the cabinet. However, the results in this book strongly suggest that this "best of both worlds" in terms of executive-legislative structure is a chimera. Premier-presidentialism may approximate this ideal balance, but as noted, it too tends to promote party presidentialization.

We count 15 cases of change of constitutional regime format – including changes from one semi-presidential subtype to the other – since 1946. Obviously the main conclusion one can draw from 15 changes in 88 countries over more than 60 years is that such fundamental alterations of democratic constitutional format are very rare (see also Rahat 2008). Nonetheless, even such small numbers may tell us something about trends in democratic institutional design. Figure 9.1 indicates each reform according to the direction of change across the continuum of regime-types from pure parliamentary through each of the various hybrids to pure presidentialism. Of these 15 reforms, 6 represent shifts

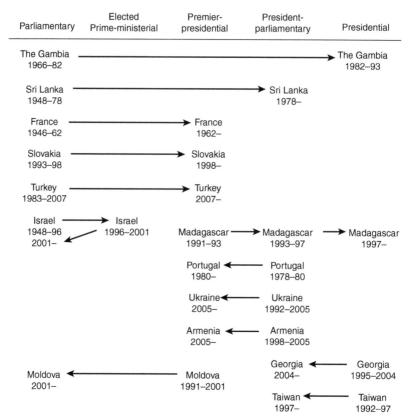

FIGURE 9.1. Reform to the Executive-Legislative Structure of Democratic
Regimes, 1946–2007.
Sources: Alemán and Schwartz (2006); Berry, Burden, and Howell (2009); Cooper
(2005); Nicholas (2009); Rahat (2008); Roper (2008).

away from parliamentarism toward a regime with a directly elected executive; 7 represent a move from one form of presidentialism to another;
and only 2 represent shifts away from a system with a directly elected
executive toward pure parliamentarism.

First, consider the two shifts to pure parliamentarism: Israel, which
we discussed at length in Chapter 6, and Moldova. Moldova's reform
came after the Communist Party regained electoral hegemony following
a period of unstable legislative majorities and nonpartisan presidents.
With the shift to pure parliamentarism, the Communists could ensure
that their chairman would occupy the (unelected) presidency (Roper
2008), eliminating the risk that another party or independent might pre-
vail in a direct popular election. These two countries combined had only

about 15 years of experience under direct elections before shifting (back) to pure parliamentarism, but the other countries in our data have over 1,000 years of accumulated experience with direct executive elections, suggesting a striking empirical regularity: *once adopted, separate executive elections are almost never abandoned.*

Returning to Figure 9.1, we see that apart from Israel's 2 changes and Moldova's 1, there are a total of 12 other structural constitutional reforms: 5 that *enter* one of the categories of separate executive authority and 7 moves *within* the categories of separate powers. The five cases of moves toward separately elected presidents include The Gambia, which is the only case to span the entire space in Figure 9.1, and one case that moved to president-parliamentarism, Sri Lanka. The other three are cases of the adoption of premier-presidentialism: France, Slovakia, and Turkey.[3]

As for the cases of moves from one form of separation of powers to another, having only seven cases restricts our ability to generalize. With that caveat in mind it is striking that only two of these cases – both of which occurred in Madagascar – represent moves toward the "president-dominated" end of the spectrum in Figure 9.1. The other five cases all represent efforts to weaken presidents' formal powers while remaining within a separate-powers framework. These cases deserve further attention, as they represent a desire to limit the presidentializing tendencies we have argued are a fundamental feature of separate-powers systems. Three of these cases switched from president-parliamentarism to premier-presidentialism: Portugal, Ukraine, and Armenia. The other two entered the semi-presidential category from pure presidentialism: Georgia and Taiwan. In these five cases, institutional reforms sought to strengthen the independence of prime ministers vis-à-vis presidents, at least in terms of the formal lines of authority.

Thus Figure 9.1 shows that while we see almost no shifts to parliamentarism and some shifts away from parliamentarism, movement within nonparliamentary cases is almost entirely away from pure presidentialism, toward the "parliamentary" end of the continuum.[4] In light

---

[3] The Turkish move refers to a constitutional amendment passed at the end of 2007, and thus the country did not enter as a semi-presidential system in our analysis of biographical data in Chapters 3 and 4, which concluded with that year.

[4] Still other cases that we know of have seen moves that do not amount to a change of type or subtype but represented either actual moves (in Finland) or serious but failed proposals (in Sri Lanka, for example) to weaken the agency relationship of the presidency over the cabinet within semi-presidential systems.

of these patterns, and anticipating future interest in similar reforms in other presidential or president-parliamentary systems, it is worth asking whether such efforts really "parliamentarize" separate-powers systems. Our research offers a qualified support for premier-presidentialism – the qualification being that parliamentarization is likely to be quite limited even where presidents have relatively weak constitutional authority. After all, we have shown repeatedly that even in premier-presidential systems, the existence of separate origin and survival tends to create fundamentally "presidentialized" parties. There are exceptions, of course, but one should be careful about designing constitutions, or recommending changes, under the assumption that the country in question would be one of the few exceptions.

Still, we do see some potential advantages to premier-presidentialism, one of which is that no premier-presidential democracy has ever been replaced by an authoritarian regime – at least not after having met the criteria we use throughout this book to identify cases of democracy. Each of the other regime-types has experienced democratic collapse.[5]

However, the most important potential advantage is the prospect of cohabitation, which does not necessarily offer parties the "best of both worlds" but at least offers the possibility to oscillate between the presidential and parliamentary worlds (see the discussion in Linz 1994). Under cohabitation, the opposition party (or parties) gains control over the cabinet, the president is relegated to a secondary political position, and the prime minister is no longer an agent of the president but rather of the parliamentary majority – as in pure parliamentarism. Still, any argument in favor of premier-presidentialism should not be based entirely on the possibility of "parliamentarization" as a counterweight to the presidency, because this phase of premier-presidentialism represents only about 20% of the total democratic experience under this format. Moreover, even under cohabitation, considerable presidentialization of the parties remains: the party that holds the premiership has every incentive to seek the presidency at the next opportunity and thus faces the electoral and governing dilemmas of presidentialization that we have detailed.

---

[5] We record breakdowns of parliamentary democracy in Malaysia and Somalia in 1969 and Pakistan in 1999; neither has returned to democracy for five or more years (although Pakistan could be in the process of doing so). Presidential democracy broke down in The Gambia in 1993, without a return thus far. Breakdowns in four other presidential democracies (Brazil 1964, Philippines 1969, Uruguay 1971, Chile 1973) and one president-parliamentary democracy (Peru 1992) have been followed by subsequent redemocratizations.

In short, this book suggests that none of the hybrid formats truly combines the "best of both worlds." Parties in all systems with directly elected executives face dilemmas of adverse selection, incentive incompatibility, and moral hazard. If reformers truly want parliamentarized parties, they should keep or adopt parliamentarism. However, if they want to combine popular election of the executive with parliamentary confidence, they should consider premier-presidentialism over the alternatives. Premier-presidentialism at least gives parties an incentive to bridge the two elected institutions more effectively than pure presidentialism or president-parliamentarism. Party presidentialization tends to occur even under premier-presidentialism, but at least parties in opposition to the president can regain control of the cabinet if an election result or a shift in the interparty balance in parliament allows them to forge a cohabitation situation. Moreover, seeking to avert cohabitation, parties seeking the presidency under premier-presidentialism have relatively weaker incentives to downplay assembly elections as their counterparts do in many president-parliamentary and pure presidential systems.

Premier-presidentialism is also more promising than the elected prime-ministerial hybrid. The adoption of this format in Israel immediately revealed the extent to which separate election forces parties to become presidentialized, even though the elected prime minister remained dependent on parliamentary confidence to survive in office. If constitutional engineers want the perceived advantages of separate election, they are better off with a dual executive, rather than trying to combine features of both presidentialism and parliamentarism in a single executive. We thus concur with Sartori's view that Israel's single-executive hybrid may very well have represented the *worst* of both worlds.[6]

Moreover, despite periodic claims that parliamentarism offers superior government performance in this way or that – a claim scholars have made since at least Woodrow Wilson's day – we also warn against shifts that emulate Moldova's elimination of its elected presidency. Sartori (1994, 112) has argued that the lack of parties with a "parliamentary fit" might make moves to parliamentarism difficult for parties to navigate. That is, although we have argued that parties take on characteristics derived from the executive-legislative structure in which they operate, presidentializing existing parliamentary parties may be much easier than

---

[6] Sartori (quoted in Hazan 2001, 351) called the Israeli system "the most incredibly stupid system ever designed."

parliamentarizing parties that have always operated in a system with a directly elected presidency.

In any case, there is certainly no empirical support for the idea that parliamentarism represents a viable reform option in countries that lack a parliamentary tradition, however desirable scholars may think it would be. Besides, regionally diverse and economically divided societies may simply be more governable with presidentialism of some form (Shugart 1999). Whatever scholars have to say about these issues, the real world has spoken, and it has said that there is an increasing desire over the long sweep of democratization since the middle of the 20th century for systems with separate presidencies. This real-world fact cannot be overlooked, and academic theories have simply not kept up. We have sought to address that gap in this book. If we have a normative case to advance for one pure or hybrid regime-type over another, it is cautiously in favor of premier-presidentialism. However, the case for that hybrid comes with the recognition that having a prime minister and cabinet accountable to the assembly, and even having the formal powers reduce the president's role within the executive, is in no way equivalent to adopting parliamentarism.

THE RESEARCH AGENDA

Our theoretical framework offers several avenues for future research. All else equal, parties that emerge under presidential institutions will face different dilemmas from those of parties in parliamentary systems. To our knowledge, only Leon Epstein (1967) ever addressed this issue, and then only briefly in order to debate Duverger's hypothesis that the "mass" party was the modern norm. We suggest not only that Epstein's insight should hold regardless of the historical context but also that presidentialized parties are the contemporary norm – for institutional, not sociological, reasons. For example, scholars have argued that presidentialism affects the *number* of political parties. To the extent that this argument is true, it is likely that presidentialism also affects the *nature* of political parties – how and why they form and develop, and what their internal politics look like, under different constitutional regimes.

Scholarly explorations of party emergence have not addressed the question of the strategic, "psychological" incentives that presidential elections generate, either in terms of intra- or interparty politics, and whether from the party's or the voter's strategic perspective. For example, given the dominance of presidentialism in many newly emerging party systems and the worldwide decline of the salience of sociocultural cleavages, political scientists could certainly benefit by placing the separation or fusion of powers more centrally in their explanations for party-system emergence and consolidation (see Geddes 2004; Hicken and Stoll 2007).

Similarly, if we accept that presidentialism affects party and party-system emergence, we should also accept the hypothesis that the incentives created by the separation of origin and survival affect parties' organizational evolution. Much of the party-development literature has an organizational sociology bent that pays little attention to the potential impact of electoral and other institutions. Even so, prominent sociologically oriented scholars recognize that institutional environments can affect parties' evolutionary trajectory. Panebianco (1988), for example, held that the shape a party takes early in its development largely explains its later developmental path. If parties take on a "presidential" character, they will retain these characteristics over time – an idea that may go a long way toward explaining why political reforms away from any form of presidentialism to parliamentarism are almost unknown.

Likewise, scholars have yet to consider many of the potential ways that the separation of powers shapes party behavior. To what extent do presidents and their parties go their separate ways? We have some research on the impact of presidents on cabinet composition (e.g. Amorim Neto 2002), but scholars should turn their attention to election campaigns, coalitional strategies, campaign organization, and the allocation of resources. Do presidents and their parties campaign on different issues or themes; receive votes from different groups of voters; or advocate different policies in the legislature? Scholars have recently confirmed that presidents and their parties often differ in terms of placement on the left-right spectrum, whether measured using published campaign manifestos (see Bruhn 2004 on Mexico, e.g.) or expert surveys (Wiesehomeier and Benoit 2009). However, no comprehensive comparison of presidents' and parties' locations in policy space using manifestos exists either across countries or over time, and thus far experts have been surveyed only once, meaning we lack a clear picture of the evolution of separation of purpose in any way beyond our aggregate electoral data. Scholars have also made little use of surveys to explore how voters think about presidents and parties differently.

Finally, our results in Chapter 8 suggest that party responsibility is unlikely when presidents' parties lack a legislative majority. "Responsible" parties are likely under *all* political conditions in parliamentary regimes, but only under fairly uncommon situations in separate-powers systems: single-party majority government. And even in that situation, responsible parties are unlikely because the separation of survival gives the executive the autonomy to deviate from the party line, free of any threat of discipline. The findings suggest that scholars should explore presidential influence in representation in far greater detail. Powell (2004) concurs in noting that scholarly consideration of the interaction between parties and voter behavior in systems with both executive and legislative elections has not advanced very far. Do voters hold presidents *personally* accountable, or do they see presidents as agents of their parties? Only additional survey research, perhaps using the Comparative Study of Electoral Systems, can help answer these sorts of questions. We hope that our theoretical framework, derived from principal-agent theory, can help advance scholarly understanding of party politics in new and important ways across the world's democracies.

References

Agence France-Presse. 1991. "Ruling party expels two more dissidents." December 7 (accessed through Factiva, June 4, 2007).

1997a. "SKorean workers reject lay-offs, accuse president-elect of backpedalling." December 27 (accessed through Factiva, June 4, 2007).

1997b. "South Korean president-elect eases stance over layoffs." December 22 (accessed through Factiva, June 4, 2007).

Alcántara Sáez, Manuel, and Flavia Freidenberg, eds. 2001a. *Partidos Políticos de América Latina: Cono Sur.* Salamanca: Ediciones Universidad Salamanca.

2001b. *Partidos Políticos de América Latina: Países Andinos.* Salamanca: Ediciones Universidad Salamanca.

2001c. *Partidos Políticos de América Latina: Centroamérica, México y República Dominicana.* Salamanca: Ediciones Universidad Salamanca.

Alchian, Armen, and Harold Demsetz. 1972. "Production, Information Costs, and Economic Organization." *American Economic Review* 62(5): 777–95.

Aldrich, John. 1995. *Why Parties? The Origin and Transformation of Party Politics in America.* Chicago: University of Chicago Press.

Alemán, Eduardo, and Thomas Schwartz. 2006. "Presidential Vetoes in Latin American Constitutions." *Journal of Theoretical Politics* 18(1): 98–120.

Alford, Peter. 1997. "Kim Dae-jung takes over Korea crisis." *The Australian* (Queensland), December 26, p. 6.

Altman, David. 2001. "The Politics of Coalition Formation and Survival in Multiparty Presidential Regimes." PhD dissertation, Department of Government, University of Notre Dame, Notre Dame, IN.

Alves, Carlos Eduardo. 1997. "Petista faz exigências e partido cobra dos aliados." *Folha de São Paulo*, November 18, p. 6.

1998a. "Frente define cúpula da campanha de Lula." *Folha de São Paulo*, May 26, p. 11.

1998b. "Esquerda dá commando de campanha a Lula." *Folha de São Paulo*, May 27, p. 8.

1998c. "Ex-radicais tocarão campanha de Lula." *Folha de São Paulo*, June 3, p. 5.

Amaral, Ricardo, and Natuza Nery. 2007. "PT tem de ceder espaços ou vai se isolar, diz Tarso." *O Estado de São Paulo*, January 8. www.estadao. com.br.

American Political Science Association. 1950. "Toward a More Responsible Two-party System: A Report of the Committee on Political Parties." *American Political Science Review* 44(3): 1–14 (supplement, part 2).

Amorim Neto, Octavio. 2002. "Presidential Cabinets, Electoral Cycles, and Coalition Discipline in Brazil." In *Legislative Politics in Latin America*, ed. Scott Morgenstern and Benito Nacif. Cambridge: Cambridge University Press, 48–78.

2006a. *Presidencialismo e Governabilidade nas Américas*. Rio de Janeiro: Editora FGV.

2006b. "The Presidential Calculus: Executive Policy-Making and Cabinet Formation in the Americas." *Comparative Political Studies* 39(4): 415–40.

Amorim Neto, Octavio, and Marina Costa Lobo. 2009. "Portugal's Semi-Presidentialism (Re)considered: An Assessment of the President's Role in the Policy Process, 1976–2006." *European Journal of Political Research* 48(2): 234–55.

Amorim Neto, Octavio, and Kaare Strøm. 2006. "Breaking the Parliamentary Chain of Delegation: Presidents and Non-Partisan Cabinet Members in European Democracies." *British Journal of Political Science* 36(4): 619–43.

Andeweg, R. B. 1997. "Institutional Reform in Dutch Politics; Elected Prime Minister, Personalized PR, and Popular Veto in Comparative Perspective." *Acta Politica* 32: 227–57.

Árabe, Carlos Henrique Goulart. 2001. "A evolução programática do Partido dos Trabalhadores." [The Programmatic Evolution of the Workers' Party] *Conjuntura Política* #29. On file with the authors.

Ard, Michael. 2003. *An Eternal Struggle: How the National Action Party Transformed Mexican Politics*. Westport, CT: Praeger.

Azevedo, Clóvis Bueno de. 1995. *A Estrela Partida ao Meio: Ambigüidades do Pensamento Petista* [The Star Split Down the Middle: Ambiguities of PT Thought]. São Paulo: Editora Entrelinhas.

Bacque, Raphaelle. 2000. "L'Elysée estime que le calendrier actuel sert Jacques Chirac." *Le Monde* electronic edition, November 30.

Baker, M. 1997. "Kim's victory a landmark for Korea." *Courier Mail* (Queensland, Australia), December 20, p. 17.

Bartels, Larry. 2008. *Unequal Democracy: The Political Economy of the New Gilded Age*. Princeton, NJ: Princeton University Press.

Baumgartner, Jody C., and Naoko Kada, eds. 2003. *Checking Executive Power: Presidential Impeachment in Comparative Perspective*. Westport, CT: Praeger.

BBC Monitoring Europe. 2004a. "Premier-delegate announces Romanian Humanist Party joins government." *Rompres news agency*, Bucharest. December 23.

2004b. "Romania presidential candidate seeks cooperation with victorious rival." *Radio Romania Actualitati*, Bucharest. December 13.

2004c. "Terms of new Romanian political alliance outlined." Rompres news agency, Bucharest. September 9.

2005. "Romania's ruling coalition signs governance agreement." *Pro TV,* Bucharest. February 16.

2007. "Romanian premier declares ruling alliance 'dead.'" March 27.

BBC news online. 2005. "Deal to end crisis in Nicaragua." October 11, http://news.bbc.co.uk/2/hi/americas/4329688.stm (accessed June 4, 2007).

Beer, Samuel. 1953. "Les parties politiques [Political Parties]." *Western Political Quarterly* 6(3): 512–17.

Bell, David S., and Byron Criddle. 2002. "Presidentialism Restored: The French Elections of April-May and June 2002." *Parliamentary Affairs* 55(4): 643–63.

Benoit, Kenneth, and Michael Laver. 2006. *Party Policy in Modern Democracies.* London: Routledge.

Berry, Christopher R., Barry C. Burden, and William G. Howell. 2009. "The President and the Distribution of Federal Spending." Unpublished.

Beuve Mery, Alain. 2000a. "Le PCF refuse un changement 'dangereux pour la démocratie.'" *Le Monde* electronic edition, November 30.

2000b. "Les Verts 'piégés' par leur base sur la question du mode de scrutin." *Le Monde* electronic edition, November 2.

Bick, E. 1998. "Sectarian Party Politics in Israel: The Case of Yisrael Ba'Aliya, the Russian Immigrant Party." In *Israel at the Polls,* ed. Daniel Elazar and Shmuel Sandler. London: Frank Cass, 121–45.

Blondel, Jean. 1984. "Dual Leadership in the Contemporary World: A Step Towards Regime Stability?" In *Comparative Government and Politics: Essays in Honor of S. E. Finer,* ed. Dennis Kavanagh and Gillian Peele. Boulder, CO: Westview Press, 73–91.

Blondel, Jean, and Ferdinand Müller-Rommel. 2001. *Cabinets in Eastern Europe.* Baskingstoke, UK: Palgrave.

Bobbio, Norberto. 1989. *Democracy and Dictatorship.* Minneapolis: University of Minnesota Press.

Boix, Carles. 2007. "The Emergence of Parties and Party Systems." In *The Oxford Handbook of Comparative Politics,* ed. Carles Boix and Susan Stokes. New York: Oxford University Press, 499–521.

Bollard, Alan. 1994. "New Zealand." In *The Political Economy of Policy Reform,* ed. J. Williamson. Washington, DC: Institute for International Economics, 73–110.

Briones Loásiga, William. 2002. "Pugna Alemán-Bolaños." *La Prensa* on-line. June 17. http://www.ni.laprensa.com.ni/cronologico/2002/junio/17/nacionales/nacionales-20020617–19.html (accessed June 4, 2007).

Bruhn, Kathleen. 2004. "Globalization and the Renovation of the Latin American Left: Strategies of Ideological Adaptation." Presented at the Annual Meeting of the Midwest Political Science Association, Chicago.

2006. "Party Ideology and Issue Stability in Mexico." Presented at the Annual Meeting of the American Political Science Association, Philadelphia.

Bryce, James. 1888. *The American Commonwealth.* New York: Macmillan.

Burden, Barry, and David Kimball. 2002. *Why Americans Split Their Tickets.* Ann Arbor: University of Michigan Press.

Burger, Angela S. 1992. "Changing Civil-Military Relations in Sri Lanka." *Asian Survey* 32(8): 744–56.

Burnham, Walter Dean. 1979. "Party Systems and the Political Process." In *The American Party Systems: Stages of Political Development*, ed. W. N. Chambers and W. D. Burnham. New York: Oxford University Press, 277–308.

Burton, John. 1997. "S Korea candidates skirt round realities." *Financial Times*, November 10, p. 4.

Busch, Andrew. 1997. *Outsiders and Openness in the Presidential Nominating System*. Pittsburgh: University of Pittsburgh Press.

Cain, Bruce, John Ferejohn, and Morris Fiorina. 1987. *The Personal Vote: Constituency Service and Electoral Independence*. Cambridge, MA: Harvard University Press.

Campbell, James E. 1997. *The Presidential Pulse of Congressional Elections*. Lexington: University Press of Kentucky.

Carey, John. 1996. *Term Limits and Legislative Representation*. New York: Cambridge University Press.

   2009. *Legislative Voting and Accountability*. New York: Cambridge University Press.

Carey, John M., and Matthew S. Shugart. 1995. "Incentives to Cultivate a Personal Vote: A Rank-Ordering of Electoral Formulas." *Electoral Studies* 14(4): 417–39.

Carroll, Royce. 2007. "The Electoral Origins of Governing Coalitions." PhD dissertation, University of California, San Diego.

Carroll, Royce, and Gary Cox. 2007. "The Logic of Gamson's Law: Pre-Electoral Coalitions and Portfolio Allocations." *American Journal of Political Science* 52(2): 300–13.

Carroll, Royce, and Matthew Soberg Shugart. 2007. "Neo-Madisonian Theories of Latin American Institutions." In *Regimes and Democracy in Latin America, Volume I: Theories and Agendas*, ed. G. L. Munck. New York: Oxford University Press, 51–104.

Ceaser, James. 1979. *Presidential Selection: Theory and Development*. Princeton, NJ: Princeton University Press.

Cháirez, Angelle Hernández. 2006. "Reconoce Calderón que hay distancia con el PAN." *El Financiero* electronic edition, March 2.

Chambraud, Cecile, and Beatrice Gurrey. 2002. "Lionel Jospin déclenche la polémique sur le calendrier electoral de 2002." *Le Monde* electronic edition, November 28.

Chandler, Clay. 1997a. "Fear grows that Seoul will renege on reform promise; despite IMF deal, analysts and investors sense a reluctance to dismantle 'Korea Inc.'" *Washington Post*, December 10, p. C13.

   1997b. "S. Korea's Kim proves mettle in financial crisis; president-elect gains support for savvy economic strategy." *Washington Post*, December 29, p. A1.

Cheibub, José Antonio. 2002. "Minority Governments, Deadlock Situations, and the Survival of Presidential Democracies." *Comparative Political Studies* 35(3): 284–312.

2007. *Presidentialism, Parliamentarism, and Democracy.* Cambridge: Cambridge University Press.

Cheibub, José Antonio, and Fernando Limongi. 2002. "Modes of Government Formation and the Survival of Democratic Regimes: Presidentialism and Parliamentarism Reconsidered." *Annual Review of Political Science* 5: 151–79.

Cheibub, José Antonio, Adam Przeworski, and Sebastian Saiegh. 2004. "Government Coalitions and Legislative Success under Presidentialism and Parliamentarism." *British Journal of Political Science* 34(4): 565–87.

Chhibber, Pradeep, and Ken Kollman. 2004. *The Formation of National Party Systems: Federalism and Party Competition in Canada, Great Britain, India, and the United States.* Princeton, NJ: Princeton University Press.

Clark, Terry D., and Diana Jurgelevičiūtė. 2008. " 'Keeping Tabs on Coalition Partners': A Theoretically Salient Case Study of Lithuanian Coalitional Governments." *Europe-Asia Studies* 60(4): 631–42.

Clark, Terry D., and Jill Wittrock. 2005. "Presidentialism and the Effect of Electoral Law in Postcommunist Systems." *Comparative Political Studies* 38(2): 171–88.

Clift, Ben. 2005. "Dyarchic Presidentialization in a Presidentialized Polity: The French Fifth Republic." In *The Presidentionalization of Politics: A Comparative Study of Modern Democracies,* ed. Thomas Poguntke and Paul Webb. Oxford: Oxford University Press, 221–45.

CNN. 2007. "Left Tempers Sarkozy's Poll Win." June 18. http://www.cnn.com/2007/WORLD-/europe/06/17/france.votes.conservatives.reut/index.html (accessed June 18, 2007).

Cohen, Marty, David Karol, Hans Noel, and John Zaller. 2008. *The Party Decides: Presidential Nominations Before and After Reform.* Chicago: University of Chicago Press.

Cole, A. 1990a. "The Evolution of the Party System, 1974–1990." In *French Political Parties in Transition,* ed. Alistair Cole. Aldershot: Dartmouth, 3–24.

    1990b. "The Return of the Orleanist Right: The Union for French Democracy." In *French Political Parties in Transition,* ed. Alistair Cole. Aldershot: Dartmouth, 106–39.

    1993. "The Presidential Party and the Fifth Republic." *West European Politics* 16(2): 49–66.

Cole, A., and P. Campbell. 1989. *French Electoral Systems and Elections since 1789.* Aldershot: Gower.

Colton, Timothy. 1995. "Superpresidentialism and Russia's Backward State." *Post-Soviet Affairs* 11(2): 144–48.

Condon, Christopher, and Stefan Wagstyl. 2007. "Romanian parliament suspends president." *Financial Times* online edition. http://cachef.ft.com/cms/s/0/d3be5f1a-ee6e-11db-b5e9-000b5df10621.html?nclick_check=1 (accessed August 21, 2008).

Converse, Philip, and Roy Pierce. 1986. *Political Representation in France.* Cambridge, MA: Belknap Press of Harvard University Press.

Cooper, Philip J. 2005. "George W. Bush, Edgar Allan Poe, and the Use and Abuse of Presidential Signing Statements." *Presidential Studies Quarterly* 35(3): 515–32.

Coppedge, Michael. 1994. *Strong Parties and Lame Ducks: Presidential Partyarchy and Factionalism in Venezuela*. Stanford, CA: Stanford University Press.

2002. *Presidential Runoffs Do Not Fragment Legislative Party Systems*. Unpublished manuscript: University of Notre Dame.

Corrales, Javier. 2002. *Presidents without Parties: The Politics of Economic Reform in Argentina and Venezuela in the 1990s*. State College, PA: Penn State Press.

2005. "Expresidents and Newcomers Running for President ... and Winning Recent Elections in Latin America." Presented at the Annual Conference of the Society for Latin American Studies, Leiden, The Netherlands.

Courtney, John C. 1995. *Do Conventions Matter? Choosing National Party Leaders in Canada*. Montreal: McGill-Queen's University Press.

Courtois, Gerard, and Cecille Chambraud. 2000. "L'avenir du quinquennat dépendra du calendrier électoral." *Le Monde* electronic edition, September 24.

Cox, Gary W. 1987. *The Efficient Secret*. New York: Cambridge University Press.

1997. *Making Votes Count: Strategic Coordination in the World's Electoral Systems Political Economy of Institutions and Decisions*. New York: Cambridge University Press.

Cox, Gary W., and Mathew D. McCubbins. 1993. *Legislative Leviathan: Party Government in the House*. Berkeley: University of California Press.

2001. "The Institutional Determinants of Policy Outcomes." In *Presidents, Parliaments, and Policy*, ed. Stephan Haggard and Matthew McCubbins. New York: Cambridge University Press, 27–89.

2005. *Setting the Agenda: Responsible Party Government in the U.S. House of Representatives*. New York: Cambridge University Press.

Cox, Karen E., and Leonard Schioppa. 2002. "Interaction Effects in Mixed-Member Systems." *Comparative Political Studies* 35(9): 1027–53.

Crisp, Brian F. 2000. *Democratic Institutional Design: The Powers and Incentives of Venezuelan Politicians and Interest Groups*. Stanford, CA: Stanford University Press.

Crow, David. 2005. "Crossing Party Lines: Volatility and Ticket Splitting in Mexico (1994–2000)." *Bulletin of Latin American Research* 24(1): 1–22.

Cutler, Lloyd. 1980. "To Form a Government." *Foreign Affairs* 59(1): 126–43.

Dahl, Robert. 1971. *Polyarchy: Participation and Opposition*. New Haven, CT: Yale University Press.

1990. "Myth of the Presidential Mandate." *Political Science Quarterly* 105(3): 355–72.

Dalton, Russell, ed. 2008. *Citizen Politics: Public Opinion and Political Parties in Advanced Industrial Democracies,* 5th ed. Washington, DC: Congressional Quarterly Press.

Dalton, Russell, Ian McCallister, and Martin Wattenberg. 2000. "The Consequences of Partisan Dealignment." In *Parties without Partisans: Political Change in Advanced Industrial Democracies*, ed. R. Dalton and M. Wattenberg. Oxford: Oxford University Press, 37–63.

Davis, James W. 1992. *The President as Party Leader.* New York: Greenwood Press.

1998. *Leadership Selection in Six Western Democracies.* Westport, CT: Greenwood Press.

Diamond, Larry, and Richard Gunther, eds. 2001. *Political Parties and Democracy.* Baltimore: Johns Hopkins University Press.

Diehl, Jackson. 1982. "Populist Lightens Staid Colombian Politics." *Washington Post*, November 20, p. A14.

Diskin, A., and R. Y. Hazan. 2002. "The 2001 Prime-ministerial Election in Israel." *Electoral Studies* 21(4) (December): 659–64.

Dix, Robert H. 1989. "Cleavage Structures and Party Systems in Latin America." *Comparative Politics* 22(1): 23–37.

Döring, Herbert. 2001. "Parliamentary Agenda Control and Legislative Outcomes in Western Europe." *Legislative Studies Quarterly* 26: 145–65.

Douglas, Roger. 1980. *There's Got to Be a Better Way.* Wellington: Fourth Estate Books.

Dow Jones International Newswires. 1999. "Romania's dismissed prime min submits resignation – radio." December 17.

Duhamel, Olivier. 1991. *Le Pouvoir Politique en France* [Political Power in France]. Paris: Presses Universitaires de France.

Duhamel, Olivier, and Gérard Grunberg. 2001. "Système de partis et Ves Républiques [Party Systems and Fifth Republics]." *Commentaire* 95 (Automne): 533–44.

Duverger, Maurice. 1954. *Political Parties: Their Organization and Activity in the Modern State.* London: Methuen.

1980. "A New Political-System Model: Semi-Presidential Government." *European Journal of Political Research* 8(2): 165–87.

East European Constitutional Review. 1999. "Constitution Watch." Volume 8 Number 3, summer 1999. http://www.law.nyu.edu/eecr/vol8num3/constitutionwatch/lithuania.html (accessed August 8, 2008).

Economist. 1991. "President Challenged with Impeachment." September 7.

Edwards, George C. III. 1989. *At the Margins: Presidential Leadership of Congress.* New Haven, CT: Yale University Press.

EFE News Service. 2005. "Sandinistas halt impeachment steps against Nicaraguan president." September 12 (accessed through Factiva, June 4, 2007).

Ehrlich, Sean. 2000. "Presidentialism and the Effective Number of Parties: Executive Power's Encouragement of Cross-District Linkages." Presented at the meeting of the Midwest Political Science Association, Chicago.

Elgie, Robert, ed. 1999. *Semi-Presidentialism in Europe.* Oxford: Oxford University Press.

Epstein, Leon. 1967. *Political Parties in Western Democracies.* New York: Praeger.

1986. *Political Parties in the American Mold.* Madison: University of Wisconsin Press.

Escudero, Laura. 2001. "Argentina." In *Partidos Politicos en América Latina: Cono Sur* [Political Parties in Latin America: Southern Cone], ed. M. Alcántara Saez and F. Freidenberg. Salamanca: Ediciones Universidad de Salamanca, 33–116.

Ferejohn, John, and Randall Calvert. 1984. "Presidential Coattails in Historical Perspective." *American Journal of Political Science* 28(1): 127–46.

Figueiredo, Marcus. 1994. "Competição Eleitoral: Eleições Casadas, Resultados Solteiros [Electoral Competition: Married Elections, Divorced Results]." *Monitor Público* 2: 21–27.

Filippov, Mikhail, Peter Ordeshook, and Olga Shvetsova. 1999. "Party Fragmentation and Presidential Elections in Post-Communist Democracies." *Constitutional Political Economy* 10(1): 3–26.

Fiorina, Morris P. 1988. "Party Government in the United States: Diagnosis and Prognosis." In *Party Governments: European and American Experiences*, ed. R. S. Katz. Berlin: Walter de Gruyter, 270–300.

Fish, M. Steven. 1998. "Mongolia: Democracy without Prerequisites." *Journal of Democracy* 9(3): 127–41.

2000. "The Executive Deception: Superpresidentialism and the Degradation of Russian Politics." In *Building the Russian State: Institutional Crisis and the Quest for Democratic Governance*, ed. Valerie Sperling. Boulder, CO: Westview, 177–92.

2005. *Democracy Derailed in Russia.* New York: Cambridge University Press.

Fitzmaurice, John. 1993. "The Estonian Elections of 1992." *Electoral Studies* 12, 2 (June): 168–73.

Frears, J. 1991. *Parties and Voters in France.* New York: St. Martin's Press.

Freidenberg, Flavia, and Francisco Sánchez López. 2001. "Partidos políticos y métodos de selección de candidatos en América Latina: Una discusión sobre reglas y prácticas." Presented at the 23rd meeting of the Latin American Studies Association, Washington, DC.

Gaffney, J. 1990. "The Emergence of a Presidential Party: The Socialist Party." In *French Political Parties in Transition*, ed. A. Cole. Aldershot: Dartmouth, 61–90.

Geddes, Barbara. 1999. "What Do We Know about Democratization after Twenty Years?" *Annual Reviews of Political Science* 2: 115–44.

2004. "The Development of Party Systems in Latin America." Presented at the Annual Meeting of the Western Political Science Association, Portland, Oregon.

Gerring, John, and Strom Thacker. 2004. "Political Institutions and Corruption: The Role of Unitarism and Parliamentarism." *British Journal of Political Science* 34(2): 295–330.

Giniger, Henry. 1962. "Pompidou named French premier." *New York Times,* April 15, p. 3.

Ginsburg, Tom. 1998. "Mongolia in 1997: Deepening Democracy." *Asian Survey* 38, 1 (January): 64–68.

Global Insight Daily Archives. 2005. "Nicaraguan Congress Ends Impeachment Effort." October 27 (accessed through Factiva, June 4, 2007).

Goldberg, G. 1998. "The Electoral Fall of the Israeli Left." In *Israel at the Polls 1996*, ed. Daniel Elazar and Shmuel Sandler. London: Frank Cass, 53–72.

Golder, Matt. 2006. "Presidential Coattails and Legislative Fragmentation." *American Journal of Political Science* 50(1): 34–48.

Golder, Sona. 2006. *The Logic of Pre-Electoral Coalition Formation.* Columbus: Ohio State University Press.

Gunther, Richard, José Ramón Montero, and Juan Linz, eds. 2002. *Political Parties: Old Concepts and New Challenges.* New York: Oxford University Press.

Gurrey, Beatrice, and Jean Baptiste de Montvalon. 2000. "Le gouvernement ne paraît pas disposé à modifier le calendrier électoral de 2002." *Le Monde* electronic edition, October 6.

Hagopian, Frances. 2007. "Parties and Voters in Emerging Democracies." In *The Oxford Handbook of Comparative Politics*, ed. Carles Boix and Susan Stokes. New York: Oxford University Press, 582–603.

Hale, Henry. 2005. "Party Development in a Federal System: The Impact of Putin's Reforms." In *The Dynamics of Russian Politics: Putin's Reform of Federal-Regional Relations* 2, ed. Peter Reddaway and Robert Orttung. Boulder, CO: Rowman and Littlefield, 179–211.

Hamilton, Alexander, James Madison, John Jay, and Roy P. Fairfield. [1787] 1937. *The Federalist Papers: A Collection of Essays Written in Support of the Constitution of the United States: From the Original Text of Alexander Hamilton, James Madison, John Jay.* New York: Random House.

Hazan, Reuven. 1997. "Executive-Legislative Relations in an Era of Reform: Reshaping Government in Israel." *Legislative Studies Quarterly* 22(3): 329–50.

1999. "The Electoral Consequences of Political Reform." In *The Elections in Israel 1996*, ed. Asher Arian and Michal Shamir. Albany: State University of New York Press, 163–85.

2001. "The Israeli Mixed Electoral System: Unexpected Cumulative and Reciprocal Consequences." In *Mixed-Member Electoral Systems: The Best of Both Worlds?* ed. Matthew S. Shugart and Martin P. Wattenberg. New York: Oxford University Press, 351–79.

2005. "The Failure of Presidential Parliamentarism: Constitutional versus Structural Presidentialization in Israel's Parliamentary Democracy." In *The Presidentialization of Politics: A Comparative Study of Modern Democracies*, ed. Paul Webb and Thomas Poguntke. Oxford: Oxford University Press, 287–310.

Hazan, Reuven, Ofer Kenig, and Gideon Rahat. 2005. "The Political Consequences of the Introduction and the Repeal of the Direct Elections for the Prime Minister." In *The Elections in Israel 2003*, ed. Asher Arian and Michal Shamir. New York: Transaction Publishers, 33–61.

Hazan, Reuven, and Gideon Rahat. 2000. "Representation, Electoral Reform, and Democracy: Theoretical and Empirical Lessons from the 1996 Elections in Israel." *Comparative Political Studies* 33(10): 1310–36.

Heffernan, R. 2005. "Why the Prime Minister Cannot Be a President: Comparing Institutional Imperatives in Britain and America." *Parliamentary Affairs* 58(1): 53–70.

Hellwig, Timothy, and David Samuels. 2008. "Electoral Accountability and the Variety of Democratic Regimes." *British Journal of Political Science* 38(1): 65–90.

Helmke, Gretchen. 2006. "Dividing to Democratize? Uncertainty and Ticket-Splitting in the Mexico 2000 Elections." Presented at the conference titled "Democracy, Divided Government and Split-Ticket Voting," Harvard University.

Helms, E. Allen. 1949. "The President and Party Politics." *Journal of Politics* 11(1): 42–64.

"Helsinki cabinet quits; Majority coalition due." *New York Times.* 1977, May 12, p. 16.

Herron, Erik, and Misa Nishikawa. 2001. "Contamination Effects and the Number of Parties in Mixed-Superposition Electoral Systems." *Electoral Studies* 20(1): 63–86.

Hershey, Marjorie Randon. 2008. *Party Politics in America*, 13th ed. New York: Longman.

Hicken, Alan, and Heather Stoll. 2007. "Presidents, Powers and Parties: The Sources of Legislative Electoral Coordination in Presidential Regimes." Presented at the Annual Meeting of the American Political Science Association, Chicago.

Hickman, John. 1999. "Explaining the Two-Party System in Sri Lanka's National Assembly." *Contemporary South Asia* 8(1): 29–40.

Hochstetler, Kathryn. 2006a. "Organized Civil Society in Lula's Brazil." Paper prepared for presentation at the Latin American Studies Association 2006 Conference, San Juan, Puerto Rico.

2006b. "Rethinking Presidentialism: Challenges and Presidential Falls in South America." *Comparative Politics* 38(4): 401–18.

Huber, John, Georgia Kernell, and Eduardo Leoni. 2005. "Institutional Context, Cognitive Resources and Party Attachments across Democracies." *Political Analysis* 13(4): 365–86.

Huber, John, and Cecilia Martínez-Gallardo. 2008. "Replacing Cabinet Ministers: Patterns of Ministerial Stability in Parliamentary Democracies." *American Political Science Review* 102(1): 169–80.

Hunter, Wendy. 2007. "The Normalization of an Anomaly: The Workers' Party in Brazil." *World Politics* 59(3): 440–75.

Hunter, Wendy, and Timothy Power. 2005. "Lula's Brazil at Midterm." *Journal of Democracy* 16(3): 127–40.

Hunter, Wendy, and Timothy J. Power. 2007. "Rewarding Lula: Executive Power, Social Policy, and the Brazilian Elections of 2006." *Latin American Politics and Society* 49(1): 1–30.

Huntington, Samuel. 1991. *The Third Wave: Democratization in the Late 20th Century*. Norman: University of Oklahoma Press.

Inglehart, Ronald. 1987. "Value Change in Industrial Societies." *American Political Science Review* 81(4): 1289–303.

Ishiyama, J. T., and R. Kennedy. 2001 "Superpresidentialism and Political Party Development in Russia, Ukraine, Armenia and Kyrgyzstan." *Europe-Asia Studies* 53(8): 1177–91.

Ito, Mazami. 2006. "Koizumi leaves LDP factions in tatters." *Japan Times Online*, June 26. http://search.japantimes.co.jp/print/nn20060626f1.html (accessed December 30, 2008).

Janda, Kenneth. 1992. "The American Constitutional Framework and the Structure of American Political Parties." In *The Constitution and American Political Development: An Institutional Perspective*, ed. P. F. Nardulli. Urbana: University of Illinois Press, 179–206.

_____ 1993. "Comparative Political Parties: Research and Theory." In *Political Science: The State of the Discipline II*, ed. A. W. Finifter. Washington, DC: American Political Science Association, 163–92.

Janda, Kenneth, and Tyler Colman. 1998. "Effects of Party Organization on Performance during the 'Golden Age' of Parties." *Political Studies* 46(3): 611–32.

Jérôme, Bruno, Véronique Jérôme-Speziari, and Michael S. Lewis-Beck. 2003. "Reordering the French Election Calendar: Forecasting the Consequences for 2002." *European Journal of Political Research* 42(3): 425–40.

Jones, Charles O. 1999. *Separate but Equal Branches: Congress and the Presidency*, 2nd ed. New York: Chatham House.

Jones, Mark P. 1995. *Electoral Laws and the Survival of Presidential Democracies*. Notre Dame: University of Notre Dame Press.

Joynes, Kate. 2005. "Judge Ends Trial Proceedings against Accused Nicaraguan Ministers." *Global Insight Daily Archives*. October 26 (accessed through Factiva, June 4, 2007).

Kada, Naoko. 2003. "Impeachment as Punishment for Corruption? The Cases of Brazil and Venezuela." In *Checking Executive Power: Presidential Impeachment in Comparative Perspective*, ed. Jody Baumgartner and Naoko Kada. Westport, CT: Praeger, 113–36.

Kasuya, Yuko. 2004. "Presidentialism and Legislative Party System Formation: The Philippines as a Crucial Case." Presented at the Annual Meeting of the American Political Science Association, Chicago.

Katz, Richard S. 1987. "Party Government and Its Alternatives." In *Party Governments: European and American Experiences,* ed. R. S. Katz. Berlin: Walter de Gruyter, 1–27.

Katz, Richard S., and William Crotty, eds. 2006. *Handbook of Party Politics*. London: Sage.

Katz, Richard S., and Robin Kolodny. 1994. "Party Organization as an Empty Vessel: Parties in American Politics." In *How Parties Organize: Change and Adaptation in Party Organizations in Western Democracies*, ed. R. S. Katz and P. Mair. London: Sage, 23–50.

Katz, Richard S., and Peter Mair. 1995. "Changing Models of Party Organization and Party Democracy: The Emergence of the Cartel Party." *Party Politics* 1(1): 5–28.

Keck, Margaret. 1992. *The Workers' Party and Democratization in Brazil*. New Haven, CT: Yale University Press.

Kelley, Stanley. 1983. *Interpreting Elections*. Princeton, NJ: Princeton University Press.

Kenig, Ofer. 2006. "The Selection of Party Leaders in Parliamentary Democracies: A Classification." Hebrew University of Jerusalem, Unpublished manuscript.

Kenig, Ofer, Gideon Rahat, and Reuven Hazan. 2005. "The Political Consequences of the Introduction and the Repeal of the Direct Elections for the Prime Minister." In *The Elections in Israel – 2003*. New Brunswick, NJ: Transaction Publishers, 33–62.

Kernell, Samuel. 2003. "The True Principles of Republican Government: Assessing James Madison's Political Science." In *James Madison: The Theory and Politics of Republican Government*, ed. S. Kernell. Stanford, CA: Stanford University Press, 92–125.

Key, V. O. 1952. *Politics, Parties, and Pressure Groups*. New York: Crowell.

Kiewiet, D. Roderick, and Mathew D. McCubbins. 1991. *The Logic of Delegation*. Chicago: University of Chicago Press.

Kimball, David C., and Cassie A. Gross. 2007. "The Growing Polarization of American Voters." In *The State of the Parties*, ed. John C. Green. Boulder, CO: Rowman & Littlefield, 265–78.

Kirchheimer, Otto. 1966. "The Transformation of Western European Party Systems." In *Political Parties and Political Development*, ed. J. LaPalombara and M. Weiner. Princeton, NJ: Princeton University Press, 177–200.

Kitschelt, Herbert. 1994. *The Transformation of European Social Democracy*. New York: Cambridge University Press.

2007. "Party Systems." In *The Oxford Handbook of Comparative Politics*, ed. Carles Boix and Susan Stokes. New York: Oxford University Press, 522–54.

Kitschelt, Herbert, Zdenka Mansfeldova, Gabor Toka, and Radoslaw Markowski. 1999. *Post-Communist Party Systems: Competition, Representation, and Inner-Party Cooperation*. Cambridge: Cambridge University Press.

Klingeman, Hans-Dieter, Richard I. Hofferbert, and Ian Budge. 1994. *Parties, Policies, and Democracy Theoretical Lenses on Public Policy*. Boulder, CO: Westview Press.

Klinkner, Philip. 1994. *The Losing Parties: Out-Party National Committees, 1956–1993*. New Haven, CT: Yale University Press.

Knapp, A. 1990. "Un parti comme les autres: Jacques Chirac and the Rally for the Republic." In *French Political Parties in Transition*, ed. A. Cole. Aldershot: Dartmouth, 140–84.

Kolodny, Robin. 1998. *Pursuing Majorities: Congressional Campaign Committees in American Politics*. Norman: University of Oklahoma Press.

Krauss, Ellis S., and Benjamin Nyblade. 2005. "'Presidentialization' in Japan? The Prime Minister, Media and Elections in Japan." *British Journal of Political Science* 35: 357–68.

Krupavicius, Algis. 2007. "Lithuania." *European Journal of Political Research* 46: 1019–31.

LaPalombara, Joseph, and Myron Weiner. 1966. *Political Parties and Political Development*. Princeton, NJ: Princeton University Press.

Latin American Weekly Report (LAWR). 2004. "Nicaragua: Assembly takes first step towards impeachment." October 19 (accessed through Factiva, June 4, 2007).

Latinnews Daily On-Line, 2005. "Nicaragua: Opposition unites against Bolaños." January 10 (accessed through Factiva, June 4, 2007).

Laver, Michael. 1999. "Divided Parties, Divided Government." *Legislative Studies Quarterly* 24(1): 5–29.

Laver, Michael, and Kenneth Shepsle. 1996. *Making and Breaking Governments: Cabinets and Legislatures in Parliamentary Democracies*. New York: Cambridge University Press.

Lee, Youngjae. 2005. "Law, Politics and Impeachment: The Impeachment of Roh Moo-hyun from a Comparative Constitutional Perspective." NYU School of Law, Public Law and Legal Theory Working Paper #4. Available at http://lsr.nellco.org/nyu/plltwp/papers/4 (accessed June 1, 2007).

Leoni, Eduardo. 2002. "Ideologia, Democracia e Comportamento Parlamentar: A Câmara dos Deputados (1991–1998)" [Ideology, Democracy and Parliamentary Behavior: The Chamber of Deputies (1991–1998)]. *DADOS – Revista de Ciências Sociais* 45(3): 361–86.

Lijphart, Arend. 1984. *Democracies: Patterns of Majoritarian and Consensus Government in Twenty-One Countries*. New Haven, CT: Yale University Press.

ed. 1992. *Parliamentary versus Presidential Government*. Oxford: Oxford University Press.

1994. *Electoral Systems and Party Systems: A Study of Twenty-Seven Democracies, 1945–1990*. Oxford: Oxford University Press.

1999. *Patterns of Democracy: Government Forms and Performance in Thirty-Six Countries*. New Haven, CT: Yale University Press.

Linz, Juan J. 1990. "The Perils of Presidentialism." *Journal of Democracy* 1: 51–69.

1994. "Presidential or Parliamentary Democracy: Does It Make a Difference?" In *The Failure of Presidential Democracy, Volume 2: The Case of Latin America*, ed. J. Linz and Arturo Valenzuela. Baltimore: Johns Hopkins University Press, 3–90.

Lipset, Seymour Martin, and Stein Rokkan. 1967. *Party Systems and Voter Alignments: Cross-National Perspectives*. New York: Free Press.

Loaeza, Soledad. 1999. *El Partido Acción Nacional, la larga marcha 1934–1994: oposición leal y partido de protesta*. [PAN, the long march 1934–1994: loyal opposition and protest party]. Sección de obras de política y derecho. México D.F.: Fondo de Cultura Económica.

Long, Norton E. 1951. "Party Government and the United States." *Journal of Politics* 13(2): 187–214.

Lupia, Arthur. 2003. "Delegation and Its Perils." In *Delegation and Accountability in West European Parliamentary Democracies*, ed. Torbjörn Bergman, Wolfgang C. Müller, and Kaare Strøm. Oxford: Oxford University Press, 33–54.

Machin, H. 1989. "Stages and Dynamics in the Evolution of the French Party System." *West European Politics* 12(4): 59–81.

Mackie, Thomas T., and Richard Rose. 1991. *The International Almanac of Electoral History*. Washington, DC: Congressional Quarterly.

Maddens, Bart, and Stefaan Fiers. 2004. "The Direct PM Election and the Institutional Presidentialisation of Parliamentary Systems." *Electoral Studies* 23, 4 (December): 769–93.

Mahler, G. S. 1997. "The forming of the Netanyahu government: coalition-formation in a quasi-parliamentary setting." *Israel Affairs* 3, 3–27.

Mainwaring, Scott. 1993. "Presidentialism, Multipartism, and Democracy: The Difficult Combination." *Comparative Political Studies* 26(2): 198–228.

　1995. "Brazil: Weak Parties, Feckless Democracy." In *Building Democratic Institutions: Party Systems in Latin America*, ed. Scott Mainwaring and Timothy Scully. Stanford, CA: Stanford University Press, 354–98.

Mainwaring, Scott P. 1999. *Rethinking Party Systems in the Third Wave of Democratization: The Case of Brazil*. Stanford, CA: Stanford University Press.

Mainwaring, Scott, and Mark Jones. 2003. "The Nationalization of Parties and Party Systems: An Empirical Measure and an Application to the Americas." *Party Politics* 9(2): 139–66.

Mainwaring, Scott, and Timothy Scully. 1995. "Introduction: Parties and Party Systems in Latin America." In *Building Democratic Institutions: Party Systems in Latin America*, ed. Scott Mainwaring and Timothy Scully. Stanford, CA: Stanford University Press, 1–37.

Mainwaring, Scott, and Matthew S. Shugart. 1997. "Juan Linz, Presidentialism, and Democracy: A Critical Appraisal." *Comparative Politics* 29(4): 449–71.

Mainwaring, Scott, and Mariano Torcal. 2006. "Party System Institutionalization and Party System Theory after the Third Wave of Democratization." In *Handbook of Party Politics*, ed. R. Katz and William Crotty. London: Sage, 204–27.

Manin, Bernard, Adam Przeworski, and Susan Stokes. 1999. "Elections and Representation." In *Democracy, Accountability, and Representation*, ed. A. Przeworski, S. C. Stokes, and B. Manin. New York: Cambridge University Press, 29–54.

Maravall, José María. 2008. "The Political Consequences of Internal Party Democracy." In *Controlling Governments: Voters, Institutions and Accountability*, ed. José María Maravall and Ignacio Sánchez-Cuenca. New York: Cambridge University Press, 157–201.

Marshall, Monty, and Keith Jaggers. 2008. "POLITY IV Project: Political Regime Characteristics and Transitions, 1800–2007." Dataset and User's Manual. Center for Global Policy, School of Public Policy, George Mason University.

Marsteintredet, Leiv, and Einar Berntzen. 2008. "Latin American Presidentialism: Reducing the Perils of Presidentialism through Presidential Interruptions." *Comparative Politics* 41(3): 83–102.

Martin, L. W., and G. Vanberg. 2004. "Policing the Bargain: Coalition Government and Parliamentary Scrutiny." *American Journal of Political Science* 48(1): 13–27.

Martz, John. 1966. *Acción Democrática*. Princeton, NJ: Princeton University Press.

Mayhew, David R. 1974. *Congress, the Electoral Connection*. New Haven, CT: Yale University Press.

McCarty, Nolan, Keith T. Poole, and Howard Rosenthal. 2006. *Polarized America: The Dance of Ideology and Unequal Riches*. Cambridge, MA: MIT Press.

McCormick, Richard. 1966. *The Second American Party System: Party Formation in the Jacksonian Era*. Chapel Hill: University of North Carolina Press.

   1979. "Political Development and the Second Party System." In *The American Party Systems: Stages of Political Development*, ed. W. N. Chambers and W. D. Burnham. New York: Oxford University Press, 152–81.

Medding, Peter. 2000. "From Government by Party to Government Despite Party." In *Parties, Elections and Cleavages: Israel in Comparative and Theoretical Perspective*, ed. Reuven Hazan and Moshe Maor. London: Frank Cass, 172–208.

Meleshevich, Andrey. 2007. *Party Systems in Post-Soviet Countries*. New York: Palgrave Macmillan.

Mendilow, Jonathan. 1999. "The Likud's Double Campaign: Between the Devil and the Deep Blue Sea." In *The Elections in Israel 1996*, ed. A. Arian and M. Shamir. Albany: State University of New York Press, 187–210.

Mi-young, Ahn. 1997. "Former dissident Kim vows to lead South Korea out of economic crisis." Deutsche Presse Agentur, December 19.

Michels, Roberto. [1911] 1962. *Political Parties: A Sociological Study of the Oligarchical Tendencies of Modern Democracy*, trans. E. A. C. Paul. New York: Free Press.

Milkis, Sidney. 1993. *The President and the Parties: The Transformation of the American Party System since the New Deal*. New York: Oxford University Press.

Miller, Warren. 1955. "Presidential Coattails: A Study in Myth and Methodology." *Public Opinion Quarterly* 19: 353–68.

Miller, Warren, and Donald Stokes. 1966. "Constituency Influence in Congress." In *Elections and the Political Order*, ed. A. Campbell, P. Converse, W. Miller, and D. Stokes. New York: Wiley, 351–72.

Mizrahi, Yemile. 2003. *From Martyrdom to Power: The Partido Acción Nacional in Mexico*. Notre Dame: University of Notre Dame Press.

Mommsen, Wolfgang J. 1984. *Max Weber and German Politics, 1890–1920*, trans. Michael S. Steinberg. Chicago: University of Chicago Press.

Morgenstern, Scott, and Steven Swindle. 2005. "Are Politics Local? An Analysis of Voting Patterns in 23 Democracies." *Comparative Political Studies* 38(2): 143–70.

Moser, Robert, and Ethan Scheiner. 2004. "Mixed Electoral Systems and Electoral Systems Effects: Controlled Comparison and Cross-National Analysis." *Electoral Studies* 23(4): 575–99.

Müller, Sean. 2006. "Presidential Power in Semi-Presidential Systems – The Case of Romania." Lizentiatsarbeit, eingereicht bei der Philosophischen Fakultät der Universität Freiburg (CH).

Müller, Wolfgang C. 1999. "Austria." In *Semi-Presidentialism in Europe*, ed. Robert Elgie. Oxford: Oxford University Press.

Muñoz, Náfer. 2002. "Politics – Nicaragua: Alemán already preparing return to power." *Inter-Press Service/Global Information Network*. January 11 (accessed through Lexis-Nexis Academic, June 4, 2007).

Myerson, Roger. 1999. "Political Economics and the Weimar Disaster." Discussion Paper No. 1216, Center for Mathematical Studies in Economics and Management Science, Northwestern University.

Nachmias, D., and I. Sened. 1999. "The Bias of Pluralism: The Redistributive Effects of the New Electoral Law in Israel's 1996 Election." In *The Elections in Israel 1996,* ed. Asher Arian and Michal Shamir. Albany: State University of New York Press, 269–94.

Nacif, Benito. 2002. "Understanding Party Discipline in the Mexican Chamber of Deputies: The Centralized Party Model." In *Legislative Politics in Latin America,* ed. Scott Morgenstern and Benito Nacif. New York: Cambridge University Press, 254–86.

Nagel, Jack H. 1998. "Social Choice in a Pluralitarian Democracy: The Politics of Market Liberalization in New Zealand." *British Journal of Political Science* 28: 223–67.

Neustadt, Richard E. 1960. *Presidential Power: The Politics of Leadership.* New York: Wiley.

Nicholas, Peter. 2009. "Obama's party may not toe line." *Los Angeles Times,* March 8, pp. A1, A6.

Nixon, Richard. 1974. "Address on the energy crisis followed by excerpts from a question and answer period with the press." Recording Source: WKAR-FM, February 23. Vincent Voice Library, Michigan State University Libraries, http://vvl.lib.msu.edu/record.cfm?recordid=5272 (accessed February 26, 2009).

Northcutt, W. 1989. "The 1988 French Presidential Election: François Mitterand's Campaign Strategy." *Proceedings of the Annual Meeting of the Western Society for French History* 16: 291–301.

Nousiainen, Jaako. 2000. "The Consolidation of Parliamentary Governance." In *Coalition Governments in Western Europe,* ed. Wolfgang C. Müller and Kaare Strøm. Oxford: Oxford University Press, 264–99.

Olson, Mancur. 1965. *The Logic of Collective Action: Public Goods and the Theory of Groups.* Cambridge, MA: Harvard University Press.

Onishi, Norimitsu. 2007. "World Briefing Asia: South Korea: President Quits His Party." *New York Times,* Feb. 23, p. 6.

Ordeshook, Peter. 1995. "Institutions and Incentives." *Journal of Democracy* 6: 46–60.

Ostrogorski, Moisei. [1902] 1964. *Democracy and the Organization of Political Parties, Volume II: The United States,* ed. S. M. Lipset. Garden City, NY: Doubleday Anchor.

Paloheimo, Heikki. 2005. "Finland: Let the Force Be with the Leader – But Who Is the Leader?" In *The Presidentialization of Politics. A Comparative Study of Modern Democracies,* ed. Thomas Poguntke and Paul Webb. Oxford: Oxford University Press, 246–68.

Panebianco, Angelo. 1988. *Political Parties: Organization and Power.* Cambridge, UK: Cambridge University Press.

Partido dos Trabalhadores. 1998. *Resoluções de Encontros e Congressos: 1979–1998* [Resolutions of Meetings and Congresses, 1979–1998]. São Paulo: Partido dos Trabalhadores.

Pensamiento, Daniel. 2005. "Cierran filas los panistas y candidato." *Mural,* December 7.

Pérez-Liñan, Aníbal. 2007. *Crisis without Breakdown: Presidential Impeachment and the New Political Instability in Latin America.* New York: Cambridge University Press.

Persson, Torsten, and Guido Tabellini. 2002. *Political Economics: Explaining Economic Policy.* Cambridge, MA: MIT Press.

Pierce, Roy. 1995. *Choosing the Chief: Presidential Elections in France and the United States.* Ann Arbor: University of Michigan Press.

2005. "The Executive Divided against Itself: Cohabitation in France, 1986–1988." *Governance* 4(3): 270–94.

Pierson, Paul. 2000. "Increasing Returns, Path Dependence, and the Study of Politics." *American Political Science Review* 94(2): 251–68.

Pitkin, Hannah. 1967. *The Concept of Representation.* Berkeley: University of California Press.

Poguntke, Thomas, and Paul Webb, eds. 2005a. *The Presidentialization of Politics.* New York: Oxford University Press.

Poguntke, Thomas, and Paul Webb. 2005b. "The Presidentialization of Politics in Democratic Societies: A Framework for Analysis." In *The Presidentialization of Politics: A Comparative Study of Modern Democracies,* ed. Thomas Poguntke and Paul Webb. New York: Oxford University Press, 1–25.

Political Database of the Americas. http://pdba.georgetown.edu/Elecdata/Para/para.html (accessed June 4, 2007).

Poole, Keith. 2006. "Presidents, and House and Senate Means, 1st Dimension of Joint Space" and "Figure 3A: House, First Dimension." www.voteview.org (accessed November 15).

Powell, G. Bingham, Jr. 2000. *Elections as Instruments of Democracy: Majoritarian and Proportional Visions.* New Haven, CT: Yale University Press.

Powell, G. Bingham. 2004. "Political Representation in Comparative Politics." *Annual Reviews of Political Science* 7: 273–96.

Power, Timothy J. 2006. "Some Further Observations on the October 3 Results." Center for Brazilian Studies, Oxford University. Unpublished.

Punnett, Robert M. 1992. *Selecting the Party Leader: Britain in Comparative Perspective.* London: Harvester Wheatsheaf.

Radu, Alexandru. 2003. "The Romanian Constitution: Main Changes." *Sfera Politicii* 102–03: 13–17.

Rae, Douglas. 1971. *The Political Consequences of Electoral Laws.* New Haven, CT: Yale University Press.

Rae, Nicol. 2006. "Exceptionalism in the United States." In *Handbook of Party Politics,* ed. R. Katz and W. Crotty. London: Oxford University Press, 196–203.

Rahat, Gideon. 2004. "The Study of the Politics of Electoral Reform in the 1990s: Theoretical and Methodological Lessons." *Comparative Politics* 36(4): 461–79.

   2008. *The Politics of Regime Structure Reform in Democracies: Israel in Comparative and Theoretical Perspective*. Albany: State University of New York Press.

   N.d. "The Politics of Electoral Reform Abolition: The Informed Process of Israel's Return to Its Previous System." Hebrew University of Jerusalem, Unpublished manuscript.

Rahat, Gideon, and Reuven Hazan. 2005. "Israel: The Politics of Extreme Proportionality." In *The Politics of Electoral Reform,* ed. Michael Gallagher and Paul Mitchell. Oxford: Oxford University Press, 333–51.

Remington, Thomas. 2002. "Putin, the Duma, and Political Parties." In *Putin's Russia: Past Imperfect, Future Uncertain,* ed. Dale R. Herspring. New York: Rowan and Littlefield, 39–59.

   2006. "Presidential Support in the Russian State Duma." *Legislative Studies Quarterly* 31(1): 5–32.

Reuters News. 2004. "Senegal president fires prime minister." April 21.

Rigger, Shelley. 2002. "The Education of Chen Shui-bian: Taiwan's Experience of Divided Government." *Journal of Contemporary China* 11(33): 613–24.

Riker, William. 1982. "The Two-Party System and Duverger's Law: An Essay on the History of Political Science." *American Political Science Review* 76(4): 753–66.

   1987. *The Development of American Federalism*. Boston: Kluwer Academic.

Rohde, David. 1991. *Parties and Leaders in the Postreform House*. Chicago: University of Chicago Press.

Romero, Vidal. 2005. "Presidents and Their Parties in the New Mexican Context: Explaining Vicente Fox and the PAN's Relationship." Presented at the conference titled "Democratic Institutions in Latin America: Implications for Mexico's Evolving Democracy," University of California, San Diego.

Roper, Steven D. 2008. "From Semi-Presidentialism to Parliamentarism: Regime Change and Presidential Power in Moldova." *Europe-Asia Studies* 60(1): 113–26.

Rosa, Vera, Clarissa Oliveira, and Vanice Cioccari. 2006. "PT articula reaproximação com o presidente." *O Estado de São Paulo*, October 31.

Rose, Richard, Neil Munro, and Tom Mackie, 1998. "Elections in Central and Eastern Europe since 1990." *Studies in Public Policy* 300. Glasgow: Centre for the Study of Public Policy, University of Strathclyde.

Rose, Richard, N. Munro and T. Mackie. 1998. "Elections in Central and Eastern Europe Since 1990." *Studies in Public Policy* 300. Glasgow: Center for the Study of Public Policy, University of Strathclyde.

Sallum, Brasilio Jr., and Eduardo Kugelmas. 2004. "Sobre o Modo Lula de Governar" [On Lula's Mode of Governing]. In *Brasil e Argentina Hoje: Política e Economia*, ed. Brasilio Sallum Jr. Baurú: Editora EDUSC, 255–88.

Samath, Feizal. 1991a. "Public Support Key in Campaign to Impeach Sri Lankan President." Reuters News Service, September 1 (accessed through Factiva June 4, 2007).

1991b. "Sri Lankan President Wins Support from His Party" Reuters News Service, September 2 (accessed through Factiva June 4, 2007).

Samuels, David. 1999. "Incentives to Cultivate a Party Vote in Candidate-Centric Electoral Systems: Evidence from Brazil." *Comparative Political Studies* 32(4): 487–518.

2000. "The Gubernatorial Coattails Effect: Federalism and Congressional Elections in Brazil." *Journal of Politics* 62: 240–53.

2002. "Presidentialized Parties: The Separation of Powers and Party Organization and Behavior." *Comparative Political Studies* 35(4): 461–83.

2003. *Ambition, Federalism, and Legislative Politics in Brazil.* New York: Cambridge University Press.

2004. "From Socialism to Social Democracy? The Evolution of the Workers' Party in Brazil." *Comparative Political Studies* 37(9): 999–1024.

2006. "Sources of Mass Partisanship in Brazil." *Latin American Politics and Society* 48(2): 1–27.

2007. "Separation of Powers." In *The Oxford Handbook of Comparative Politics*, ed. Carles Boix and Susan Stokes. New York: Oxford University Press, 703–26.

2008a. "The Evolution of *Petismo*, 2002–2008." *Opinião Pública* 14(2): 302–18.

2008b. "Brazilian Democracy under Lula and the PT." In *Constructing Democratic Governance in Latin America*, 3rd ed., ed. Michael Shifter and Jorge Dominguez. Baltimore: Johns Hopkins University Press, 152–76.

Samuels, David, and Matthew Soberg Shugart. 2003. "Presidentialism, Elections and Representation." *Journal of Theoretical Politics* 15(1): 33–60.

Samuels, David, and Richard Snyder. 2001. "The Value of a Vote: Malapportionment in Comparative Perspective." *British Journal of Political Science* 31(3): 651–71.

Sandoval, Consuelo. 2004. "Legislativo invita a Poderes a discutir reformas," *La Prensa* on-line. February 18. http://www-ni.laprensa.com.ni/archivo/2004/febrero-/18/politica/politica-20040218–02.html (accessed June 4, 2007).

Sartori, Giovanni. 1976. *Parties and Party Systems: A Framework of Analysis.* New York: Cambridge University Press.

1987. *The Theory of Democracy Revisited.* Chathan, NJ: Chatham House.

1994. "Neither Presidentialism nor Parliamentarism." In *The Failure of Presidential Democracy, Vol. 1: Comparative Perspectives*, ed. Juan J. Linz and Arturo Valenzuela. Baltimore: Johns Hopkins University Press, 106–18.

Saúl, Lilia. 2005. "AN se reúne para aprobar plataforma electoral." *El Universal*, November 12.

Saux, Jean Louis. 2000. "Charles Pasqua souhaite à son tour que la présidentielle précède les legislatives." *Le Monde* electronic edition, September 27.

Schattschneider, E. Elmer. 1942. *Party Government.* New York: Farrar and Rinehart.

Schlesinger, Joseph. 1984. "On the Theory of Party Organization." *Journal of Politics* 46(2): 369–400.

　　1991. *Political Parties and the Winning of Office.* Chicago: University of Chicago Press.

Schmidt, Vivien A. 1996. *From State to Market? The Transformation of French Business and Government.* New York: Cambridge University Press.

Schmitter, Philippe, and Terry Lynn Karl. 1991. "What Democracy Is … and Is Not." *Journal of Democracy* 2(3): 75–88.

Schumpeter, Joseph. 1942. *Capitalism, Socialism and Democracy.* London: Harper and Brothers.

Scott, Robert. 1969. "Political Parties and Policy-Making in Latin America." In *Political Parties and Political Development,* ed. Joseph LaPalombara and Myron Weiner. Princeton, NJ: Princeton University Press, 331–68.

Scully, Timothy. 1992. *Rethinking the Center: Party Politics in 19th- and 20th-century Chile.* Stanford, CA: Stanford University Press.

Sedelius, Thomas. 2006. "The Tug-of-War between Presidents and Prime Ministers: Semi-Presidentialism in Central and Eastern Europe." PhD dissertation, Orebro University.

Severinghaus, Sheldon R. 1996. "Mongolia in 1995: Gearing Up for the 1996 Elections." *Asian Survey* 36(1): 95–99.

　　2000. "Mongolia in 1998 and 1999: Past, Present, and Future at the New Millennium." *Asian Survey* 40(1): 130–39.

Shirk, David. 2005. *Mexico's New Politics: The PAN and Democratic Change.* Boulder, CO: Lynne Rienner.

　　2006. "Choosing Mexico's 2006 Presidential Candidates." Presented at the Working Group Meeting on Mexico's 2006 Elections, hosted by the Weatherhead Center for International Affairs, Harvard University.

Shugart, Matthew. 1988. "Duverger's Rule, District Magnitude, and Presidentialism." PhD dissertation, University of California, Irvine.

Shugart, Matthew S. 1995. "The Electoral Cycle and Institutional Sources of Divided Presidential Government." *American Political Science Review* 89: 327–43.

　　1999. "Presidentialism, Parliamentarism and the Provision of Collective Goods in Less-Developed Countries." *Constitutional Political Economy* 10(1): 53–88.

　　2005. "Semi-Presidentialism: Dual Executive and Mixed Authority Patterns." *French Politics* 3(3): 323–51.

　　2006. "Comparative Executive-Legislative Relations." In *The Oxford Handbook of Political Institutions,* ed. R. A. W. Rhodes, S. A. Binder, and B. A. Rockman. New York: Oxford University Press, 344–65.

Shugart, Matthew S., and John M. Carey. 1992. *Presidents and Assemblies: Constitutional Design and Electoral Dynamics.* New York: Cambridge University Press.

Shugart, Matthew S., and Stephan Haggard. 2001. "Institutions and Public Policy in Presidential Systems." In *Presidents, Parliaments, and Policy,* ed. Stephan Haggard and M. D. McCubbins. New York: Cambridge University Press, 64–104.

Shugart, Matthew S., Melody Ellis Valdini, and Kati Suominen. 2005. "Looking for Locals: Voter Information Demands and Personal Vote-Earning Attributes of Legislators under Proportional Representation." *American Journal of Political Science* 29, 2 (April): 437–49.

Siavelis, Peter, and Scott Morgenstern, eds. 2008a. *Pathways to Power*. College Station: Pennsylvania State University Press.

Siavelis, Peter, and Scott Morgenstern. 2008b. "Introduction: Political Recruitment and Candidate Selection in Latin America: A Framework for Analysis." In *Pathways to Power in Latin America*, ed. Peter Siavelis and Scott Morgenstern. College Park: Penn State University Press.

Skach, Cindy. 2005. *Borrowing Constitutional Designs: Constitutional Law in Weimar Germany and the French Fifth Republic*. Princeton, NJ: Princeton University Press.

2007. "The 'Newest' Separation of Powers: Semipresidentialism." *International Journal of Constitutional Law* 5(1): 93–121.

Skowronek, Steven. 1997. *The Politics Presidents Make: Leadership from John Adams to Bill Clinton*. Cambridge: Belknap Press of Harvard University Press.

Smith, Peter H. 1979. *Labyrinths of Power: Political Recruitment in Twentieth-Century Mexico*. Princeton, NJ: Princeton University Press.

Sorauf, Frank. 1968. *Party Politics in America*. Boston: Little, Brown.

Stark, Leonard P. 1996. *Choosing a Leader: Party Leadership Contests in Britain from Macmillan to Blair*. London: Macmillan.

Stellman, H. 1996. "Electing a Prime Minister and a Parliament: The Israeli Election of 1996." *Parliamentary Affairs* 41(4): 648–60.

Stirk, Peter. 2002. "Hugo Preuss, German Political Thought and the Weimar Constitution." *History of Political Thought* 23(3): 497–516.

Stokes, Susan C. 1999. "Political Parties and Democracy." *Annual Review of Political Science* 2: 243–67.

2001. *Mandates and Democracy: Neoliberalism by Surprise in Latin America*. Cambridge: Cambridge University Press.

Straits Times (Singapore). 1991. "Eight MPs expelled over bid to impeach president." September 8 (accessed through Factiva June 4, 2007).

Strøm, Kaare. 1990. "A Behavioral Theory of Competitive Political Parties." *American Journal of Political Science* 34(2): 565–98.

2003. "Parliamentary Democracy and Delegation." In *Delegation and Accountability in Parliamentary Democracies*, ed. Kaare Strøm, Wolfgang C. Müller, and Torbjorn Bergman. Oxford: Oxford University Press, 55–106.

Strøm, Kaare, and Wolfgang Müller, eds. 1999. *Policy, Office or Votes? How Political Parties in Western Europe Make Hard Decisions*. New York: Cambridge University Press.

Subramanian, Nirupama. 1999. "Sri Lanka's presidency – The most powerful job in the world." *Indian Express*, December 16.

Sundquist, James. 1992. *Constitutional Reform and Effective Government*. Washington, DC: Brookings Institution.

Taagepera, Rein. 2007. *Predicting Party Sizes: The Logic of Simple Electoral Systems*. Oxford: Oxford University Press.

Taagepera, Rein, and Matthew Soberg Shugart. 1989. *Seats and Votes: The Effects and Determinants of Electoral Systems*. New Haven, CT: Yale University Press.

Tam Cho, Wendy K., and Brian J. Gaines. 2004. "The Limits of Ecological Inference: The Case of Split-Ticket Voting." *American Journal of Political Science* 48: 152–71.

Tavits, Margit. 2009. "Direct Presidential Elections and Turnout in Parliamentary Contests." *Political Research Quarterly* 62(1): 42–54.

Tegos, Alexandros. 2007. "Until Death Do Us Part – On the Assumption that Leaders Act to Survive in Office." University of Mannheim. Unpublished.

Thies, M. F. 2001. "Keeping Tabs on Partners: The Logic of Delegation in Coalition Governments." *American Journal of Political Science* 45(3): 580–98.

Torcal, Mariano, and Scott Mainwaring. 2003. "The Political Recrafting of Social Bases of Party Competition: Chile 1973–95." *British Journal of Political Science* 33: 55–84.

Torgovnik, E. 2000. "Strategies under a New Electoral System: The Labor Party in the 1996 Israeli Elections." *Party Politics* 6(1): 95–106.

Tsebelis, George. 2002. *Veto Players: How Political Institutions Work*. Princeton, NJ: Princeton University Press.

Tsebelis, George, and Tatiana Rizova. 2007. "Presidential Conditional Agenda Setting in the Former Communist Countries." *Comparative Political Studies* 40(10): 1155–82.

UNDP. 2003. *Atlas do Desenvolvimento Humano no Brasil* [Atlas of Human Development]. Version 1.0.0 United Nations Development Program for Brazil.

Van Biezen, Ingrid. 2004. "How Political Parties Shape Democracy." Center for the Study of Democracy, University of California, Irvine. Available at http://escholarship.org/uc/item/17p1modx (accessed November 3, 2009).

Ware, Alan. 1996. *Political Parties and Party Systems*. New York: Oxford University Press.

Warwick, Paul. 1994. *Government Survival in Parliamentary Democracies*. New York: Cambridge University Press.

Weber, Max. [1917] 1978. *Parliament and Government in a Reconstructed Germany, Volume 3 of Economy and Society: An Outline of Interpretive Sociology*, ed. R. Guenther and C. Wittich. Berkeley: University of California Press.

 [1919] 1958. "Politics as a Vocation." In *From Max Weber: Essays in Sociology*, ed. Hans Gerth and C. Wright Mills. New York: Oxford University Press, 77–128.

Weinbaum, Marvin, and Dennis Judd. 1970. "In Search of a Mandated Congress." *Midwest Journal of Political Science* 14: 276–302.

Wiesehomeier, Nina, and Kenneth Benoit. 2009. "Presidents, Parties and Policy Competition." *Journal of Politics* 71(4): 1435–47.

Willey, Joseph. 1998. "Institutional Arrangements and the Success of New Parties in Old Democracies." In *Parties and Democracy*, ed. R. Hofferbert. Oxford: Blackwell, 229–46.

Wilson, Woodrow. 1908. *Constitutional Government in the United States.* New York: Columbia University Press.

Wolinetz, Steven. 2002. "Beyond the Catch-all Party: Approaches to the Study of Parties and Party Organization in Contemporary Democracies." In *Political Parties: Old Concepts and New Challenges*, ed. R. Gunther, J. R. Montero, and J. Linz. Oxford: Oxford University Press, 136–65.

World Bank. 2007. "World Development Indicators" (online resource). Washington, DC: World Bank.

Index